CONFRONTING
CREATION

CONFRONTING CREATION

How Judaism Reads Genesis

An Anthology of Genesis Rabbah

by Jacob Neusner

University of South Carolina Press

For
Joshua and Lynn Bell

Co-workers for many years
in the making of many books

People of pride and professionalism
patience and good will
who learn from their own mistakes
and teach others to do the same

A token of thanks for many years of
loyal and excellent collaboration

Published in Columbia, South Carolina, by the
University of South Carolina Press

Manufactured in the United States of America

Library of Congress Cataloging-in-Publication Data

Midrash, rabbah. Genesis. English. Selections.
    Confronting creation: how Judaism reads Genesis : an anthology of
Genesis rabbah / by Jacob Neusner.
       p.   cm.
    Includes index.
    ISBN 0–87249–732–1
    1. Midrash rabbah. Genesis—Commentaries. 2. Bible. O.T.
Genesis—Commentaries. I. Neusner, Jacob, 1932–   . II. Title.
BM517.M65A3   1991
296.1′4—dc20   90–48548

Contents

Contents

Preface

While the world at large treats Judaism as "the religion of the Old Testament," the fact is otherwise. Judaism inherits and makes the Hebrew scriptures its own, just as does Christianity. And just as Christianity rereads the entire heritage of ancient Israel in the light of "the resurrection of Jesus Christ," so Judaism understands the Hebrew scriptures as only one part, the written one, of "the one whole Torah of Moses, our rabbi." In this book I show how the sages of Judaism in the early centuries of the common era read scripture—the written part of the Torah for Judaism, "the Old Testament" for Christianity—as Torah, that is, as an expression of God's word, seamless, whole, and harmonious.

Here we see how, in one of the writings of ancient Israel, Genesis Rabbah, the written Torah was remade into a medium for expression of that "whole Torah," oral and written, that our sages of blessed memory—the correct way of referring to the ancient rabbis of Judaism—gave to all Israel, the Jewish people. Scripture formed a principal component of the Torah, but only one part, and here we see how scripture was recast as (part of the) Torah.

In Genesis Rabbah we see how the received scriptures formed an instrumentality for the expression of a writing bearing its own integrity and cogency, appealing to its own conventions of intelligibility, and, above all, making its own points. Any notion therefore that the authorships of Judaism proposed a systematic exegesis of scripture conducted in terms of the original or historical program of scripture, or appealed to scripture for validation or vindication of doctrine or practice perceived as independent of scripture, distorts the character of the discourse of Judaism. Scripture formed part of the Torah. The authorships of Judaism, particularly in late antiquity, also participated in the discourse and statement of the Torah. They did not write *about* scripture, they wrote *with* scripture, for scripture supplied the syntax and grammar of their thought, hence, "writing with scripture."

The Judaism of the dual Torah, oral and written, which people ordinarily mean when they speak of "Judaism," commonly makes its appearance as a "biblical religion." That is to say, people ordinarily take for granted that that Judaism (like all other Judaisms) appeals for validation to the Hebrew scriptures or Old Testament. Consequently, we tend to compare Judaism to Christianity, regarding both of them, each in its own way, as biblical: appealing to scripture, whether the written Torah (Judaism) or the Old Testament (Christianity). But when we adopt such a perspective upon the two great religions of the European West, we treat as distinct and independent what for both religions forms part of an integrated whole. That is to say, we see scripture (written Torah, Old Testament) not as part of an integral revelation, in which each part illuminates all others (oral Torah, New Testament). Rather, we address one part on its own, ignoring the perspective of faith altogether. But if we read the written Torah/Old Testament distinct from the oral Torah/New Testament, what we do is deny the fundamental conviction of the faith of Judaism or Christianity.

We do just that when we describe as exegetical ("midrashic") the relationship of the oral to the written Torah or the New to the Old Testament. That is to say, we deem one document to be essentially autonomous of the other, then establishing its relationship to the other through processes of rereading and reinterpretation. On that basis we develop the conception that the original scriptures (again: written Torah/Old Testament) enjoy an existence independent of the faith and the synagogue or church that preserve them. These original scriptures bear an autonomous meaning, determined by the criteria of initial context and historical circumstance, and that meaning stands in judgment, so to speak, upon the meanings imputed to these scriptures by the Judaism of the dual Torah or by the Christianity of the Bible, Old and New Testaments alike. Viewed historically, the collection of writings we know as the Hebrew scriptures or Old Testament obviously bear meaning determined by the original setting and intent of authors or authorships (individual, collective writers).

But that meaning never made a profound impact, prior to the nineteenth century, upon the reception and reading of the Israelite scriptures. What did make its mark was the uses of those scriptures for the makers of the Judaism of the dual Torah, on the one side, and the Christianity we now know as orthodox: the Christianity of the Bible, Old and New Testaments, on the other. And what mattered to those system-builders concerned the revelation of God as they received it: the Torah of Moses, our rabbi, for the Judaism of the dual Torah; the person of Jesus Christ, God incarnate, for Christianity. To those protean conceptions, scripture served, as did all else, as testimony and testament. It formed part of a larger, wholly cogent statement. It served important purposes in the formation and expression of that statement. But it constituted a subordinated and merely instrumental entity, not the court of last appeal and final judgment, not the ultimate source of truth and validation, except—of course—after the fact. The fact found expression in the figure of the sage, in the model of Moses, our rabbi, or in the person, as the church received him, of Christ Jesus.

People commonly suppose that when Judaic or Christian authorships turned to Israelite scripture, it was in search of proof-texts. The relationship was exegetical or eisegetical. The representation of either religion as forming an essentially exegetical relationship to Israelite writings, however, vastly distorts the nature of that religion. When Judaic and Christian authorships proposed to compose their statements, they of course appealed to scripture. But it was an appeal to serve a purpose defined not by scripture but by the faith—the Judaic or Christian system—under construction and subject to articulation. Scripture formed a dictionary, providing a vast range of permissible usages of intelligible words. Scripture did not dictate the sentences that would be composed through the words found in that (limited) dictionary. Much as painters paint with a palette of colors, authorships wrote with scripture. The paint is not the picture. Matthew's Gospel of Jesus is not (merely) a reprise of Isaiah. But the picture cannot be painted without the pigments on the palette, and Matthew's Gospel cannot have been created without the verses of Isaiah and other prophetic passages that provided Matthew's framework for the gospel story of Jesus

Christ. And when the church in its first three centuries framed its scriptures—as everybody knows—it received the Israelite writings because of the church's reading of those writings. It spoke through those writings. It appealed to their facts. It responded, in the formation of its imagination and metaphoric reality, to those writings. Its life and being were nourished by those writings. But the church came first, then the scriptures, and, ultimately, the Bible, Old and New Testaments forming one complete and wholly harmonious, seamless statement and document. And so it was with the Judaism of the dual Torah, in its framework and within its inner logic and discipline.

What follows from these propositions is clear. If we wish to understand the place and power of the Israelite scriptures in the Judaism of the dual Torah and in the writings of nascent Christianity, we must begin by freeing ourselves of one conception and exploring the implications of another. Genesis Rabbah is an ideal place in which to begin that liberating process of reading scripture as (part of) the Torah. The negative is this: we must abandon any notion of a perceived distinction between the oral and the written Torahs, or between the New and Old Testaments. The positive is that we must see the two Torahs as the one whole Torah of Moses, our rabbi. We must see the two Testaments as "the Bible." The negative: we cannot take for granted that the appearance of a verse of the Israelite scriptures in a rabbinic composition or a New Testament writing serves a single, determinate purpose—for example, as a "proof-text," as a source of vindication or validation for a statement a later author wishes to prove. The positive: we have to undertake an inductive inquiry into the uses and authority of the received scriptures of ancient Israel, allowing diverse documents to provide, each its own indication of where and how the inherited, authoritative writings serve the purposes of an author or authorship.

My translation of Genesis *(Bereshit)* Rabbah takes as its text and systematic commentary J. Theodor and Ch. Albeck, *Midrash Bereshit Rabba. Critical Edition with Notes and Commentary* (Berlin and Jerusalem, 1893–1936) I-III. That text is authoritative, so far as contemporary Judaic scholarship can produce a critical text, and I have treated it as authoritative in every detail. I have furthermore had the advantage of an excellent translation, already available, and have made ample use of it. I systematically consulted H. Freedman, *Genesis*, in *Midrash Rabbah. Translated into English with Notes, Glossary, and Indices*, edited by H. Freedman and Maurice Simon (London: Soncino Press, 1939) I-II. Where I have adopted Freedman's translation verbatim or nearly so, I have indicated by adding his name in square brackets. (Readers who want to follow this up may simply turn to the clearly marked counterpart in his translation.) But I have taken full account of his rendering of nearly every line. I learned from him on each occasion on which I consulted him. It is a splendid piece of work. As to the translation of verses of scripture, I took an eclectic approach, sometimes copying Freedman's, sometimes relying on the fine English of the RSV, and sometimes making my own translation. Readers will do well to keep at hand a copy of the English translation of the Hebrew scriptures they find the most clear and accessible. To me they all have merits.

I have devised a reference system for Genesis Rabbah to allow us to identify the components of each chapter. For this purpose, I use the existing chapter numbers, given in the Hebrew text and in the English translation. These are in Roman numerals. I then subdivide each chapter into its principal units of thought, e.g., its main points. These subdivisions are marked with another Roman numeral. Each subsection of a subdivision, a completed thought, for example, is marked with an Arabic number. Finally, I mark each sentence with a letter. So I:I.1.A is the first chapter, the first principal unit of thought in that chapter, the first subsection of that unit of thought, and the first sentence of that subsection. In this way we see clearly the principal parts of which the entire document is composed and can refer to them very conveniently. It is the equivalent of assigning to sentences of the Bible numbers, e.g., Gen. 1:1. For the rabbinic literature, mine is the first reference system to do more than indicate either the chapter of a large document or the page on which a given sentence appears; and it is, further, the only reference system that makes possible at a glance a clear analysis of how a given chapter is put together.

I have selected from my translation of Genesis Rabbah passages I believe especially striking and compelling for Jews today. I have introduced each passage with a brief statement of the point to which I believe the passage is relevant, and concluded each with a remark on what I think is important in the citation. In this way I hope to enrich the weekly study of the Torah lection by making available what the great rabbis of the third and fourth century, who framed Judaism as we now know it, had to say about important episodes in the book of Genesis. What would give me special joy would be use of this book in synagogue study and also worship, as a companion to the reading of the book of Genesis in synagogue services. That is a merit to which I permit myself to aspire—but only because I serve merely as faithful and accurate mediator of the text to my own time.

CONFRONTING CREATION

Introduction

In this book we read the Hebrew scriptures—the written Torah of Judaism, the Old Testament of Christianity—in the way in which the sages of Judaism of the formative age, the first six centuries of the common era [= A.D. to Christianity] thought we should read them. I deal in particular with the book of Genesis and follow how the sages of Judaism—called "our sages of blessed memory"—understood the account of the creation of the world and the formation of holy Israel, the Jewish people, in relationship to its land, the land of Israel. Judaism from that time to our own day has studied this part of the Torah in the light of our sages' guidance. The issues they thought important, the way in which they thought scripture should be read and understood, the conclusions they found compelling—these modes of Torah study told faithful Jews what was important in scripture. In the pages of this anthology, I give a large sample of how "our sages of blessed memory" made out of the book of Genesis an urgent statement to Jews in all ages.

In the book of Genesis, as the sages who composed Genesis Rabbah see things, God set forth to Moses the entire scope and meaning of Israel's history among the nations and salvation at the end of days. In a few words let me restate the conviction of the framers of the document:

"We now know what will be in the future. How do we know it? Just as Jacob had told his sons what would be in time to come, just as Moses told the tribes their future, so we may understand the laws of history if we study the Torah. The Torah tells us not only what happened but why. The Torah therefore permits us to discover the laws of history. Once we know those laws, we may also peer into the future and come to an assessment of what is going to happen to us—and, especially, of how we shall be saved from our present existence. Because everything exists under the aspect of a timeless will, God's will, and all things express one thing, God's program and plan, in the Torah we uncover the workings of God's will. Our task as Israel is to accept, endure, submit, and celebrate."

Now that message must strike you as surprising. For the world reads the book of Genesis as the story of the beginnings of the world and of Israel: creation of the world, humanity from Adam to Noah, then from Noah to Abraham, and finally the story of the three patriarchs and four matriarchs of Israel, Abraham, Isaac, Jacob, Sarah, Rebecca, Leah, and Rachel, and finally, Joseph and his brothers. But to the rabbis who created Genesis Rabbah, the book of Genesis tells the story of Israel, the Jewish people, in the here and now. The principle? What happened to the patriarchs and matriarchs signals what will happen to their descendants: the model of the ancestors sends a message for the children. So the importance of Genesis, as the sages of Genesis Rabbah read the book, derives not from its lessons about the past but from its message for Israel's present—and, especially, future.

So their conviction is that what Abraham, Isaac, and Jacob did shaped the future history of Israel. If, therefore, we want to know the meaning of events now and tomorrow, we look back at yesterday to find out. Why did the sages of the Jewish people, in the land of Israel, come to Genesis with the questions of their own day? Because, they maintained, the world reveals not chaos but order, and God's will works itself out not once but again and again. If we can find out how things got going, we also can find meaning in today and method in where we are heading. So did our sages believe. And that is why they looked to a reliable account of the past and searched out the meaning of their own days. Bringing to the stories of Genesis that conviction that the book of Genesis told not only yesterday but also the tale of tomorrow, the sages whose words are before us in this anthology transformed a picture of the past into a prophesy for a near tomorrow.

What made Israel's sages look longingly at the beginnings of the world and of Israel? Because in their own day they entertained deep forebodings about Israel's prospects. To understand why, we have to ask where and when our book reached its conclusion. We want also to know who stands behind the work, its authorship and—in particular—how the authorship expressed itself.

When we know the answer to that question, we also can say, why the message proved urgent and immediate, why, in other words, the sages before us turned to Genesis with the questions they found compelling, rather than with other questions. Since, in our own day, the book of Genesis forms the battlefield among Protestant theologians, some of whom wish to read it as a work in geology and others of whom do not, we have to assess what brings readers to this holy book, before we try to understand what they find in it.

Now, all scholars agree, Genesis Rabbah came to closure around the year 400, give or take a half a century either way— that is, some time between 350 at the earliest and 450 at the latest. Taking as fact the conclusions of scholars who have worked hard on the problem, we can place the document in one location—time, country—and not some other. Once we know where and when the document reached its conclusion, we also can see more clearly to whom its message made a difference. And the answer of the question of where and when is simple: in the land of Israel, toward the end of the fourth century of the common era. What made that particular time crucial in the life of Israel, the Jewish people, in the land of Israel, is an event that also shaped the entire history of Western civilization. We may, in fact, locate the sages' rereading of the Torah's account of the beginnings, the beginnings of the world and of Israel— that is, the book of Genesis—at exactly that moment at which Western civilization also came to its genesis. That is, the fourth century marked the beginning of the West as it reached its continuing and enduring definition.

What made all the difference, and what happened in that turning point in time? It was, first, the conversion of Constantine, the emperor of Rome, to Christianity and the legalization of Christianity, then its designation as the state's favored religion, and finally, by the end of the century, the establishment of Christianity as the religion of Rome. To the Christians, it was an age of vindication and validation. Some of the church's leading figures had met persecution and imprisonment in the decades just prior to Constantine's conversion, and then ended their lives as high officials of the Roman empire at his court. If the great German rabbi, Leo Baeck, had been taken out of the

3

concentration camp where he was in 1945 and by the end of 1947 had become prime minister of Germany under the successor of Adolph Hitler, we could begin to imagine the power of events, as Christians experienced them. The triumph of Christianity changed the history of the West, because, from that point onward, the principal institutions of politics, culture, and social organization in Western civilization found definition and meaning in the Christian religion—pure and simple. Since Rome encompassed the greater part of then-known civilization in the West, the fourth century therefore encompassed the redefinition of the West. What happened may be summarized very simply: Rome became Christian, and a formerly despised and illicit religious group took power.

But that event, by itself, need not greatly have confounded Israel and its sages. A second event, at the same critical time, mattered more. To understand it, we have to recall that Israel, the Jewish people, had hoped, from the destruction of the temple in 70, to witness its rebuilding, together with the restoration of Israel's government in its land and the advent of Israel's righteous and correct ruler, the Messiah. Reason for that hope derived from the destruction of the first temple, when, after the passage of a few generations, Israel returned to its land, the Levites to their platform, and the priests to the altar of God. So hope persisted that the same pattern would find renewal, and the prophets' promises of redemption—which the Christians claimed had already been kept in the restoration after 586— would once more be kept. Then Israel's faith as the ancient prophets had formed it would find the vindication that Christianity (from Israel's viewpoint, momentarily) now enjoyed.

As the years passed, from Constantine's conversion in 312 onward, Israel's thinkers may well have pondered the meaning of events. We know that the counterparts in the Christian world found they had to revise and rewrite the entire history of the world, from creation onward, to provide an explanation of the new age in the continuity of time. It would be speculative to claim that Israel as a whole expected the Messiah just now, as the claim so long rejected that Jesus had been Christ and that Christ now triumphed made its way. For Christians claimed, quite plausibly for many, that the conversion of the hated Rome

4

to Christianity validated and vindicated their original conviction about Jesus as the Christ.

Whether or not Israel in its land worried over that matter we do not know. But we do know one stunning fact. In 360, just a generation beyond Constantine's conversion, an emperor came to the throne who threw off Christianity and reaffirmed paganism. Julian, whom Christians called from then to now "the apostate," reestablished overthrown idols, reopened the philosophical schools of pagan tradition, and presented paganism in its elegant and cultured form to a startled empire. At the same time Julian undertook to embarrass and humiliate the Christians. Since the Christians had by no means gained a majority of the population when Julian managed this stunning turn in world history, the Christian dream seemed to turn into a nightmare. For the worst thing that can happen, beyond remission, is a new growth of cancer, and, for those who recalled the miracle of Constantine's conversion and the consequent upward move of Christianity, the moment foreboded a miserable end.

Why all this affected Israel is simple. As part of his program to embarrass Christianity and disprove its claims, Julian announced that the Jews might go back to Jerusalem and rebuild their temple. The Gospels represent Jesus as predicting that no stone on stone would remain, for the temple would be destroyed and never rebuilt. Well, no stone did remain on another. But now, it appeared, Jesus' prediction would be shown a lie. Then what would result from the rest of his claims, as they circulated in the New Testament and in the church? And how would the Christians now disprove the Jews' insistence that the prophets' promises of old would yet be kept?

Since the Christians had long pointed to the destruction of the temple and the loss of Jerusalem as mark of Israel's punishment for rejecting the Christ, Julian's action certainly pointed toward a malicious intent. Here, in Julian's mind, people could find yet another cause to reject Christianity and all its claims. For the Jews, of course, Julian's move stood for something quite the opposite: the vindication of Israel's patience, endurance, and hope. Now it all seemed to come true—and that on the eve of the three hundredth anniversary of the destruction. By the Jews' reckoning, the temple had been destroyed in the year 68, so if it took a few years, from 360 onward, by the year 368, Israel would regain its holy altar and sacred city, the sacrifices so long suspended, and—by Israel's hopeful reckoning—the world would conclude the sorry history and celebrate the coming of the Messiah.

But it was not to be. Within the year, Julian died on a battlefield in far-off Iran, near the waters of Babylon where so large a portion of Israel then lived. Christians reported that on his lips, as he breathed his last, were the words, "Galilean, thou hast triumphed." Whatever he said—if anything—hardly matters. That was precisely what the Christian world concluded. Julian's death in his campaign against the Iranian empire under its most brilliant ruler, Shapur II, of the dynasty known as the Sasanian (hence, in the history books, Sasanian Iran), for all time wiped out the last hope of pagan renaissance in Rome. For Israel in its land, the disappointment proved only the least problem.

For ahead, over the next generation, lay a trial the Jewish people in the Roman empire had never before known. Judaism in Rome from the beginnings of Roman rule in the Middle East had enjoyed the status of a protected, completely licit religion. Jews enjoyed freedom to practice their religion. They could not, for example, be forced to violate the Sabbath. Buildings built for Judaic worship enjoyed the protection of the state. Constantine had done little to limit the Jews' rights, either as citizens or as believers in their faith. But now that freedom for the first time faced abridgment—and worse. What was happening was simple. After Julian, the initial policy of tolerance of both paganism and Judaism shifted. The Roman government, once more Christian, determined to make certain that the Christian grasp on power never again would weaken. So laws against paganism in all its forms went forth from Constantinople to the entire empire, placing severe restraints on all forms of pagan worship and imposing heavy penalties on those who fostered paganism.

When Christian zealots attacked pagan temples, just as, in times past, pagan zealots had harassed and murdered Christians, they went after synagogues and Jews as well. For in the counterattack on paganism, the net that was cast caught Israel too. Before Constantine, of course, Christianity had no politics;

therefore, by the way, no policy for Israel, the Jewish people, either. Afterward in a matter of a few generations Christianity had to develop a politics, a view of history, and a policy of a political character governing Israel, the Jewish people. As a matter of theology, there had been a Christian policy of toleration for Israel, meant to await the second coming and the last judgment as witness to the truth of Christianity. That, in general, yielded a political policy that Jews were not to be exterminated, as pagans in time to come would be exterminated, and Judaism was not to be extirpated, as, in the future, paganism would be destroyed. But that was to be the general policy for the long haul. What in particular happened now—toward the end of the fourth century, from Julian's death after 260 to the turn of the fifth century? A policy, drawn from the program against paganism, limited Israel's right to the security and freedom that the nation had enjoyed, in its land, with only a few (if bitter) periods, from the coming of Roman governance and rule in the first century B.C.E. Specifically, synagogues were destroyed, Jews lost the right to convert slaves whom they purchased, Jews who became Christians enjoyed the protection of the state, and in various other ways, Jews' former privileges and rights were abridged or revoked. By the turn of the fifth century, around 410, the Jews' institution of self-government in the land of Israel, the rule by their patriarch, came to an end. In all, it was a very difficult time, not because of trouble alone, not even because of the unprecedented character of the new laws and outrages, but because of the disappointment and despair that followed the high hopes kindled by Julian's abortive scheme.

To revert to our sad analogy, if in 1937 Hitler had given way to a democratic government that restored Jewish rights, and in 1939 a new Nazi government had come back to power and annulled those rights again, we might have a relevant analogy to the awful dread that affected despairing Israel. What now? And what of the brief hope of yesterday? In consequence of the restoration of Christian rule and the disappointment attached to the failure of Julian's scheme to rebuild the temple, Israel's hope for the restoration of the holy temple and the near coming of the Messiah turned into disaster. Not only would the temple not be rebuilt, but the Christian claim that Israel's hope was

7

lost, its land beyond its grasp, its future in doubt enjoyed renewed self-evidence for those who believed it, and they were
now many. Historians tell us that by the end of the fourth century the land of Israel, now the Holy Land, possessed a Christian, not a Jewish majority. Whether or not that is so, I cannot
say, but it does suggest what happened.

To conclude this tale and move on to the question of why I
have had to tell it: the fourth century in fact presented the
West, including Israel, with its first Christian century. While
the Jewish people had managed on the whole to ignore the
Christians' slow but steady rise to power, they no longer could
pretend Christianity constituted a temporary setback in the
journey to the end of time. It was not temporary, it was far
more than a setback, and it had to be dealt with. Genesis Rabbah came to closure, all scholars generally concur, toward the
end of the fourth century. And that fact matters for one reason:
the land of Israel now found itself in the domain of Christianity,
an enormous and historical shift in the status of the land and of
the Jewish people—therefore also of the Torah. In Genesis
Rabbah every word is to be read against the background of the
world-historical change that had taken place in the time of the
formation of the document. The persons who compiled the materials we shall now see made a statement through what they
selected and arranged. This then is their collage, their creation.
Genesis Rabbah in its final form emerges from that momentous
first century in the history of the West as Christian, the century
in which the Rome empire passed from pagan to Christian rule,
and, in which, in the aftermath of the Emperor Julian's abortive
reversion to paganism in 360, Christianity adopted that policy of
repression of paganism that rapidly engulfed Judaism as well.

Before proceeding, let me give one concrete example of
how our sages responded. Their doctrine of Rome must prove
critical. Rome now claims to be Israel—that is, Christian and
heir to the testament of the founders. How do the sages of Genesis Rabbah deal with this new definition of who is Rome?
They do not deny it, they affirm it: Rome is Esau, or Moab, or
Ishmael. And we? We are Israel. So in a concrete way Genesis
talks about us, here and now, about us, Israel, and about *our
sibling*, Rome. That concession—Rome is a sibling, a close rel-

8

ative of Israel—represents an implicit recognition of Christianity's claim to share the patrimony of Judaism, to be descended from Abraham and Isaac. So how are we to deal with the glory and the power of our brother, Esau? And what are we to say about the claim of Esau to enthrone Christ? And how are we to assess today the future history of Israel, the salvation of God's first, best love? It is not by denying Rome's claim but by evaluating it, not by turning a back to the critical events of the hour but by confronting those events forcefully and authoritatively.

That is the power of Genesis Rabbah. That is why, if we listen to its messages, we hear something remarkable. It is how Israel's sages reopened the book of Genesis and reconsidered its story of beginnings. Why? Because in that story they hoped to find, and they did find, the counterpart—namely, the story of the day at hand, which, they anticipated, would indeed form the counterpart and conclusion to the story of beginnings. From creation to conclusion, from the beginnings of salvation in the patriarchs and matriarchs to the ending of salvation and its fulfilment in their own day: this is what our sages sought to discover. And in the book of Genesis, in the doings of the founders, they found models for deeds of the descendants.

That, in a few words, tells us the setting of Genesis Rabbah. Brought into being in the age of crisis, the work, which presents comments on successive verses in the book of Genesis, told Israel the meaning of its day and of many days to come. For Genesis Rabbah, the first statement of Judaism on the meaning of the book of Genesis to be written down, formed the source for centuries to follow. When for the coming, difficult centuries Israel would turn to Genesis, the Jewish people would encounter that book through the eyes of the sages who originally assembled the passages before us. And when Israel faced disappointment in its messianic hope, when Israel wondered where things were heading, when Jews asked why they should go on and what their duties were, they found answers to their questions in the book of Genesis. That was because the sages of Genesis Rabbah had turned that book into a message for Israel's living history. No longer about long-dead ancestors, the genealogy and family history of the book of Genesis, imposed on the house and destiny of Israel, explained not a distant past but an immediate moment: today, tomorrow, the near coming of redemption. Let me state quite simply that, as I was working my way through Genesis Rabbah, with the understanding I have just given of whom I heard and what I witnessed, I found myself deeply moved by the human triumph of our sages. I do not mind saying, there are passages in Genesis Rabbah that have moved me to tears.

Genesis told about beginnings so as to point to happy endings, and in reading the book of Genesis Israel could find reason to hope for its future in the certain facts of a long-ago past. That, in a single sentence, states the power of Genesis Rabbah, the astonishing achievement of the sages who brought together the paragraphs they chose and formed them into the message at hand. We who live out our lives as survivors of the worst catastrophe in the history of Israel, the Jewish people, must find special relevance in the gift to us of these ancient sages. So, to conclude, Genesis Rabbah forms part of the great labor of presenting the one whole Torah of Moses, our rabbi, revealed by God to Israel at Mount Sinai. Genesis Rabbah forms an important component of the complete Torah worked out by the rabbis of ancient times, from the publication of the Mishnah at ca. 200 to the completion of the Babylonian Talmud at ca. 600. At ca. 400 C.E., Genesis Rabbah comes midway in the unfolding of the Torah—the one whole Torah of Moses, our rabbi.

Let me now deal with some further questions. Why should Genesis Rabbah make a difference today? Genesis Rabbah matters to us for two reasons. First, it presents us with a model we can emulate. It teaches us to exercise freedom in responding to the written Torah, scripture. Why? Because it shows us how the sages of ancient times read scripture in light of their own concerns. We too can follow their model and emulate their example. Second, it also presents important lessons on the deeper meaning of scripture—namely, the meaning of scripture for the Jewish people, for Israel, through the ages. So Genesis Rabbah shows us a method and teaches us a message, and in both aspects it speaks directly to us. For the deepest conviction of our sages is that scripture speaks to us—that is, to Israel, in all ages and all the time. Accordingly, they recognize no single and original meaning that dictates for all time to come what scripture is permitted to say. To the contrary, they exercised a freedom of interpretation, by insisting that God speaks through the Torah to Israel everywhere and continually. So they exemplify for us how to read scripture, and they also teach us some lessons that scripture has to offer them and us. The power of Genesis Rabbah is not only its message, therefore, but also its method. What is the method? To take up scriptures, bring to the written Torah the deepest anguish of the age. Allow the Torah to speak to us here and now.

What is the message? Address the circumstance of historical crisis. In its own day, this message generated remarkable renewal, a rebirth of intellect in the encounter with scripture, not in quest of the rules of sanctification—these had already been found by the framers of the Mishnah and its successor documents in the Tosefta, Sifra, and the like—but of salvation. So the book of Genesis, which portrays how all things had begun, would testify to the message and the method of the end: the coming salvation of patient, hopeful, enduring Israel. The deepest conviction of Judaism today imparts relevance to that same message. It is to come once more to the written Torah, as much as to the oral one, following the model and example of the sages: to bring our burden and our crisis to scriptures, and to Genesis in particular, where it all began. There we shall seek the lessons of the coming salvation of eternal Israel.

That is why the interest and importance of our sages' reading of Genesis transcend the age in which the sages did their work. For how the great Judaic sages of that time taught the interpretation of the stories of Genesis would guide later Judaic exegetes of the same biblical book. So when we follow the work before us, we gain entry into the way in which Judaism in its normative and classical form, from that day to this, would understand the stories of the creation of the world. These concern Adam's sin, Noah, and, especially, the founding family of Israel, in its first three generations, Abraham, Isaac, and Jacob, as well as Joseph. Once we have read Genesis the way "our sages of blessed memory" teach us to, we gain the freedom to follow our imagination as they arouse it. We no longer need to deal with those who claim to dictate how in what they deem a literal and fundamental sense we must receive the story of

11

the creation of the world and of Israel. What to some proves fundamental, to us, having heard the story as the third- and fourth-century sages of Israel retell it, appears shallow. What these sages find in the text opens our minds to possibilities beyond imagining.

Sages' way of reading the first book of the Bible shows that faithful exegetes may uncover deep layers of meaning and discover truth entirely consonant with the concerns of a given age. That is so, whether it is the fourth century, in which our sages did their work, or the twenty-first century, to which, with God's help, I hope to hand on these books of mine.

Prologue:
Studying the Torah with the Sages as Our Teachers

Genesis Rabbah's authors express their ideas in a way that is not familiar to us, and we shall have to learn how to read in a different idiom from the everyday. Specifically, our writers make use of verses of scripture to express their thoughts. They will cite two or more verses together, what I call a "base verse," which is to say, a verse of the book of Genesis, followed by some other verse. This other verse is understood by the writers and the readers of our document to shed light on the base verse. In the interplay between the one and the other, the meaning that our writers wish to elicit then emerges. Since the authors of Genesis Rabbah are expressing what they conceive to be the Torah—that is, God's word to Israel, the Jewish people—we may say that they are (re)writing the Torah by means of verses of scripture: writing with scripture the way we write with words. We have then to learn how they make use of verses of scripture—citing one in connection with some other—in order to convey their meanings. When you understand how this works, then you can derive enormous wisdom and deep understanding of the Torah through the study of scripture (the written part of the Torah) alongside our sages of blessed memory.

The basic means of putting forth ideas in Genesis Rabbah, then, is in the linking of a verse of Genesis with some other verse. Only after that linkage has allowed us to set forth the main proposition we wish to express will other kinds of discussions be introduced. So the main point will always come at the outset—as it does with any good writer—in the interplay of two scriptural verses.

With that in mind, let us now turn to the literary character
of our book. It is a composite of paragraphs, not a sustained
essay. Each paragraph takes up a verse of the book of Genesis
in sequence, so the whole book is organized around the order of
another book—that is, Genesis Rabbah (as its name tells us)
follows the sequence of verses of the book of Genesis. Let us
examine the opening statement of Genesis Rabbah and see
both what our sages of blessed memory are saying and how they
are delivering their message. Once we have followed their discussion here, we can see the rules that will guide us in following their treatment of other passages.

> *I:I.1.A.* "In the beginning God created" (Gen. 1:1): *[handwritten: Base Verse]*
>
> *B.* R. Oshaia commenced [discourse by citing the fol-
> lowing verse:] "Then I was beside him like a little child, and
> I was daily his delight [rejoicing before him always, rejoicing *[handwritten: cited Verse]*
> in his inhabited world, and delighting in the sons of men]"
> (Prov. 8:30–31).
>
> *C.* The word for 'child' uses consonants that may also
> stand for 'teacher,' 'covered over,' and 'hidden away.'
>
> *D.* "Some hold that the word also means 'great.'
>
> *E.* "The word means 'teacher,' in line with the follow-
> ing: 'As a teacher carries the suckling child' (Num. 11:12).
>
> *F.* "The word means 'covered over,' as in the following:
> 'Those who were covered over in scarlet' (Lam. 4:5).
>
> *G.* "The word means 'hidden,' as in the verse, 'And he
> hid Hadassah' (Est. 2:7).
>
> *H.* "The word means 'great,' in line with the verse,
> 'Are you better than No-Ammon?' (Nah. 3:8). This we trans-
> late, 'Are you better than Alexandria the Great, which is lo-
> cated between rivers.' "
>
> *2. A.* Another matter:
>
> *B.* The word means "workman."
>
> *C.* [In the cited verse] the Torah speaks, "I was the
> work plan of the Holy One, blessed be he."
>
> *D.* In the accepted practice of the world, when a mortal
> king builds a palace, he does not build it out of his own head,
> but he follows a work plan.

E. And [the one who supplies] the work plan does not build out of his own head, but he has designs and diagrams, so as to know how to situate the rooms and the doorways.

F. Thus the Holy One, blessed be he, consulted the Torah when he created the world.

G. So the Torah stated, "By means of 'the beginning' [that is to say, the Torah] did God create" (Gen. 1:1).

H. And the word for "beginning" refers only to the Torah, as Scripture says, "The Lord made me as the beginning of his way" (Prov. 8:22).

The opening lines show us a kind of reading of scripture that we do not regularly see. We are used to reading several lines at once and seeing the sense of the whole, but here we have only a clause. When, moreover, we see a commentary to the scriptures, there will be amplification of a verse or a phrase. But here the phrase "In the beginning . . ." stands by itself. Then comes a named authority, R. Oshaia, who cites another verse of scripture. This second verse is cited so as to help us read the initial verse in a fresh way. The cited verse, Prov. 8:30–31, is spoken, in the context of the book of Proverbs, by "wisdom," which our sages of blessed memory take to be identical with the Torah. When he cites Prov. 8:30 in connection with Gen. 1:1, what then does R. Oshaia have in mind? Finding the answer draws us back to the verse at hand, "In the beginning." The word "in" can stand also for "by," and what R. Oshaia understands is, "by means of 'the beginning' God created. . . ." Then what is this "beginning" by means of which, or by reference to which, God created? Proverbs 8:30–31 is, then, the answer: it was by wisdom, which is to say, the Torah, that God created the heaven and the earth. But that lesson is not spelled out. Rather, we work on that intersecting verse of Proverbs. The word for "child" is important, because "wisdom," that is, the Torah, says, "Then (that is, at creation] I [that is, the Torah] was beside him like a little child." The word for "child" is made of consonants in Hebrew that yield a variety of other words, and these are specified teacher, covered over, hidden away, and great. Several verses are cited to show how these letters bear the stated meanings.

15

This seems somewhat academic, and, at this point, it is. What happens now is a second go-around on the same matter of the meanings imputed to the letters at hand, and now the real action starts. For "workman" is the meaning our sage wishes to develop. When the verse of Proverbs says, "Then I was beside him like a little child, and I was daily his delight [rejoicing before him always, rejoicing in his inhabited world, and delighting in the sons of men]" (Prov. 8:30–31), the meaning of what the Torah, which is speaking, says is, "I was the work plan of the Holy One." That is to say, "when God created the heaven and the earth, I, the Torah, provided the plan by which God made the world." God consulted the Torah when he created the world, and that point is then made explicitly at F-G. The message of R. Oshaia is very clear, and it is a message concerning what he thinks is critical about the story of creation: God designed the world in the model of the Torah. If, then, people want to know how the world is supposed to be, they should consult the Torah.

Let me restate what I think is happening here. I:I.1 begins with the introduction of an intersecting verse, Prov. 8:30, which will be carefully expounded and only then brought into relationship to the base verse. No. 1 spells out the several meanings of the letters used in the word "child," that is, simply explaining the intersecting verse in its own terms. Then no. 2 interrelates the intersecting verse with the base verse. How so? The intersecting verse is made to speak for the Torah, in line with Prov. 8:22. At what point in the intersecting verse—Prov. 8:30, not Prov. 8:22—do we then find the pertinent meaning? I take for granted it is at the first of the meanings imputed to the word for tutor—namely, teacher. Thus the Torah speaks, announcing, "Then I was with him as the tutor" in the process of the creation of the world. What is curious, then, in no. 2 is that the original intersecting verse is not cited at the end. I am inclined to suspect that in the mind of the framer of the passage the cited verse should then begin with Prov. 8:22 and conclude with Prov. 8:30, so we have an exceptionally long intersecting verse. Otherwise the intersecting verse before us makes no sense. There can be no doubt, of course, that nos. 1 and 2 form a single statement, since in this way, without no. 2, no. 1 serves no purpose.

What, then, is important about the opening verse of the story of creation? It is the message that creation attests to the lessons of the Torah. That is proven by R. Oshaia by appeal to the meanings of words and phrases, but, as with all great readings of the holy scriptures, it is the theology of the Torah that has dictated the interpretation of the Torah—in that order. First we begin with theological truth, and then, in scripture, we identify the sense and meanings of verses, in line with that fundamental affirmation.

Let me now give a second example, also from the very opening lines, of the same way of setting forth a message. Here the message that the sage wishes to set forth is that we know only a very little about the creation of the world; the Torah tells us how the world was made, but much that is in the Torah we are not going to grasp. It is humility that ought to characterize us in facing with awe and wonder the mysteries of creation—a peculiarly modern message indeed. The way in which this message is laid out will be indirect. We begin with a new intersecting verse—that is, a verse other than Gen. 1:1, which forms the foundation of our passge—and it is Ps. 31:19. We once more commence with a word study, this time with a word that means "dumb," "silence," "bound." The point now is, in speaking about creation, there is good reason to say less than we know or think:

I:V.1.A. R. Huna in the name of Bar Qappara commenced [discourse by citing the following verse]: "Let the lying lips be made dumb [which arrogantly speak matters kept secret against the righteous]" (Ps. 31:19).

B. "[Translating the Hebrew word for dumb into Aramaic one may use words meaning] 'bound,' 'made dumb,' or 'silenced.'

C. " 'Let [the lying lips] be bound,' as in the following verse: 'For behold, we were binding sheaves' (Gen. 37:7).

D. " 'Let the lying lips be made dumb,' as in the usage in this verse: 'Or who made a man dumb' (Ex. 4:11).

17

E. " 'Let them be silenced' bears the obvious meaning of the word.

F. "Which arrogantly speak matters kept secret against the righteous (Ps. 31:19):

G. ". . . which speak against the righteous, the Life of the Ages, matters that he kept secret from his creatures [Freedman: the mysteries of creation].

H. "With pride (Ps. 31:19):

I. That is so as to take pride, saying 'I shall expound the work of creation.'

J. "And contempt (Ps. 31:19): Such a one treats with contempt the honor owing to me.

K. For R. Yose b. R. Hanina said, "Whoever gains honor through the humiliation of his fellow gains no share in the world to come.

L. "For one does so through the honor owing to the Holy One, blessed be he, how much the more so!"

M. And what is written after the cited verse [Ps. 31:19]?

N. "How abundant is your goodness, which you have stored away for those who revere you (Ps. 31:20).

O. Rab said, "Let one [who reveals the mysteries of creation] not have any share in your abundant goodness.

P. "Under ordinary circumstances, if a mortal king builds a palace in a place where there had been sewers, garbage, and junk, will not whoever may come and say, 'This palace is built on a place where there were sewers, garbage and junk,' give offense? So too, will not whoever comes and says, 'This world was created out of chaos, emptiness, and darkness' give offense?

Q. R. Huna in the name of Bar Qappara: "Were the matter not explicitly written in scripture, it would not be possible to state it at all: 'God created heaven and earth' (Gen. 1:1)—from what? From the following: 'And the earth was chaos' (Gen. 1:2). [Freedman: God first created chaos and emptiness, and out of these he created the world, but this is not to be taught publicly.]"

A new intersecting verse is presented. The pertinent theme of the verse is the notion that there are things about which one must not speak, hence, in the repertoire of meanings attributed to the key word—be dumb—the important one is "silenced." The continuation of the same verse carries forward the same idea—namely, that one should not speak arrogantly against the righteous, meaning God. The combination of the two ideas is then clear. That is, it is arrogant to expound the works of creation, and these are matters about which one must remain silent. J then carries forward the exposition of Prov. 31:20, the matter of contempt. The same point is made over again. There are matters one must not call to mind. Then Huna-Bar Qappara completes the matter and makes the main point. It is stunning and fresh, yet fully prepared: one could not say about creation what scripture itself says. That is that the world began unformed and void. Once more it is clear that we deal with a unified and cogent statement, so that A-I and J to the end, while on the surface distinct from one another, are formed to make a single, exceedingly surprising point, which comes only at the end.

That I:I and I:V follow a single pattern is quite clear. The exposition of the intersecting verse takes place in stages, with a philological exercise on the meaning of a fundamental word at hand, following by a secondary expansion on the sense of the verse as a whole. That is the point that the base verse enters the frame of reference, and that is not in a philological but in a theological aspect. So if we may characterize the intention of the framers of the two compositions, it is to move from philological to theological issues (using theological in a broad sense). The philological exercise, moreover, introduces precisely those themes that become important later on—that is, keeping the mouth bound up and closed, not lying, and above all, silence. Then we move on to silence concerning creation—that is, not admitting that what God worked with was garbage.

Let us now try to see both units as forming a single, continuous statement. What we have is a cogent and pointed statement, beginning, middle, and end. If we go back to I:I, moreover, we see that the philological exercise, with its interest in the meanings of "tutor, covered over and hidden," moves us right to the direction the author wants us to take. That is, he is interested in making the point that God looked into the Torah and made the world, so the Torah contains the secrets of creation. Then I:V makes the further point, surely deliberate and in the right order, that the secrets of creation, as the Torah contains them, are not to be spelled out. So before us, thus far, is a remarkably cogent composition, making a single point through the selection and organization of distinct materials. May we say that the things chosen themselves have been written for the present purpose? That question does not carry a self-evident answer. We do not have a verse-by-verse exposition. Instead we have discursive essays, taking up such questions as meanings of words and propositions of a philosophical order.

So if this is a commentary, it is a different sort of commentary from the sort of verse-by-verse, phrase-by-phrase exercise in exposition, analysis, and secondary expansion, that we might have anticipated. The text finds its meaning in the association of whole units of thought with individual verses, and these units of thought concern themes or topics, not merely meanings of words or phrases (though on the surface the philological interest proves paramount). Did the compositors of the whole also make up the several units? That we cannot now say. In later passages we shall see strong evidence that the compositors chose from available materials, not making them up, and revising them only in superficial ways. In the present passage it does appear that the one who proposed to put together a sequence of expository passages on the opening verses of Genesis also made up the passages at hand. Why so? Because, despite the original impression of prolixity and diversity, in fact the composition hangs together so cogently as it does only because it depends for sense and deep meaning on the base verse itself(!). Out of contact with the statement, "In the beginning God created . . . ," the two compositions—both I:I and I:V—make little sense. If that reading of the whole is sound, then we are in the hands of remarkably subtle and brilliant authors, not merely redactors, selectors, compositors, and the like. And the nature of the authorship, the mode of creativity—these will not prove at all simple to uncover and define.

Then who speaks through the book before us? I hear two different voices, first, the voice of the author of the paragraph; second, the voice of the one who selected the paragraph and put it in the document, so speaking through the paragraph but not in it. It is as if you determined to write a book by selecting paragraphs from letters you have received. Your book would have two voices, the voice of your correspondents, and, as the one who selected and arranged their messages, your voice too. It is like the place of the artist in creating a collage. The artist does not create the materials, but the artist sees and conveys the message. So Genesis Rabbah speaks through selection and arrangement, and also through what is chosen.

That is why, for our part, when we want to know from whom we hear in this book, we turn first of all to the people who made the choices and arranged the book's materials as we now have them. We do not know who wrote the paragraphs before us, where, when, or why someone composed them as we have them. But we do have the document itself, and the document as a matter of fact accurately represents the selection and arrangement of the writings—therefore the mind and imagination of those who made the selections and accomplished their arrangement.

Let me generalize on the two passages we have read and ask, how, exactly, does Genesis Rabbah work? Various verses of scripture come to illuminate one another. A favorite exercise of our sages is to draw upon one verse to tell us the meaning of an entirely distinct and separate passage. For example, in many passages we shall begin with a verse from one of the prophetic books or the writings and only then work our way back to the verse of the book of Genesis that concerns us. This effort to see one verse in light of another provides a model of the mind of the sages. They see one verse in light of another because they are used to seeing one thing in light of another, today in the aspect of yesterday and tomorrow, one of the patriarchs in the aspect of Israel, the Jewish people, embodied in that man's life and times. The principal mode of thinking demonstrated here requires us to look deeply at something, for, in the depths, we find something else, as each thing stands for another, and all things possess a potentiality of meaning never close to the surface, always in the depths. To explain too much diminishes the surprise of what is to come. Following these three points— expecting to see many verses amassed in the inquiry into a given proposition, prepared to take note of diverse opinions and the names of the important authorities, above all ready to loose the bonds of our imagination so that we can see many things in one thing—we shall do well in the wonderful work at hand.

Part One

BERESHIT:
Genesis Rabbah
Parashiyyot I–XXIX

1 Creation

God Looked into the Torah and Created the World

What Did God Find in the Torah?

"Creationists," who hold that the book of Genesis reports exactly what happened when God made the world, claim to report the fundamental message of scripture. Our sages, by contrast, advance the same claim but produce a different message. They take the view that the importance of the Torah's account of creation is to establish the credentials of the Torah itself. They ask, how do we know how the world was created? They answer, because the Torah tells us. And what is it that the Torah tells us? The story of creation. How, further, did God know how to create the world? Because God looked into the Torah. So the upshot? Humanity knows about creation because the Torah reports it. The message readers find in Gen. 1:1 is this: God looked into the Torah and created the world. What follows for them—and I think, for us too—is this. We too can find in the Torah the principles of being. On to our first encounter.

I:I.1.A. "In the beginning God created" (Gen. 1:1):

B. R. Oshaia commenced [discourse by citing the following verse:] "Then I was beside him like a little child, and I was daily his delight [rejoicing before him always, rejoicing in his inhabited world, and delighting in the sons of men]" (Prov. 8:30–31).

C. "The word for 'child' uses consonants that may also stand for 'teacher,' 'cover over,' and 'hidden away.'

D. "Some hold that the word also means 'great.'

E. "The word means 'teacher,' in line with the following: 'As a teacher carries the suckling child' (Num. 11:12).

F. "The word means 'covered over,' as in the following: 'Those who were covered over in scarlet' (Lam. 4:5).

G. "The word means 'hidden,' as in the verse, 'And he hid Hadassah' (Est. 2:7).

H. "The word means 'great,' in line with the verse, 'Are you better than No-Ammon?' (Nah. 3:8). This we translate, 'Are you better than Alexandria the Great, which is located between rivers.' "

2.A. Another matter:

B. The word means "work plan."

C. [In the cited verse] the Torah speaks, "I was the work plan of the Holy One, blessed be he."

D. In the accepted practice of the world, when a mortal king builds a palace, he does not build it out of his own head, but he follows a work plan.

E. And [the one who supplies] the work plan does not build out of his own head, but he has designs and diagrams, so as to know how to situate the rooms and the doorways.

F. Thus the Holy One, blessed be he, consulted the Torah when he created the world.

G. So the Torah stated, "By means of 'the beginning' [that is to say, the Torah] did God create" (Gen. 1:1).

H. And the word for "beginning" refers only to the Torah, as scripture says, "The Lord made me as the beginning of his way" (Prov. 8:22).

Let us begin by noticing a literary matter, then turning to the substance of the passage. We start with two verses, Gen. 1:1, as we expect. But then we have another verse, Prov. 8:30–31. What is the meaning of that other reference? What the sage proposes to do here is read one verse in the light of another, just as, many times over, our sages will read one situation—that of our own day—in light of another, that of the patriarchs' and matriarchs' day. So in a literary form the same mode of seeing the world emerges: we read one verse in light of another, and we work our way through the interpretation of the language of that verse, in no. 1, prior to making the point we wish to make, which is at no. 2.

When we speak of what is fundamental in our encounter with the Torah, we do well to listen to our sages. What is it that we find in the Torah? Our sages do not refer to the physics of creation, or the chemistry of the making of woman and man. They refer to the purpose of creation, later on finding the principle of humanity as representing God's likeness, in God's image. Those convictions about the holiness of creation and ultimate human value demand credence. And they form the message and define the meaning of scripture's account of the creation of the world.

There Are Things We Shall Never Know about Creation

What precisely does the scriptural picture of creation tell us? It is that the world came from the raw materials round about us. We see chaos and disorder. God worked with chaos and disorder. We see formlessness, void, emptiness. These traits of human existence served God in making the wonder of wonders, the world itself. And we, like God, can make use of what is empty and formless and void—a lesson yet to be learned.

I:V.1.A. R. Huna in the name of Bar Qappara commenced [discourse by citing the following verse]: "Let the lying lips be made dumb matters kept secret [that is, lips which arrogantly speak against the righteous things that should not be revealed]" (Ps. 31:19).

B. "Translating the Hebrew word for dumb into Aramaic one may use words meaning] 'bound,' 'made dumb,' or 'silenced.'

C. " 'Let [the lying lips] be bound,' as in the following verse: 'For behold, we were binding sheaves' (Gen. 37:7).

D. " 'Let the lying lips be made dumb,' as in the usage in this verse: 'Or who made a man dumb' (Ex. 4:11).

E. " 'Let them be silenced' bears the obvious meaning of the word.

F. " 'Which arrogantly speak matters kept secret against the righteous' (Ps. 31:19):

G. " '. . . which speak against the Righteous,' the Life of the Ages, matters that he kept secret from his creatures [Freedman: the mysteries of creation].

H. " 'With pride' (Ps. 31:19):

I. That is so as to take pride, saying, 'I shall expound the work of creation.'

J. " 'And contempt' (Ps. 31:19): Such a one treats with contempt the honor owing to me.

K. For R. Yose b. R. Hanina said, "Whoever gains honor through the humiliation of his fellow gains no share in the world to come.

L. "For one does so through the honor owing to the Holy One, blessed be he, how much the more so!"

M. And what is written after the cited verse [Ps. 31:19]?

N. " 'How abundant is your goodness, which you have stored away for those who revere you' (Ps. 31:20).

O. Rab said, 'Let one [who reveals the mysteries of creation] not have any share in your abundant goodness.'

P. "Under ordinary circumstances, if a mortal king builds a palace in a place where there had been sewers, garbage, and junk, will not whoever may come and say, 'This palace is built on a place where there were sewers, garbage and junk,' give offense? So too, will not whoever comes and says, 'This world was created out of chaos, emptiness, and darkness' give offense?

Q. R. Huna in the name of Bar Qappara: "Were the matter not explicitly written in scripture, it would not be possible to state it at all: 'God created heaven and earth' (Gen. 1:1)—from what? From the following: 'And the earth was chaos' (Gen. 1:2). [Freedman: God first created chaos and emptiness, and out of these he created the world, but this is not to be taught publicly.]"

God in the Torah reveals only part of the whole truth about creation. There are parts to be kept concealed. There are things about which one must not speak, hence, in the repertoire of meanings attributed to the key word—be dumb—the important one is "silenced." The continuation of the same verse carries forward the same idea—namely, that one should not speak arrogantly against the righteous, meaning God. The combination of the two ideas is then clear. That is, it is arrogant to expound the works of creation, and these are matters about which one must remain silent. There are matters one must not call to mind. Why not? The secret of creation follows. It is stunning and fresh, yet fully prepared: one could not say about creation what scripture itself says. That is that the world began unformed and void. Keeping the mouth bound up and closed, not lying, and above all, silence are required. But not for the reason you would expect. Silence concerning creation means not admitting that what God worked with was garbage. "What is humanity that you are mindful of us" indeed.

God's Record of Creation is True: Only One God Made the World

Our sages speak not about our time, which they could never have imagined. They address issues about their own day. Here we see how they did so—and how they give us a model for ourselves. Specifically, in their day they confronted people who maintained that creation had been botched. Then, these same people maintained, the God who created the world was incompetent, foolish, evil. There must, then, be a God we cannot or do not know, at least, not from the record of the Torah, a God above the world, an unknown God, who rules, but who is not revealed. That is the God to be worshiped. Our sages rejected this view. They did so in countless ways. One of them was to celebrate creation. Another was to prove, systematically, that the basic notion of two dominions, one subject to the creator-God, the other subject to the unknown God, is wrong. So scripture indeed formed the battleground. Through systematic study of scripture our sages proved the truth. That is because they and the ones with whom they argued shared scripture as a body of fact. In our own day we have to draw upon scriptures of a greater variety, including scriptures of science and philosophy. But our sages held the same: the seal of God is truth, Torah encompasses all truth.

I.VII.1.A. R. Isaac commenced [discourse by citing the following verse]: " 'The beginning of your word is truth [and all your righteous ordinance endures forever]' (Ps. 119:16)."

B. Said R. Isaac [about the cited verse], "From the beginning of the creation of the world, 'The beginning of your word was truth.'

C. " 'In the beginning God created' (Gen. 1:1).

D. " 'And the Lord God is truth' (Jer. 10:9).

E. "Therefore: 'And all your righteous ordinance endures forever' (Ps. 119:16).

F. "For as to every single decree which you lay down for your creatures, they accept that degree as righteous and receive it in good faith, so that no creature may differ, saying, 'Two powers gave the Torah, two powers created the world.'

G. "[Why not?] Because here it is not written, 'And gods spoke,' but rather, 'And God spoke' (Ex. 20:1).

H. " 'In the beginning [gods] created is not written, but rather, 'in the beginning [God] created' [in the singular]."

What we have is a proposition proved by argument based on facts, that there are not two gods or two dominions. What then is the role of the verse of scripture here? Our base verse, that is, the verse cited from Genesis, supplies a fact for the proof of that syllogism. Then there is another, a second verse. It is the one that is cited along with the verse of Genesis that is subject to discussion. I call this "the intersecting verse." The interest is in a proposition, namely, that matters are so formulated as to give the lie to those who hold there are two powers or dominions. That is proven by a number of verses—for example, Ex. 20:1, and not only by Gen. 1:1. The purpose then is to make the theological point that is expressed, namely, to prove that there is only a single dominion.

The Place of Israel in Creation

Our sages speak always to and for Israel, the Jewish people. The Torah came from God through Moses to Israel. So the passage of scripture—so our sages maintain—does not ignore what is the main topic always and everywhere. That is Israel. It must follow that everything in the Torah will tell us something important for Israel. Is this the case even when we learn about the very beginnings of the world? It indeed is true even here.

I.II.1.A. R. Joshua of Sikhnin in the name of R. Levi commenced [discourse by citing the following verse]: " 'He has declared to his people the power of his works, in giving them the heritage of the nations' (Ps. 111:6).

B. "What is the reason that the Holy One, blessed be he, revealed to Israel what was created on the first day and what on the second?

C. "It was on account of the nations of the world. It was so that they should not ridicule the Israelites, saying to them, 'Are you not a nation of robbers [having stolen the land from the Canaanites]?'

D. "It allows the Israelites to answer them, 'And as to you, is there no spoil in your hands? For surely: "The Caphtorim, who came forth out of Caphtor, destroyed them and dwelled in their place" (Deut. 2:23)!'

E. " 'The world and everything in it belongs to the Holy One, blessed be he. When he wanted, he gave it to you, and when he wanted, he took it from you and gave it to us.'

F. "That is in line with what is written, '. . . in giving them the heritage of the nations, he has declared to his people the power of his works' (Ps. 111:6). [So as to give them the land, he established his right to do so by informing them that he had created it.]

G. "He told them about the beginning: 'In the beginning God created . . .' (Gen. 1:1)."

What does the creation story tell us? It answers Israel's question: What right have we to the land? The answer is that God made the world, and told humanity about creation so as to establish God's right to give the world to whom God willed. And that small pocket of earth God gave to Israel, God had the right to give—for God made it all. The purpose of the passage is to demonstrate Israel's right to the land. The point at hand is that God informed Israel of his power (Ps. 111:6) so as to give them a valid claim on the land of Israel. Then Gen. 1:1 is cited only to validate the claim at hand, so the joining of Ps. 111:6 to Gen. 1:1 is for the purpose of expounding the principle of divine ownership of the land—that is, Israel's valid claim— and not the meaning of either verse. Once again we see that scripture supplies facts, as much as, today, science and philosophy and history supply facts. The purpose of these facts is to allow us to demonstrate propositions and learn more about the rules by which, in creation and in history, we are governed. So in that sense our sages read scripture the way scientists read nature.

God Made the World for Israel

The story of creation concerns Israel in yet another way. Sages' view of Israel transcends all imagining. They see Israel as holy, the climax of humanity. When you consider the state of Israel in their day—a defeated and brokenhearted nation, its Torah taken over by a triumphant sibling—you must find extraordinary the act of faith, hope, and fantasy taken in what follows. Yet that act of faith and fantasy will appear well founded, when you think about the further fact that we are here—despite it all, after all that has happened. So maybe our sages are right—at least about what we may become.

I.IV.1.A. ["In the beginning God created" (Gen. 1:1):] Six things came before the creation of the world, some created, some at least considered as candidates for creation.

B. The Torah and the throne of glory were created [before the creation of the world].

C. The Torah, as it is written, "The Lord made me as the beginning of his way, prior to his works of old" (Prov. 8:22).

D. The throne of glory, as it is written, "Your throne is established of old" (Ps. 93:2).

E. The patriarchs were considered as candidates for creation, as it is written, "I saw your fathers as the first-ripe in the fig tree at her first season" (Hos. 9:10).

F. Israel was considered [as a candidate for creation], as it is written, "Remember your congregation, which you got aforetime" (Ps. 74:2).

G. The temple was considered [as a candidate for creation], as it is written, "You, throne of glory, on high from the beginning, the place of our sanctuary" (Jer. 17:12).

H. The name of the Messiah was kept in mind, as it is written, "His name exists before the sun" (Ps. 72:17).

I. R. Ahbah bar Zeira said, "Also [the power of] repentance.

J. "That is in line with the following verse of Scripture: 'Before the mountains were brought forth' (Ps. 90:2). From that hour: 'You turn man to contrition and say, Repent, you children of men' (Ps. 90:3)."

K. Nonetheless, I do not know which of these came first, that is, whether the Torah was prior to the throne of glory, or the throne of glory to the Torah.

L. Said R. Abba bar Kahana, "The Torah came first, prior to the throne of glory.

M. "For it is said, 'The Lord made me as the beginning of his way, before his works of old' (Prov. 8:22).

N. "It came prior to that concerning which it is written, 'For your throne is established of old' (Ps. 93:2)."

2.A. R. Huna, R. Jeremiah in the name of R. Samuel b. R. Isaac: "Intention concerning the creation of Israel came before all else.

B. "The matter may be compared to the case of a king who married a noble lady but had no son with her. One time the king turned up in the marketplace, saying, 'Buy this ink, inkwell, and pen on account of my son.'

C. "People said, 'He has no son. Why does he need ink, inkwell, and pen?'

D. "But then people went and said, 'The king is an astrologer, so he sees into the future and he therefore is expecting to produce a son!'

E. "Along these same lines, if the Holy One, blessed be he, had not foreseen that, after twenty-six generations, the Israelites would be destined to accept the Torah, he would never have written in it, 'Command the children of Israel.' [This proves that God foresaw Israel and created the world on that account.]"

3.A. Said. R. Benaiah, "The world and everything in it were created only on account of the merit of the Torah.

33

B. " 'The Lord for the sake of wisdom [Torah] founded the earth' (Prov. 3:19)."

C. R. Berekiah said, "It was for the merit of Moses.

D. " 'And he saw the beginning for himself, for there a portion of a ruler [Moses] was reserved' (Deut. 33:21)."

4.A. R. Huna in the name of Rab repeated [the following]: "For the merit of three things was the world created, for the merit of dough offerings, tithes, and firstfruits.

B. "For it is said [translating Gen. 1:1 in a new way], 'On account of [the merit of] what is first, God created . . .' (Gen. 1:1).

C. "And the word 'first' refers only to dough offering, for it is written, 'Of the first of your dough' (Num. 15:20).

D. "The same word refers to tithes, as it is written, 'The first fruits of your grain' (Deut. 18:4).

E. "And the word 'first' refers to firstfruits, for it is written, 'The choicest of your land's firstfruit' (Ex. 23:19)."

The power of the exposition is to forge a link between the natural world of creation and the historical world of Israel, its life and salvation. The world was created because of Israel. That simple proposition lays down a judgment that will lead the exegete to join details of creation and of the stories of the patriarchs to details of the history of Israel, with the ultimate effect of showing the correspondence between Israel's salvific existence and the natural order of the world. We begin with the necessary catalogue of the six things and proceed at no. 2 to a secondary exposition of the same matter. Then we introduce creation for the sake of the Torah, followed by a complementary proposition on other things for the sake of which the world was created. Here is the point at which Gen. 1:1 serves as a proof-text. No. 4 is an autonomous unit, built on the notion that wherever we find the word "first/beginning," we have reference to the proposition before us.

All Creation Points toward Israel

The claim that creation aims at Israel takes shape in very specific points of correspondence between the story of creation

and the history of Israel. Our sages did not argue about generalizations, like philosophers. Nor did they merely record things
that happened, like historians. They looked for the laws of history, the generalizations emerging from the particulars of the
past, much the way social scientists look for the general in the
particular. So the mere statement of their proposition, which we
saw earlier, demands much more specific proof. That is what
we now find.

II:III.1.A. ["And the earth was unformed . . ." (Gen.
1:2):]

B. R. Judah b. R. Simon interpreted the verse as referring to coming generations, [as follows]:

C. " 'The earth was unformed' refers to Adam, who was
[Freedman:] reduced to complete nothingness [on account of
his sin].

D. " 'And void' refers to Cain, who sought to return the
world to unformedness and void.

E. " 'And darkness was upon the face of the deep'
(Gen. 1:2) refers to the generation of Enosh: 'And their works
are in the dark' (Is. 29:15).

F. " 'Upon the face of the deep' (Gen. 1:2) refers to the
generation of the flood: 'On the same day were all the fountains of the great deep broken up' (Gen. 7:11).

G. " 'And the spirit of God hovered over the face of the
water' (Gen. 1:2): 'And God made a wind pass over the earth'
(Gen. 8:1).

H. "Said the Holy One, blessed be he, 'For how long
will the world make its way in darkness. Let light come?'

I. "And God said, 'Let there be light' (Gen. 1:3). This
refers to Abraham. That is in line with the following verse of
scripture: 'Who has raised up one from the earth, whom he
calls in righteousness to his foot' (Is. 41:23).

J. " 'And God called the light day' (Gen. 1:3) refers to
Jacob.

K. " 'And the darkness he called night' (Gen. 1:30)
refers to Esau.

L. " 'And there was evening' refers to Esau.

M. " 'And there was morning' refers to Jacob.

N. " 'One day'—for the Holy One, blessed be he, gave him one day, and what is that day? It is the Day of Atonement. [Freedman, p.17, n.1: It is the one day over which Satan, symbolizing the wickedness of Esau, has no power.]"

II:IV.1.A. R. Simeon b. Laqish interpreted the verses at hand to speak of the empires [of the historical age to come].

B. " 'The earth was unformed' refers to Babylonia, 'I beheld the earth and lo, it was unformed' (Jer. 4:23).

C. " 'And void' refers to Media: 'They hastened [using the letters of the same root as the word for 'void'] to bring Haman' (Est. 6:14).

D. " 'Darkness' refers to Greece, which clouded the vision of the Israelites through its decrees, for it said to Israel, 'Write on the horn of an ox [as a public proclamation for all to see] that you have no portion in the God of Israel.'

E. " '. . . upon the face of the deep' refers to the wicked kingdom [of Rome].

F. "Just as the deep surpasses investigation, so the wicked kingdom surpasses investigation.

G. " 'And the spirit of God hovers' refers to the spirit of the Messiah, in line with the following verse of Scripture: 'And the spirit of the Lord shall rest upon him' (Is. 11:2)."

2.A. On account of what merit will the Messiah come? [It will be on account of the merit represented by the verse:] ". . . over the face of the water" (Gen. 1:2).

B. It is, specifically, on account of the merit of repentance, which is compared to water: "Pour out your heart like water" (Lam. 2:19).

3.A. R. Haggai in the name of R. Pedat: "There was a covenant made with the water, that even in the time of intense heat, a breeze will hover over it."

How should we enter into the mode of thought of our sages? Can we turn their way of reading scripture to our own task? We can, if we look at the world for the evidences of God's work, and look to scripture for propositions demanding testing and analysis. But sages begin from conviction, and so must we.

They start with the fundamental certainty that the Torah speaks about Israel. Then they go in search, in scripture, of how the story of creation finds its counterpart in the history of Israel. That is the method, the mode of thought, we see before us. Sages follow a single, cogent path of discourse, linking each of the elements of the set of verses of Genesis to other biblical figures, associated with proof-texts. So Genesis speaks of persons to come later on. Heroic or evil figures who will occur are prefigured in the elements of creation, a stunning point. It is one that we shall see many times, because the purpose of putting together Genesis Rabbah comes to expression each time our sages make that point in a specific way. Time and again the compositors introduce materials to prove that there is a close correspondence between the creation of the world and the history of Israel, or, later on, between the lives and deeds of the patriarchs and the salvation of Israel in history and at the end of time. The passage to follow takes up the same mode of interpretation—namely, reading the verse at hand in the light of other biblical passages and figures.

The next sizable composition, II:IV.1, carries forward the exegetical procedure of the foregoing entry, taking up parts of the verse at hand and assigning them to elements of a historical character. What is happening in both passages is an interest in finding the historical, human points of correspondence to the components of nature that are at issue. We move from creation to the patriarchs to the history of Israel, a complete account of the three components of time at hand. We have left out only one critical component of all being, which is the Torah. To that we now turn.

Creation and Torah: Torah and Light

The creation of light prefigures the creation of the Torah. That simple proposition completes the fundamental rereading of the story of creation accomplished by our sages.

III:V.1.A. Said R. Simon, "The word 'light' is written five times [in the same verse], to match [the five] books of his Torah.

B.   "And God said, 'Let there be light' (Gen. 1:3) matches the book of Genesis, in which the Holy One, blessed be he, was engaged when he created the world.

C.   " 'And there was light' matches the book of Exodus, which begins, 'These are the names,' in which Israel went forth from Egypt, from darkness to light.

D.   " 'And God saw the light' matches the book of Leviticus, which is rich in rules.

E.   " 'And God divided the light' matches the book of Numbers, in which God divided those who had come forth from Egypt apart from those who would enter the land.

F.   " 'And God called the light' matches the book of Deuteronomy, which is rich in many laws."

G.   They objected to him, "But is not the book of Leviticus also filled with many laws?"

H.   He said to them, "[The verse refers only to Deuteronomy, for the verse itself contains] a repetition [just as there is in the book of Deuteronomy]: '*And* God called the light day'! Now is not the light the same thing as the day?! [Of course it is.]" [Freedman: Hence it is fitting that this verse should correspond to Deuteronomy, which also contains much repetition of the previous books.]

The point of interpretation yields yet another link between the story of creation and the larger setting, the Torah as a whole, in which that story is found. So the details of the story correspond to the main frame of the Torah. The result? Creation corresponds to the Torah, and, of greater polemical weight, the Torah corresponds to creation. The upshot is that the Torah is comparable, in detail, to light. What follows is that mastery of the Torah will permit us to penetrate into the mysteries of creation. But these already present themselves to us, as we have seen. Our sages leave little to the imagination—because they wish to give us a model for the use of our imagination. In what follows they carry forward in a very concrete way the spelling out of the conviction that the Torah presents us with the story of how God made the world. The Torah's very words, the letters of which words are made, contain the method of creation.

How Exactly Did God Make the World?
With Words, With Letters That Make Words

When our sages ask the question of detail—just exactly what did God do when God made the world, What did God use?—they turn to the bed-rock of truth. There can be no truth that is not said with words. So words convey truth. Words are made of letters. So at the bedrock of creation— the thing with which God made the world—we find letters. This appeal to the alphabet as the container of the rules of creation, the laws of life, should not surprise us. First of all, the stress of Genesis is on God's saying things. God said this and such-and-so came into being. God is called "the one who spoke and brought the world into being." So the natural next step is to appeal to the power of words. And, from that point, the focus on the traits of particular letters, of the Hebrew alphabet of course, proves entirely reasonable. We too create worlds with words, so we should not be surprised that God did. If you doubt it, reflect on the power to create evil contained within a mean statement to someone you love—or hate.

I.X.1.A. ["In the beginning God created" (Gen. 1:1):] R. Jonah in the name of R. Levi: "Why was the world created with [a word beginning with the letter] B?

B. "Just as [in Hebrew] the letter B is closed [at the back and sides but] open in front, so you have no right to expound concerning what is above or below, before or afterward."

C. Bar Qappara said, " 'For ask now of the days past which were before you, since the day that God created man upon the earth' (Deut. 4:32).

D. "Concerning the day *after* which days were created, you may expound, but you may not make an exposition concerning what lies before then.

E. " 'And from one end of the heaven to the other' (Deut. 4:32).

F. "[Concerning that space] you may conduct an investigation, but you may not conduct an investigation concerning what lies beyond those points."

G.   R. Judah b. Pazzi gave his exposition concerning the story of creation in accord with this rule of Bar Qappara.

2.A.   Why with a B?

B.   To tell you that there are two ages [this age and the age to come, for the letter B bears the numerical value of two].

3.A.   Another matter: Why was the world created [with a word beginning with the letter] B?

B.   Because that is the letter that begins the word for blessing.

C.   And why not with an A?

D.   Because that is the first letter of the Hebrew word for curse.

4.A.   Another matter: Why not with an A?

B.   So as not to give an opening to the *minim* [people who claim that there are two domains, one ruled by the creator-God, another ruled by an unknown God; the one an evil, the other a beneficent, divinity] to claim, "How can the world endure, when it has been created with a word meaning curse!"

C.   Rather, said the Holy One, blessed be he, "Lo, I shall write it with a letter standing for the word 'blessing,' and may the world endure!"

5.A.   Another matter: Why with a B?

B.   Because the letter B has two points, one pointing upward, the other backward, so that [if] people say to it, "Who created you?" it will point upward.

C.   It is as if to say, "This one who is above has created me."

D.   "And what is his name?" And it points for them with its point backward: "The Lord *[Adonai]* is his name" [pointing to the first letter in the alphabet, backward from the second, which is the A, standing for the One].

6.A.   R. Eleazar bar Abinah in the name of R. Aha: "For twenty-six generations the letter A made complaint before the Holy One, blessed be he, saying to him, 'Lord of the world! I am the first among all the letters of the alphabet, yet you did not create your world by starting with me!'

B. "Said the Holy One, blessed be he, to the A, 'The world and everything in it has been created only through the merit of the Torah. Tomorrow I am going to come and give my Torah at Sinai, and I shall begin [the Ten Commandments] only with you: "I [beginning with the A] am the Lord your God" (Ex. 20:1).' "

7.A. Bar Hutah said, "Why is it called *'alef?* Because that is the word for a thousand: 'The word which he commanded for a thousand *[elef]* generations' (Ps. 105:8)."

The sequence of points about creation now can stand review. First, one must not speculate on matters not revealed in the Torah, a familiar theme. God reveals what God wants humanity to know. Second, the world is created for blessing, not for curse. There is no evil creator, exceeded by a benevolent but unknown God. The good creator made the world and has told humanity why. Israel in the Torah knows the answer: a whole and complete system, Judaism all in the opening phrases of the story of creation.

Creation out of Nothing?

So much for our sages' address to Israel. But what about discourse with the world beyond? One important argument for the existence of God, as framed by philosophers of religion, relies upon the claim that God created the world out of nothing. It is an appeal to first things.

I.IX.1.A. A philosopher challenged Rabban Gamaliel, saying to him, "Your God was indeed a great artist, but he had good materials to help him."

B. He said to him, "What are they?"

C. He said to him, "Unformed [space], void, darkness, water, wind, and the deep."

D. He said to him, "May the spirit of that man [you] burst! All of them are explicitly described as having been created by him [and not as preexistent].

E. "Unformed space and void: 'I make peace and create evil' (Is. 45:7).

F. "Darkness: 'I form light and create darkness' (Is. 45:7).

G. "Water: 'Praise him, you heavens of heavens, and you waters that are above the heavens' (Ps. 148:4). Why? 'For he commanded and they were created' (Ps. 148:5).

H. "Wind: 'for lo, he who forms the mountains creates the wind' (Amos 4:13).

I. "The depths: 'When there were no depths, I was brought forth' (Prov. 8:24)."

We have already noticed that our sages do not regard as true or at least as important the proposition that before creation there was nothing. Nonetheless, in dealing with the world of philosophy, as the following passage indicates, our sages did take up that matter. They knew how to argue with Epicurean philosophers (the "unbelievers" or *apikorsim* of which we hear in the Sayings of the Founders, Pirke Avot).

Creation and Morality

Our sages carry forward the prophets' point of insistence. What matters above all is morality. We are what we do. God judges us by our deeds. Accordingly, when they explain the meaning and message of creation, our sages investigate the question of how the very ground of being, the creation of the world, relates to the rules of goodness and right by which we are to live. At this point in our encounter with our sages, we already know what they will say. It is that the creation of the world serves to confirm the rules that govern right deeds.

III:VIII.1.A. Said R. Yannai, "At the beginning of the creation of the world the Holy One, blessed be he, foresaw the deeds of the righteous and the deeds of the wicked.

B. " 'And the earth was unformed and void' refers to the deeds of the wicked.

C. " 'And God said, 'Let there be light' refers to the deeds of the righteous.

D. " 'And God saw the light, that it was good,' refers to the deeds of the righteous.

E. " 'And God divided between the light and the darkness' means [he divided] between the deeds of the righteous and the deeds of the wicked.

F. " 'And God called the light day' refers to the deeds of the righteous.

G. " 'And the darkness he called night' refers to the deeds of the wicked.

H. " 'And there was evening' refers to the deeds of the wicked.

I. " 'And there was morning' refers to the deeds of righteous.

J. " 'One day,' for the Holy One, blessed be he, gave them one day [and what day is that]? It is the day of judgment."

2.A. ["One (unique) day" (Gen. 1:3):] Said R. Tanhum, "It was the day on which unique things were made, heaven, earth, and light."

B. Said R. Yudan, "[It was called 'one day'] because on that day, the Holy One, blessed be he, was truly unique in his world."

C. That view accords with the position of R. Yohanan and not with that of R. Hanina.

D. R. Yohanan said, "On the second day of creation, the angels were created. That is in line with this verse of Scripture: 'Who lays the beams of your upper chambers in the waters,' and it is further written, '. . . who makes spirits, your angels' (Ps. 104:3–4)."

E. R. Hanina said, "The angels were created on the fifth day: 'And let fowl fly above the earth' (Gen. 1:20), and it is written, 'And with two [wings] did the angel fly' (Is. 6:2)."

3.A. R. Luliani bar Tabari in the name of R. Isaac: "Both R. Hanina and R. Yohanan concur that nothing whatsoever was created on the first day. It was so that you should not say, 'Michael was spreading out [the heaven] at the south of the firmament, and Gabriel at the north, with the Holy One, blessed be he, measuring from the middle.'

B. "Rather: 'I am the Lord who makes all things, who stretched out the heavens alone, who spread forth the earth by myself' (Is. 44:24).

C. " 'By myself' for who was with me? So it is written, meaning, 'Who was my partner in the creation of the world?' "

God made the world perfect and without blemish. What about wicked people? Do they not blemish creation? What about the suffering of the righteous? Does that testify to a perfect world? These two issues will always call into question the profoundly world-affirming attitude of our sages. How do they respond to these concerns, one which will never cease to trouble faithful Israel? There are several answers. First, where there are marks of imperfection, they will be removed at the end of days. Second, God knew what he was doing from the beginning, creating both good and evil, as the story of creation makes clear. When, therefore, will the perfection of creation come to full realization? On that "one day," the day of judgment. The basic reading of the creation story repeatedly uncovers this single point. It is a stunning mode of argument, based on a text all parties claim to contain the truth. The negative polemic addresses those who say God was not alone in creating the world. So at each point the exegetes address positions contrary to their own, and the compositors have selected what we must find to be cogent and coherent.

What Gives Testimony to the Truth of the Torah? Nature Itself

Since our sages repeatedly claim that God made the world and rules it, that the Torah reveals the rules that the world follows, the question at hand naturally demands attention. How do we know that our sages' view is true? Is the evidence only going to come from the Torah? The answer before us turns to nature itself. Natural law and the revealed truth of the Torah together testify to the same fact: God rules, the Torah and nature together tell us the natural laws by which God rules. First, sages demonstrate that nature itself obeys God's rules. So it is natural for all creation to carry out the purpose and will of the creator. This is only the beginning of the answer to the question at hand.

V:III.1.A. Said R. Levi, "The waters were saying to one another, 'Let us go and obey the command of the Holy One, blessed be he.'

B. "That is in line with the following verse of scripture: 'The floods have lifted up their voice' (Ps. 93:3).

C. "They said, 'Where shall we go?'

D. "Scripture says, 'Let the floods take up their roaring' (Ps. 93:3)". . . .

I. R. Eliezer says, "The sea drew them in, in line with this verse of scripture: 'Have you entered into the springs of the sea' (Job 38:16). The sense is, to the place of waters absorbed by the sea."

J. Our rabbis [explain the same usage] in this way, "[The waters say,] 'We are crushed, so receive us, we are crushed, so receive us.' "

2.A. Said R. Joshua b. R. Nehemiah, "The water climbed mountains and went down into the depths until it came to the ocean. That is in line with this verse of scripture: 'They ascended the mountains, descended into valleys, to the place which you have founded for them' (Ps. 104:8).

B. "What is this 'place that you have founded for them'?

C. "It is the ocean."

Both units deal with the gathering of the water in one place. The important issue for no. 1 is the interpretation of Ps. 93:3. The verse, providing the fact that the waters obeyed God and went where they were sent, then requires an appropriate explanation on its own. No. 2 makes the same point but provides its evidence from a different text. The point of the narrative important to the exegete-compositors, then, is the obedient faith of the waters in doing what God had told them to do.

What Gives Testimony to the Truth of the Torah? Nature Carries Out God's Will for Human History

The second stage in the important argument to prove that the Torah and the natural world attest to the same rules is simple. We now have to show that nature serves God's will even in respect to the history of humanity. In what follows we show how nature—water, in particular—did what God willed for humanity.

V:I.1.A. "And God said, 'Let the waters under the heaven be gathered together into one place and let the dry land appear' " (Gen. 1:9):

B. It is written, "At your rebuke they fled" (Ps. 104:7).

C. "And God said, 'Let the waters under the heaven be gathered together into one place' " (Gen. 1:9).

2.A. ["Let the waters be gathered together into one place" (Gen. 1:9):] R. Berekhiah in the name of R. Abba bar Yama: " 'Let there be a line set for the water,' in accord with this verse of scripture: 'And a line shall be stretched forth over Jerusalem' (Zech. 1:16). [Freedman, p. 34, n. 2: The letters of the word for 'let . . . be gathered' thus derive from the word for a measuring line and are to be translated: 'let the waters be confined to a definite measure of quantity.']

B. [Explaining the language for " 'be gathered together" differently] R. Abba bar Kahana in the name of R. Levi: 'Let the water be gathered together to me [that is, in the sense of the dative, for my purpose, so that] I may do with them what I plan in the future [specifically, the flood I shall make of the waters].'

C. "The matter may be compared to the case of a king who built a palace and gave residences in it to people who lacked the power of speech. They would get up in the morning and greet the king by making appropriate gestures with their fingers and with flag-signals. The king thought to himself, 'Now if these, who lack the power of speech, get up in the morning and greet me by means of gestures, using their fingers and flag-signals, if they had full powers of speech, how much the more so!'

D. "So the king gave residences in the palace to people possessed of full powers of speech. They got up and took possession of the palace [and seized it]. They said, 'This palace no longer belongs to the king. The palace now belongs to us!'

E. "Said the king, 'Let the palace revert to its original condition.'

F. "So too, from the very beginning of the creation of the world, praise for the Holy One, blessed be he, went upward only from water. That is in line with the verse of scripture which states, 'From the roar of many waters' (Ps. 93:4). And what praise did they proclaim? 'The Lord on high is mighty' (Ps. 93:4).

G. "Said the Holy One, blessed be he, 'Now if these [waters], which have neither mouth nor power of speech, so praise me, when mortals are created, how much the more so!'

H. "The generation of Enosh went and rebelled against him, the generation of the flood went and rebelled against him, the generation of the dispersion went and rebelled against him.

I. "The Holy One, blessed be he, said 'Let these be taken away and let those [that were here before, that is, the primeval waters] come back.'

J. "That is in line with the following verse of scripture: 'And the rain was upon the earth forty days and forty nights' (Gen. 7:12)."

When God told the waters what to do, they listened and obeyed. But when man received a commandment, he disobeyed. So we contrast the obedience of the one with the rebellion of the other. Then why was man punished by the waters of the flood? Because the obedient come to punish the disobedient. The main point contrasts the gathering together of the water, done so obediently, to the rebellion of man, punished by the flood. The parable then spells the matter out. The water was originally spread over the whole earth. The water praised God. So God drew the conclusion specified in the parable, and ordered the water to draw back into one place—hence Ps. 104:7. God's purpose was to provide dwelling space for humanity. But in light of the record of humanity, God called the water back and restored it to its place over the whole earth. So the intersecting verse—Zech. 1:16—generates a subtle interpretation of the base verse. That is the purpose of the gathering together of the water. This is given a critical place in the history of humanity, and, once more, creation is shown to prefigure humans history and destiny—a dimension of the text persistently discovered by the exegetes.

What Gives Testimony to the Truth of the Torah? Nature Itself Carries Out God's Will for Israel's History in Particular

From humanity in general, affected by nature in the flood, we come to Israel. Does nature serve God's will for Israel? Indeed so, the same water that destroyed humanity for its sin correspondingly saved Israel for its redemption. The picture is whole, complete, and encompassing.

V:V.1.A. Said R. Jonathan, "The Holy One, blessed be he, made a stipulation with the sea to split open before the Israelites.

B. "That is in line with this verse of Scripture: 'And the sea returned to its former strength,' which word may be read, 'in accord with the stipulation that it had been given' (Ex. 14:27)."

C. Said R. Jeremiah b. Eleazar, "It was not with the sea alone that the Holy One, blessed be he, made such a stipulation, but he made the same stipulation with everything that was created on the six days of creation.

D. "That is in line with this verse of Scripture: 'I, even my hands, have stretched out the heavens and all their host have I commanded' (Is. 45:12).

E. " 'I commanded' the sea to divide.

F. " 'I commanded' the heaven to be silent before Moses: "Give ear, heaven" (Deut. 32:1).

G. " 'I commanded' the sun and the moon to stand still before Joshua.

H. " 'I commanded' the ravens to bring food to Elijah.

I. " 'I commanded' the fire not to harm Hananiah, Mishael, and Azariah.

J. " 'I commanded' the lions not to harm Daniel, the heaven to open before Ezekiel, the fish to vomit up Jonah."

48

Once more we see the systematic effort to interrelate the story of creation with the history of Israel, so that there is a close correspondence between the natural world and the historical world of Israel. The repertoire of historical events of course is hardly random, since it lays emphasis upon moments at which Israel was saved. So the main point is that Israel will be saved by God's intervention into its history, just as the world was brought into existence through God's act of creating the world. I take the emphasis therefore to stress the power of God to do his will in the natural and in the historical world, but, in context, that power also takes form through the obedience of the water to God's word. Time and again Israel will be compared to dirt and to water, to indicate its virtue: submission and obedience. So the message is clear.

What Gives Testimony to the Truth of the Torah? Nature Carries Out God's Will for Israel's History in Particular. Natural Law, Historical Rule, and Sages' Own Day: Israel and Rome

Sages do not leave things in terms of generalities. Quite to the contrary, it is important to them to make specific and immediate exactly the message they find in scripture. The sun and the moon stand for Esau and Jacob, Rome and Israel. And in light of that fact, what do we learn for Israel from the story of the creation of the world?

VI:III.1.A. ["And God made the two great lights" (Gen. 1:16):] R. Tanhum, R. Phineas in the name of R. Simon: "Since [God] calls them 'great,' how is it possible that he then goes and diminishes [one of] them by saying, 'the great light and the lesser light' (Gen. 1:16)?

B. "It is because [the latter] entered the territory of its fellow. [The moon sometimes appears by day, not only by night.]"

2.A. Said R. Phineas, "In reference to all offerings, it is written, 'And a he-goat for a sin offering' (Num. 28:22, 29:5).

But with reference to the offering for the new month, it is written, 'A he-goat for a sin offering for the Lord' (Num. 28:15).

B. "[What sin has the Lord committed, that a he-goat has to be brought as a sin offering in behalf of the Lord?] Said the Holy One, blessed be he, 'I am the one who made him enter the territory of his fellow.'

C. "Now if this one entered the territory of his fellow with permission nonetheless is disparaged by scripture, one who enters the territory of his fellow without permission—how much the more so!"

3.A. R. Levi in the name of R. Yose b. R. Ilai: "It is merely natural that someone who now is great should count by what is great, and someone who now is small should count by what is small.

B. "Esau [Rome] counts by the sun, because it is great, while Jacob [Israel] counts by the moon, for it is small."

C. Said R. Nahman, "That really is a good omen. Esau counts by the sun, because it is great. But just as the sun rules by day but does not rule by night, so Esau will have something in this world but nothing in the world to come.

D. "Jacob counts by the moon, which is small, and just as the moon rules by night and also by day [making its appearance both by night and day], so too will Jacob have a portion in this world and in the world to come."

E. R. Nahman made a further statement on the same matter. R. Nahman said, "So long as the light of the great luminary lasts, the light of the lesser luminary is not going to be noted. Once the light of the great light sets, then, and only then, the light of the lesser one shines forth.

F. "So too, as long as the light of Esau lasts, the light of Jacob will not be seen. Once the light of Esau sets, then the light of Jacob will shine forth.

G. "That is in line with this verse: 'Arise, shine [for behold, darkness shall cover the earth, and gross darkness the peoples, but upon you the Lord will arise, and his glory shall be seen upon you]' (Is. 60:1)."

The point of course is that Rome now is great but in the age to come will be nothing, and Israel now has something but in the world to come will have everything. The compositors of our document persistently relate the creation of the world to the history of humanity and of Israel, and here too the analogy between creation and Israel is made explicit. Not only so, but a persistent point of emphasis will remind us that the very character of the natural world testifies to the coming redemption of Israel.

What Gives Testimony to the Truth of the Torah? Nature Carries Out God's Will. Natural Law, Historical Rule, and the Moral Condition of Humanity

Sages took for granted that the moral condition of humanity affected the historical standing of societies and the private destiny of individuals. They posited a correspondence between the laws of nature, the rules of history, and the conduct of individuals. So our picture of the full meaning of creation demands that we ask sages how they relate the sun and the moon not only to Israel's historical destiny and social life, but also to individual Israelites' lives in the here and now. For Jews live out their days as individuals, not only as Israel under the aspect of eternity.

VI:IX.1.A.   "And to rule over the day and the night" (Gen. 1:18):

B.   Said R. Hilpai, "If that statement bears upon the lights, has it not already been stated, 'The great light to rule' (Gen. 1:17)?

C.   "Why then does scripture say, 'and to rule by day and by night'?

D.   "The reference is to the righteous, who enjoy the power to rule over what is created to give light by day and to give light by night, in line with the following verse of scripture: 'And the sun stood still and the moon stayed. . . . Is not this written in the book of the upright' (Joshua 10:13)?"

E. What is this "book of the upright"?

F. R. Hilpai referred the passage to the verse at hand: "And to rule by day and by night" (Gen. 1:18).

G. R. Hanina in the name of R. Samuel bar Isaac assigned the reference to the end of the book [of Genesis]: " 'But his younger brother [Ephraim] shall be greater than he [Manasseh], and his seed shall become the fulness of nations' (Gen. 48:19). Is that truly possible? Rather, the cited verse refers to Joshua, who came forth from him, and who would hold the sun and the moon in their tracks, which rule over the world from one end to the other."

H. R. Hanina in the name of R. Samuel refers to the verse at the end of the Torah: " 'His firstling bullock, majesty is his, and his horns are the horns of the wild ox, with them he shall gore the peoples all of them, even the ends of the earth' (Deut. 33:17).

I. "Is such a thing truly possible? [Surely not!] Rather, the passage refers to Joshua, who would hold the sun and the moon in their tracks, which rule over the world from one end to the other."

2.A. Said R. Simeon b. Yohai, "The book of Deuteronomy was the ensign [Freedman] for Joshua. When the Holy One, blessed be he, came to reveal himself to Joshua, he found him sitting with the book of Deuteronomy in his hand. He said to him, 'Be strong, Joshua, be of good courage, Joshua. This book of the Torah [namely, Deuteronomy, the scroll you are holding] will not be removed from your mouth' (Joshua 1:8).

B. "[Joshua] took [the scroll of Deuteronomy] and showed it to the orb of the sun, saying to it, 'I never kept silent from this [scroll of the Torah, but recited its words continually], but you will keep silent before me. Forthwith: 'And the sun stood still' (Joshua 10:13)."

C. Said R. Isaac "[What he said was,] 'You are a bad servant. Were you not purchased by father's money? Did father [Joseph, from whom I descend] not see you in a dream: 'Lo, the sun and the moon and eleven stars bowed down to me' (Gen. 37:9)? Forthwith: 'And the sun stood still' (Joshua 10:13)."

Hilpai introduces the recurrent exercise of finding a counterpart in the history of Israel to events in the creation of the world. Once we agree that the verse at hand cannot refer to the natural process of creation, its point having been made in the preceding statement of the same passage, the process of finding the appropriate counterpart in Israel's history begins. That process then moves very rapidly to a point at which rule over the sun and the moon in the heaven becomes a center of narrative. Of course, the appropriate possibility will link the Torah book, hence Joshua (rather than Deborah) to the story of creation. The main point? It is the rule of the heavens by a master of the Torah.

The Perfection of Creation

Now we have followed our sages as they work their way through the story of the creation of the world. We turn to them for a final judgment on the whole. But in advance we know it. Our sages affirm the world, celebrate nature, find in Israel's destiny evidence for the natural course of events from the beginning of the world to the end of time. Once more we recall their situation. They saw the world ruled by gentiles, the empire fall into the hands of people who read the same Torah but understood it in quite a different way. They could point to no triumph for Israel, no worldly confirmation of their faith, no historical event to attest to the truth of the Torah. But if not in history, then in nature, and if not now, then at the end of days. That was their solution to the problem at hand. History in Rome's terms had led to what sages held to be a misreading of the meaning of history and salvation. So our sages turned from that history back to creation, and forward to redemption. Creation pointed toward the salvation of Israel at the end of days. But above all, creation—nature—through its very perfection attested to the truth of the Torah.

IX:II.1.A. R. Tanhuma opened [discourse by citing the following verse of Scripture]: "He has made everything beautiful in its time" (Qoh. 3:11).

B. Said R. Tanhuma, "The world was created at the proper time. The world was not ready to be created prior to this time." [God admired the works of creation because the world was brought into being when it was ripe. Hence what has attracted the exegete's attention, once again, is the question, What is it about the world that God found to be very good? The answer here is that the world was "beautiful in its time," the right one for God to create.]

2.A. Said R. Abbahu, "On the basis of the cited verse, we learn that the Holy One, blessed be he, had created worlds and destroyed them [as unsuccessful], until he created this world. He said, 'This one pleases me, the others did not please me.' "

B. Said R. Phineas, "The scriptural verse that supports R. Abbahu's view is this: 'And God saw all that he had made [and lo, it was very good].' (Gen. 1:31)."

We see two modes of making the same point, the one through the intersecting verse and the base verse, which we may call exegetical, the other syllogistic, joined with facts supplied by scripture to prove the point. It is the perfection of creation, the best of all creations, completed at just the right moment.

Once More: If Perfect, Why the Imperfection?

Again and again our attention moves from how we wish things to be to how they are. We have therefore to ask whether God really knew what was going to happen?

IX:III.1.A. ["And God saw all that he had made, and behold, it was very good" (Gen. 1:31):] R. Yohanan and R. Simeon b. Laqish:

B. R. Yohanan said, "A mortal king builds a palace, then he examines the upper floors in one inspection and the lower ones in another, but the Holy One, blessed be he, could take in both the upper floors and the lower floors in a single look." [Freedman, p. 65, n.1: interpreting "And God saw *everything* that he had made"—in a single glance.]

C. Said R. Simeon b. Laqish, " 'Lo, it was very good' refers to this world. *'And* lo, it was very good' [with the addition of *and*] encompasses the world to come. The Holy One, blessed be he, encompassed both of them with a single look."

2.A. R. Simeon b. Laqish in the name of R. Eleazar b. Azariah: " 'Oh, Lord God, behold, you have made the heaven and the earth' (Jer. 32:17). From that moment: 'There is nothing too hard for you.' (Jer. 32:17)."

B. R. Haggai in the name of R. Isaac, " 'And you, Solomon, my son, know the God of your father and serve him with a whole heart and with a willing mind, for the Lord searches all hearts and understands all the imaginations of the thoughts' (1 Chr. 28:9). [Taking the root of the word for 'imaginations,' YSR, which serves also as the root for the word 'form' or 'create,' we interpret as follows:] Before thought is formed in the heart of man, it already is revealed before you."

C. R. Yudan in the name of R. Isaac: "Before a creature is actually created, his thought is already revealed before you."

D. Said R. Yudan in his own name, " 'For there is not a word in my tongue but lo, O Lord, you know it altogether' (Ps. 139:4). Before my tongue forms speech, already 'lo, O Lord, you know it altogether.' "

Did God not know, prior to creation, whether what he would make would be any good? Is that why he had to look at it and declare it very good? The answer of course is that God knows before human creation precisely what mortals will go and do, all the more so before his own act of creation does he know the outcome of all things. If we look back at the sequence of propositions, what do we find? First, the mystery of creation is sealed and not to be revealed. Second, it is true that God made worlds before this one. But the reason is that only with the creation of this world did God know that the world he created was very good. God fully inspected this world and found it very good. God knew full well what he was doing when he undertook to create the world. If people maintained that the creator-God was an evil bungler, the present sequence would present a systematic reply. God not only did not bungle creation but knew precisely what he was doing from beginning to end. The reference to God's inspecting creation and finding it very good, then, contains no implication that God did not know what he was doing, since he knew full well from before creation precisely what he was doing.

The Perfection of Creation

(1): "O my world, my world! May you always charm me as you charm me at this hour!"

The world, God says, is "very good." How did God feel at that moment?

IX:IV.1.A. R. Hama bar Hanina and R. Jonathan:

B. R. Hama bar Hanina said, "The matter may be compared to the case of a king who built a palace. He saw it and it pleased him. He said, 'O palace, palace! May you always charm me as you charm me at this hour!' So said the Holy One, blessed be he, to his world, 'O my world, my world! May you always charm me as you charm me at this hour!' "

C. R. Jonathan said, "The matter may be compared to the case of a king who married off his daughter and arrayed for her a marriage canopy, a house, which he plastered, paneled, and painted. He saw [what he had made] and it pleased him. He said, 'O my daughter, my daughter, may this marriage canopy always charm me as it charms me at this hour.' So said the Holy One, blessed be he, to his world, 'O my world, my world! May you always charm me as you charm me at this hour.' "

The base verse here finds amplification in the parables of God's prayer when he found the world very good. The world-affirming statements fall into the larger program of argument outlined just now. Since later on God will destroy the world through the flood, the point assumes a certain poignancy.

The Perfection of the World

(2): "It is very Good"

Once more, what can God's judgment, "it was very good," possibly mean?

IX:XII.1.A. All rabbis say the following in the name of R. Haninah, R. Phineas, R. Hilqiah in the name of R. Simon: "The word 'very' and the word for man are written with the same consonants [M'D, 'DM, respectively]. The letters for both are the same.

B. "The meaning then is as follows: 'And God saw everything that he had made, and behold, it was very good' (Gen. 1:31)—and behold, man is good."

IX:XIII.1.A. Said R. Simeon b. Laqish, " 'Behold, it is very good' refers to the kingdom of heaven. '*And* behold, it is very good' encompasses the kingdom here on earth.

B. "And can anyone say that the kingdom here on earth is 'very good'?

C. "Rather, it exacts justice of mortals: 'I, even I, have made the earth and created man upon it' (Is. 45:12). [The word for 'man,' Adam, may be read, 'Edom,' which then refers to Rome. So the point is that God affirms the legitimacy of Rome, the earthly kingdom (Freedman, p. 70, n. 2). I think it not farfetched to discern a polemic, which is that Rome is legitimate when it exacts justice and not legitimate when it does not.]"

2.A. "And there was evening, and there was morning, the sixth day" (Gen. 1:31):

B. Said R. Yudan, "[The use of the definite article, 'the,' prior to the ordinal, 'sixth,' hence, '*the* sixth day,' serves] to encompass the additional hour that people add from the weekday to the holy time [by beginning their observance of the Sabbath one hour before sunset].

C. "And during that hour the work of making the world was completed."

3.A. "The sixth" (Gen. 1:31):

B. Said R. Simon, "Now came [Freedman:] a weakening of the creation. Hitherto world time was counted [the second day, third day], but now we count by a different reckoning [first, second, third day of the week]."

IX:XII introduces the climax. The crown of creation is humanity, in the text at hand, man, and when God praises creation, the intent focuses in the end upon humanity. The purpose of the whole then leads us to conclude that the human being is "very good." IX:XIII then draws the matter to a close. The heart of the *parashah* is the sustained and most effective exposition of the problem of evil in creation.

2 Man and Woman

All Creation Worked Together in Making Man and Woman

We move from our sages' fundamental reading of creation to their philosophy of humanity: Who is man, Who is woman? To begin with they confronted the simple statement, "Let us make man." To whom did God speak?

VIII:III.1.A. "And God said, 'Let us make man' " (Lev. 1:26):

B. With whom did he take counsel?

C. R. Joshua b. Levi said, "With the works of heaven and earth he took counsel.

D. "The matter may be compared to the case of a king who had two advisers, and he would do nothing without their express approval."

E. R. Samuel b. Nahman said, "It was with the things that he had created each prior day that he took counsel.

F. "The matter may be compared to the case of a king who had a privy counselor, and he would do nothing without his express approval."

G. R. Ammi said, "He took counsel with his own heart.

H. "The matter may be compared to the case of a king, who had a palace built by an architect. When he saw it, it did not please him. To whom could he then address his complaint? Would it not be to the architect? So too: 'And it grieved him in his heart' (Gen. 6:6)."

I. Said R. Yose, "The matter may be compared to the case of a king who conducted his affairs through a trust officer and incurred a loss. To whom should he address his complaint? Is it not to the trust officer? Accordingly: 'And it grieved him in his heart' (Gen. 6:6)."

With whom did God take counsel? It was with the creations already in hand. Clearly, the sages here wish to argue against the view that more than one power made heaven and earth, including man. In this way they show us how they brought their deepest concerns to scripture and found there strong and persuasive answers.

What Is Man? A Mixture of Heaven and Earth

Now to the point: man bears within himself—and woman is no different—traits of God and traits of earth. Our sages have no choice in seeing things this way (at least, to their way of looking), because scripture does say man is like God: "in our image." And yet, man is man.

VIII:IV.1.A. Said R. Berekhiah, "When God came to create the first man, he saw that both righteous and wicked descendants would come forth from him. He said, 'If I create him, wicked descendants will come forth from him. If I do not create him, how will the righteous descendants come forth from him?'

B. "What did the Holy One, blessed be he, do? He disregarded the way of the wicked and joined to himself his quality of mercy and so created him.

C. "That is in line with this verse of scripture: 'For the Lord knows the way of the righteous, but the way of the wicked shall perish' (Ps. 1:6).

D. "What is the sense of 'shall perish'? He destroyed it from before his presence and joined to himself the quality of mercy, and so created man."

2.A. R. Hanina did not explain the cited verse in this way. Rather, [he said,] "When the Holy One, blessed be he, proposed to create the first man, he took counsel with the ministering angels. He said to them, 'Shall we make man (Gen. 1:26)?'

B. "They said to him, 'What will be his character?'

C. "He said to them, 'Righteous descendants will come forth from him,' in line with this verse: 'For the Lord knows the way of the righteous' (Ps. 1:6), meaning, the Lord reported concerning the ways of the righteous to the ministering angels.

D. "But the way of the wicked shall perish' (Ps. 1:6), for he destroyed it [to keep it away] from them.

E. "He reported to them that righteous descendants would come forth from him, but he did not report to them that wicked descendants would come forth from him. For if he had told them that wicked descendants would come forth from him, the attribute of justice would never have given permission for man to be created."

God's act of creation represented a demonstration of God's merciful and loving character. That is the critical proposition, against anyone who holds that the creator-God was evil. The positioning of the discourse makes good sense, since we continue to follow the question, With whom did God take counsel when he said, "Shall we make man?"

The Angels Contend against Man

The debate about the true character of man goes forward. Implicit is the earlier concentration on the paradox of life: the good suffer, the wicked prosper. Now the matter is deepened. How could God have so made man as to sin at all? Does this not testify to a flaw in creation?

VIII:V.1.A. Said R. Simon, "When the Holy One, blessed be he, came to create the first man, the ministering angels formed parties and sects.

B. "Some of them said, 'Let him be created,' and some of them said, 'Let him not be created.'

C. "That is in line with the following verse of scripture: 'Mercy and truth fought together, righteousness and peace warred with each other' (Ps. 85:11).

D. "Mercy said, 'Let him be created, for he will perform acts of mercy.'

E. "Truth said, 'Let him not be created, for he is a complete fake.'

F. "Righteousness said, 'Let him be created, for he will perform acts of righteousness.'

G. "Peace said, 'Let him not be created, for he is one mass of contention.'

H. "What then did the Holy One, blessed be he, do? He took truth and threw it to the ground. The ministering angels then said before the Holy One, blessed be he, 'Master of the ages, how can you disgrace your seal [which is truth]? Let truth be raised up from the ground!'

I. "That is in line with the following verse of scripture: 'Let truth spring up from the earth' (Ps. 85:2)."

L. R. Huna the elder of Sepphoris said, "While the ministering angels were engaged in contentious arguments with one another, keeping one another preoccupied, the Holy One, blessed be he, created him.

M. "He then said to them, 'What good are you doing [with your contentions]? Man has already been made!'"

In creating man, God expressed his special love for him. The location presents no problems, since the question that the passage—by being located here—answers is the same one with which we have been dealing: With whom did God take counsel? But the answer is more important than the question, here as earlier, since it produces a syllogism not provoked by the question at all. The stress is that the ministering angels opposed the creation of man; because of their divisive character, God was able to do it anyhow. The deeper proposition, now repeated several times, hardly needs restatement.

Man in God's Image: What Can that Possibly Mean?

What is this splendid thing, this human being? The angels had never seen such a creature before. He looked like God. What were they to make of this? And what are we to make of such an extraordinary vision of who we are? For the message of our sages, through the ironies and the paradoxes by which they state their message, is stunning. Man is like god, so even the angels do not know the difference. Given the world they proposed to explain and had to endure, our sages made an astonishing statement. Only the Torah, in its basic message, can have given them reason for so hopeful a view of humanity.

VIII:X.1.A. Said R. Hoshiah, "When the Holy One, blessed be he, came to create the first man, the ministering angels mistook him [for God, since man was in God's image] and wanted to say before him, 'Holy, [holy, holy is the Lord of hosts].'

B. "To what may the matter be compared? To the case of a king and a governor who were set in a chariot, and the provincials wanted to greet the king, 'Sovereign!' But they did not know which one of them was which. What did the king do? He turned the governor out and put him away from the chariot, so that people would know who was king.

C. "So too when the Holy One, blessed be he, created the first man, the angels mistook him [for God]. What did the Holy One, blessed be he, do? He put him to sleep, so everyone knew that he was a mere man.

D. "That is in line with the following verse of scripture: 'Cease you from man, in whose nostrils is a breath, for how little is he to be accounted' (Is. 2:22)."

This is simply a stunning follow-up on the foregoing. Since man is in God's image, the angels did not know man from God. Only that man sleeps distinguishes man from God. I cannot imagine a more daring affirmation of humanity. The theme derives from the verse that states, "in our image, after our likeness" (Gen. 1:26), but this passage is not cited in the present construction. We have a profoundly polemical statement about the true character and condition of man. Accordingly, "in our image" yields the view that the complete image of man is attained in a divine union between man and woman, and, further, the syllogism that what makes man different from God is that man sleeps, and God does not sleep. Given the premise of the base verse and the issues inherent in the allegation that man is in God's image, the treatment here proves extraordinary.

What Does it Mean to be in God's Image? Goodness

The prophets told humanity what God wants: to do justice, love mercy, walk humbly with God. So to be in God's image is to live life in accord with the image that God had framed for humanity. God's own profession is to practice deeds of loving kindness. To be like God is to do the deeds God does.

VIII:XIII.1.A.   Said R. Abbahu, "The Holy One, blessed be he, took the cup of blessing [for the benediction of the marriage of Adam and Eve] and said the blessing for them."

B.   Said R. Judah b. R. Simon, "Michael and Gabriel were the best men of the first man."

C.   Said R. Simlai, "We have found that the Holy One, blessed be he, says a blessing for bridegrooms, adorns brides, visits the sick, buries the dead, and says a blessing for mourners.

D.   "What is the evidence for the fact that he says a blessing for bridegrooms? As it is said, 'And God blessed them' (Gen. 1:28).

E.   "That he adorns bride? As it is written, 'And the Lord God built the rib . . . into a woman' (Gen. 2:22).

F.   "Visits the sick? As it is written, 'And the Lord appeared to him [Abraham]' (Gen. 18:1).

G.   "Buries the dead? As it is written, 'And he buried him [Moses] in the valley' (Deut. 34:6)."

H.   R. Samuel bar Nahman said, "Also he concerns himself for the mourner. It is written, 'And God appeared to Jacob again,' when he came from Paddan-aram, and blessed him [after the death of Deborah, Rebecca's nurse] (Gen. 35:9).

I.   "What was the blessing that he said for him? It was the blessing for mourners."

The particular ethical actions emphasized by sages therefore follow the model that God has provided, hence, just as rites are (merely) natural, so acts of supererogatory virtue fostered by sages, acts that produce merit, are treated as divine.

The Creation of Rain, The Creation of Man

The biblical account of the creation of man and woman begins with reference to rain. Our sages then focus upon the relationship between rain and man. They see rain as a sign of God's love for humanity. Humanity cannot live without the constant and steady blessing of God, in this context, through rain. That is the basic message our sages uncover in the narrative of God's deciding to make man and woman. So we begin with rain.

XIII:III.1.A. "For the Lord God had not yet caused it to rain on the earth" (Gen. 2:4):

B. Scripture makes mention of the entire name of God when speaking of the entire world. It likewise makes mention of the full name of God in connection with rainfall.

2.A. Said R. Simeon b. Yohai, "Three things are of equal weight with one another, and these are they: the earth, man, and rain."

B. Said R. Levi bar Hiyyatah, "And each of the three of them is written with three consonants, to teach you that if there is no earth, there can be no rain, and if there is no rain, there can be no earth, and without the two of them, then there can be no man."

XIII:IV.1.A. Said R. Hoshaiah, "The power involved in making rain is as formidable as that of all the works of creation.

B. "What is the scriptural basis for that view? 'Who does great things and unsearchable' (Job 5:9). On what count? 'By giving rain upon the earth and sending waters upon the fields' (Job 5:10)."

C. R. Aha derives proof from the following: " 'He has made the earth by his might' (Jer. 10:12). 'At the sound of his giving a multitude of waters in the heavens' (Jer. 10:13). 'Sound' means only rain, in line with this verse: 'Deep calls to deep at the sound of your cataracts' (Ps. 42:8)."

XIII:V.1.A. R. Isaac said, "[Rain] indicates that God has been propitiated just as much as the sacrifices do: 'Lord, you have been favorable to your land' (Ps. 85:2)."

B. R. Simon said, "It collects the exiles [in that it is as valuable as the restoration of the exiles to the land.] 'You have turned the captivity of Jacob' (Ps. 85:2)."

C. R. Yohanan said, "It drives away divine wrath: 'You have withdrawn all your wrath' (Ps. 85:4)."

D. R. Tanhuma bar Hanilai said, "It atones for sins, as it is said, 'You have forgiven the sin of your people' (Ps. 85:3)."

XIII:VI.1.A. R. Hiyya bar Abba said, "[Rain] is equivalent in weight to the ressurection of the dead."

B. R. Abba son of R. Hiyya said, "Indeed, the sages set the prayer for rain in the paragraph of the prayer concerning the resurrection of the dead, to indicate that the word 'hand' pertains to both, and the word 'opening' pertains to both.

C. "The word 'hand' pertains to both: 'The hand of the Lord was upon me' (Ez. 37:1) [in connection with the vision of the dry bones], and the word 'hand' applies to the other: 'You open your hand [and by giving rain provide for creation]' (Ps. 148:16).

D. "The word 'opening' pertains to both: 'The Lord will open to you his good treasure, the heaven, to give rain of your land' (Deut. 28:12), and 'opening' occurs in regard to the other: 'Behold I will open your graves' (Ez. 37:12)."

E. R. Yudan in the name of R. Eleazar, "The word 'song' occurs with respect to the one, and the word 'song' occurs with respect to the other:

F. "The word 'song' occurs with respect to the one: 'Let those who dwell in the rock sing' (Is. 42:11). And the word 'song' occurs with respect to the other: 'You have remembered the earth and watered her . . . the valleys also are covered with grain, they shout for joy, yes, they sing' (Ps. 65:10,14)."

G. R. Hiyya bar Ba said, "Rain is still greater than the resurrection of the dead, for the resurrection of the dead serves man, but this serves man and beast, and, further, the resurrection of the dead serves only Israel, while this serves both Israel and the nations of the world."

2.A. A gentile asked R. Joshua, saying to him, "You have your festivals and we have our festivals. When you rejoice, we do not rejoice, and when we rejoice, you do not rejoice. What is it that we and you rejoice together?"

B. [Joshua answered him] "It is when it rains. What is the verse of scripture that so indicates? 'The meadows are clothed with flocks' (Ps. 65:14). What occurs afterward? 'Shout to God all the earth' (Ps. 66:1).

C. "Not priests, Levites, Israelites, but rather 'all the earth'!"

3.A. Said R. Joshua b. Levi, "When it rains, cattle go into heat. What is the scriptural basis for that view?

B. " 'The rams clothe the flocks' (Ps. 66:1). That is to say, 'The rams cover the flocks,' in a more acceptable word choice."

The opening paragraph explains the use of a different name of God, not the "God" of Gen. 1:1ff. but now "Lord God." Then the exegete turns to a new matter—namely, the importance of rain, explaining therefore why the creation narrative regards it as noteworthy that God had not yet made rain, hence the specification of rain as a principal component of creation. So at issue for the exegete is the connection between "rain" and "earth" in the base verse. This interest spills over into the next paragraph. At this point we have an anthology on the power of rain. The verse at hand refers to rain and all else follows. But notice what our sages do once the theme comes up? They think once more of Israel and the correspondence of creation in nature to Israel in history. Now the creation of rain links explicitly to the concerns of Israel's life and salvation: return of the exiles, atoning, assuaging divine wrath. Creation corresponds to sacred history, so that now rain, in creation, locates its counterpart in the resurrection of the dead, in Israel's history. That Israel's history in particular is meant of course finds its proof in what follows.

Rain Serves God's Purpose

Pursuing the theme that nature and history, rain and humanity, attest to God's will, we ask, what does God do, through rain, to carry out God's will? The answer is that when it does not rain, destruction follows. So God punishes humanity by withholding rain. Then when it rains in the right way, it is God's reward. Our sages concentrate on the good in life, thus asking how to interpret not only evil and catastrophe, but also—for them more routine—goodness and blessing. Theirs is a reading of scripture for times of trouble, but also for days of serenity and good order.

XIII:XIV.1.A. Said R. Berekhiah, "When a broken [spirit] came up from the earth, then: 'It watered the whole face of the ground' (Gen. 2:6). [Freedman, p. 108, n. 2: The connection is between the word used in the cited verse for cloud, namely, *ed,* and the word for destruction, also, *ed,* so: Let there ascend from the earth the breaking of one's evil desires and then it shall water.]"

B. That view accords with the position of R. Berekhiah, who said, " 'My doctrine shall drop as rain' (Deut. 32:2) means, when men will destroy their stiff-neckedness, then rain will fall."

XIII:XV.1.A. How much rain must come down for a person to become obligated to say a blessing [in thanksgiving for the coming of the rain]?

B. R. Yose in the name of R. Judah [and] R. Jonah, R. Judah in the name of R. Samuel: "When the rain first starts to fall, it must be sufficient to fructify the earth, but, at the end, any amount at all suffices [to impose the obligation to recite a blessing]."

C. R. Hiyya in the name of R. Yohanan: "At the beginning, enough to make the ground fruitful, and at the end, enough to rinse off the surface of roof tiles."

D. R. Yannai bar Ishmael in the name of R. Simeon b. Laqish: "At the beginning enough to fructify the ground and at the end enough to dissolve the stopper of a cask [a clay stopper]."

E. But is it not the case that any amount of rain can fall without dissolving the clay stopper of a flask! Rather: enough so that it will appear as if it has been dissolved.

2.A. And how does one have to recite the blessing? It must be in accord with that which we have learned in the Mishnah:

B. For rain and for good news, one recites the blessing: "Blessed is God who is good and does good" [M. Ber. 9:2].

C. R. Berekhiah in the name of R. Levi derives proof of that proposition from the following verse: " 'As cold water to a faint soul, so is good news from a far country' (Prov. 25:25). Just as good news is the occasion for reciting, 'Blessed is God who is good and does good,' so for cold water one must recite the blessing, 'Who is good and who does good.' ' "

3.A. R. Judah said, "This is how my father, Ezekiel, would recite the blessing:

B. "May your name be blessed and exalted and magnified for each drop of rain which you bring down for us, for you keep them apart from one another [so they will not form a sheet of water and wash us away]."

C. R. Yudan bar Simeon said, "For he brings them down by measure: 'For he draws away the drops of water' (Job 36:27), with the word for 'draw away' bearing the same meaning as it does in this verse: 'And a deduction shall be made subtracted from your valuation' (Lev. 27:18)."

4.A. R. Yose bar Jacob visited R. Yudan of Magdela. Heard him reciting this blessing: "Thousands and tens of thousands of times we have to thank your name for each drop of rain which you bring down to us, for you pay back good to those who are guilty [since in strict justice you would not permit it to rain, since rain benefits the guilty and the innocent alike]."

B. He said to him, "This is how R. Simeon would recite the blessing."

5.A. Said R. Zeirah, "There they say, 'When prices are low and the river has enough water for the province, one says, "Blessed is God who is good and does good." ' "

XIII:XVI.1.A. "And watered the whole [face of the ground]" (Gen. 2:6):

    B. [Explaining the emphasis upon the *whole* face of the ground] said R. Eleazar in the name of R. Yose b. Zimra, "When it rains, *everything* enjoys the blessing. Trade is blessed, and the merchants make a profit."

    C. R. Yohanan bar Levi said, "Also the feeble are helped."

    D. R. Hiyya bar Abba said, "Also the sick are benefited. Their limbs grow softer for them [and more supple]."

    E. Abimi was a member of an association for visiting the sick. When it rained, R. Hiyya bar Abba would say to him, "How are they doing?"

    F. He would say to him, "They are relieved."

    G. Rabbi said, "Even a jewel benefits from the rain."

    H. Rabbis say, "Even fish benefit from the rain."

    G. Said R. Phineas, "There was a case in Acre that the fishermen brought up a fish which they reckoned would weigh three hundred *litras*, but when they actually weighed it, it weighed only two hundred *litras*. There was an old fisherman there, and he said to him, 'It is because it has not yet rained.'

    H. "Once it had rained, they caught a fish that they reckoned would weight two hundred *litras* but when they actually weighed it, it weighed three hundred."

The point is clear. Sages ask about how to respond not only to calamity but also, and especially, to the normal course of nature. They see a world in which rain is commonplace, drought unusual. That is how things are. So they direct Israel's attention to the way to respond to nature when nature is a blessing. The deeper message cannot escape our eye. People call on God in times of trouble: Why me? Why now? Why here? But they should ask the same questions in times of prosperity—and live up to the answers.

Dirt and Water; the Components of Man

Over and over sages recognized the dual nature of man, made up of the breath of life, that comes from God, but also of the dirt of the earth. They find the true character of humanity in the mixture of these traits—and in their union.

XIV:I.1.A. "Then the Lord God formed man [of dust from the ground and breathed into his nostrils the breath of life]" (Gen. 2:7):

B. "The king by justice establishes the land but a man of gifts overthrows it" (Prov. 29:4).

C. "The king" refers to the king of kings of kings, the Holy One, blessed be he.

D. ". . . by justice establishes the land" for he created the world in accord with the attribute of justice: "In the beginning God [the Hebrew word for God, *elohim*, is taken to represent the attribute of justice] created" (Gen: 1:1).

E. "But a man of gifts overthrows it" refers to the first man. He was the dough offering *[hallah]*, marking the completion of the world, and dough offering falls into the category of the priestly gift, as it is said, "Of the first of your dough you shall set apart dough offering for a priestly gift" (Num. 15:20). [So while God established the world through justice, the first man—in the category of a gift—overthrew it.]

F. Said R. Yose b. Qisratah, "It may be compared to the case of a woman who mixes her dough with water and, in the middle of the work, raises up her dough offering [before the dough was fully kneaded]. So too, at the beginning: 'And a mist went up from the earth' (Gen. 2:6), and afterward: 'Then the Lord God formed of dust from the earth' (Gen. 2:7)."

The exegesis rests on the interplay of Gen. 2:6, referring to water, and Gen. 2:7, referring to dust of the earth. So man is made of those two materials. What the exegete finds interesting is that the available materials for man were mud and water. What about the metaphor of the priestly gift, the dough offering? That offering is owing from dough while it is being prepared, falling due at the point at which the crust forms, that is, when the enzyme that causes the dough to rise has been killed by the heat of the baking. It is an offering presented to the priest by the housewife when she has completed the preparation of dough in the process of baking bread. Hence the creation of man is compared to mixing water and flour to create bread. Then removing man from the mixture of water and dirt is compared to the removal of dough from the mixture of water and flour. The intersecting verse supplies the pertinent metaphor. The human being then is the select offering of creation, not only in God's image but also the offering of creation to the creator.

To pursue this theme: the message is that man is the sacred component of creation, just as the part of the dough is made holy for presentation to the priest. I find the whole extraordinarily powerful, because of the author's striking union of syllogism, metaphor, and exegetical rhetoric. The syllogism, as I said, is that man was made of dirt and water, as the narrative suggests. The metaphor is between the making of man and the making of dough. The vision of man as the most holy component of creation, suitable for presentation to the priest, exploits the already available metaphor that represents man as "in our image, after our likeness." So the details of the narrative are carefully woven together. The exegetical rhetoric invokes a verse which, by itself, does not refer to the matter of dough at all. Yet by reference to the double meaning of "a man of gifts," imparted by the allusion to "gifts" with the particular word that stands also for gifts to the priests ("heave offering" [priestly rations]), the exegete is able to introduce the image he wishes to employ—namely, the comparison of man to dough.

But that does not complete his accomplishment, since the point of the whole is that God made the world, including man, in accord with the attribute of justice. Now, if we did not know that ahead of us is the story of man's sin and punishment, the rather subtle passage before us surely prepares the way. That is to say, the creation of man is the story of divine justice, not divine mercy. That will come later, indeed will be the rest of the story of humanity. It is difficult to imagine how the exegete could have introduced into the interpretation of the biblical narrative a broader range of unifying and yet subterranean images and themes than he has done.

The Creation of Woman

Up to now we have spoken only of man. But nearly everything that has been said applies also to woman. Now the account of why woman was brought into existence—to be sure,

from the perspective of the men who compose the story—
comes to the fore.

XVII:II.1.A. "It is not good" (Gen. 2:18):

B. It has been taught on Tannaite authority: Whoever
has no wife lives without good, without help, without joy,
without blessing, without atonement.

C. Without good: "It is not good for man to be alone"
(Gen. 2:18).

D. Without help: "I will make him a helper fit for him"
(Gen. 2:18).

E. Without joy: "And you shall rejoice, you and your
household" (Gen. 14:26).

F. Without atonement: "And he shall make atonement
for himself and for his house" [here house is taken by sages to
mean his wife, so if he cannot make atonement for his wife,
he also cannot make atonement for himself"] (Lev. 16:11).

G. R. Simon in the name of R. Joshua b. Levi: "Also
without peace, as it is said, 'And peace be to your house
[again, meaning wife]' (1 Sam. 25:6)."

H. R. Joshua of Sikhnin in the name of R. Levi: "Also
without life, as it is written, 'Enjoy life with the wife whom
you love' (Qoh. 9:9)."

I. R. Hiyya bar Gomedi said, "Also he is not a complete man: 'And he blessed *them* and called *their* name Adam'
(Gen. 5:2)."

J. And some say, "Such a person also diminishes the
image of God: 'For in the image of God made he man' (Gen.
9:6), after which it is written: 'And you, be fruitful and multiply' (Gen. 9:7)." [Freedman, p. 133, n. 2: God's majesty, as it
were, is impaired when man refuses to fulfil these functions.]

The main point is that where scripture speaks of "house" it
means one's wife. The rest then follows. Our sages view the
world from the viewpoint of women who maintain life by building the home, men who sustain life by keeping the household
in all ways. True, in our own day women do more than keep
the home, and men do more than make a living but also make a
contribution to the home and family. But in the sages' world the

division of labor by gender was a given. What they contribute should not be missed: the recognition that man is incomplete without woman, as much as woman without man. In this sense they see the two as complementary and essential, so they do not maintain that one gender takes priority over the other. In that context, that too was a step forward.

The Dual Quality of Woman

Our sages' appreciation for woman comes to expression in one principle. God is the one who gives a man a good wife. It is a blessing from God, and all goodness therefore depends on God. So the message of scripture comes to articulation here as everywhere else: all blessings flow from God, woman above all. I cannot imagine how our sages can have stated in their context and circumstance a more affirmative view of woman.

XVII:III.1.A. "I will make him a helper as his counterpart" (Gen. 2:18):

B. If a man has merit, the wife is a help, and if not, she is his counterpart [in opposition to him].

C. Said R. Joshua bar Nehemiah, "If one has merit, his wife will be like the wife of Hananiah son of Hakhinai, and if not, she will be like the wife of R. Yose the Galilean." [Hananiah's wife is never mentioned again.]

2.A. R. Yose the Galilean had a bad wife, who was the daughter of his sister [so it was an act of merit that he married her] but who used to embarrass him. His disciples said to him, "Master, divorce her, for she does not treat you with respect."

B. He said to them, "Her dowry is too big for me, so I cannot divorce her."

C. One time he and R. Eleazar b. Azariah were in session. When they had finished their studies, he said to him, "Master, will you allow me to go with you to your house?"

D. He said to him, "Yes."

E. When they got there, she looked down and left the house [angrily]. [Yose] looked into the pot that was standing on the stove and asked her, "Is there anything in the pot?"

F. She said to him, "In the pot there is hash." But when he went and peeked, he found chicken.

G. R. Eleazar b. Azariah understood what he was hearing. They sat down together and ate. He said to him, "My lord, did she not say that in the pot was hash, while we found chicken in it?"

H. He said to him, "It was a miracle."

I. When they had finished eating, he said to him, "My lord, divorce that woman, for she does not treat you with respect."

J. He said to him, "Sir, her dowry is too much for me to pay, so I cannot divorce her."

K. He said to him, "We [your disciples] will divide up her dowry so that you can divorce her." They did so and divided among themselves the cost of her dowry, and he divorced her and married another woman, far better than she had been.

L. The sins of that first wife caused it to happen that she went and married the town watchman. After some time trouble came upon the man, and [since he was blind] she would lead him all over town [to go begging]. But when they would come in the neighborhood in which R. Yose the Galilean lived, she led him away from it.

M. Since that man had been the town watchman and knew the entire town, he said to her, "Why do you not bring us to the neighborhood in which R. Yose the Galilean lives? I heard that he carries out his religious duties [and so will support us, since we are poor]."

N. She said to him, "I am his divorced wife, and I haven't got the strength to face him."

O. One time they came begging to the neighborhood of R. Yose the Galilean, and the husband began to beat her, and her cries brought embarrassment all over town. R. Yose the Galilean looked out and saw that the couple was being ridiculed in the marketplaces of the town. He took them and gave them housing in a room that he owned and provided them with food so long as they lived.

P. This was on the count of the verse: "And that you do not hide yourself from your own flesh" (Is. 58:7).

XVII:IV.1.A. "So out of the ground the Lord God
formed every beast of the field [and every bird of the air, and
brought them to the man to see what he would call them, and
whatever the man called every living creature, that was its
name]" (Gen. 2:19):

2.A. Said R. Aha, "When the Holy One, blessed be
he, came to create the first man, he took counsel with the
ministering angels. He said to them, 'Shall we make man?'
(Gen. 1:26).

B. "They said to him, 'What is his character?'

C. "He said to them, 'His wisdom will be greater
than yours.'

D. "What did the Holy One, blessed be he, do [in order to make his point]? He brought before them domesticated
beasts, wild beasts, and fowl. He said to them, 'As to this
creature, what is its name?' but they did not know.

E. " 'What is its name?' But they did not know.

F. "Then he brought them before man. He said to him,
'As to this, what is its name?' 'Ox.' 'And as to this, what is its
name?' 'Camel.' 'And as to this, what is its name?' 'An ass.'
'And as to this, what is its name?' 'Horse.'

G. "That is in line with this verse: 'And whatever man
called every living creature, that was its name' (Gen. 2:19).

H. "He said to him, 'And what is your name?'

I. "He said to him, 'As for me, what is proper is to call
me "Adam" for I have been created from the earth [which in
Hebrew is called *adamah*].'

J.. " 'And as for me, what is my name?' He said to him,
'As for you, it is fitting for you to be called, "The Lord," for
you are the Lord of all that you have created.' "

3.A. Said R. Hiyya, " 'I am the Lord, that is my name'
(Is. 42:8). That is my name, which the first man called me."

4.A. [Reverting to the story interrupted by Hiyya's
statement:] "He then went and brought before the first man
each beast with its mate. He said, 'Every creature has a mate,
but I have no mate.' 'But for the man will there not be found
a helper fit for him?' (Gen. 2:20).

B. "And why did not he create her for him to begin with? The Holy One, blessed be he, foresaw that later on man would complain to him about [his wife, Eve], so he did not create her until [man] himself had asked for her on his own.

C. "When he asked for her on his own, forthwith: 'So the Lord God caused a deep sleep to fall upon the man, and while he slept [took one of his ribs and closed up its place with flesh]' (Gen. 2:21)."

The power of the passage lies at no. 2, the debate on the value of the human being between God and the angels. The power of humanity lies in the knowledge of the world that the angels did not have, but humanity did and does. To know the names of things is to exercise power. For it means that you understand what is about you. Then the creation of woman comes to the fore. In his review of the creatures of the world, man found none with whom to share life, until God made woman. The point of the whole then is to link the details of man's knowing the names of all the beasts and God's creating Eve for man. When we ask about our sages' basic view of woman, the answer is before us.

3 The Sabbath

The Sabbath at the Climax of Creation

The story of the creation of the world in six days aims at the climactic moment of sanctification and blessing of the world on the eve of the Sabbath. What is the blessing of the Sabbath? It is a day of joy and not sorrow—a simple blessing. Our sages speak of real people, a real world.

XI.I.1.A. "And God blessed the seventh day" (Gen. 2:3).

B. "The blessing of the Lord makes one rich [and grief adds nothing]" (Prov. 10:22).

C. This refers to the Sabbath: "And God blessed . . ." (Gen. 2:3).

D. "And grief adds nothing" (Prov. 10:22) refers to mourning [which is not to be done on the Sabbath], in line with this verse: "For the king was grieved on account of his son" (2 Sam. 19:3).

The intersecting verse answers the question of what blessing God gave to the Sabbath and finds in the prohibition of mourning on that day a particular blessing. Our sages proceed to spell out the kind of blessings the Sabbath brings.

The Sabbath of Creation, the Life of Israel

What our sages now do is discover in the very creation of the world full reason to account for Israel's own holy way of life. So what each Jew does week by week corresponds to and carries out the purpose of creation. Reading scripture in light of contemporary concerns leads our sages deep into the everyday reality of the Jewish people—a daring and fundamental assertion on the part of our sages.

XI:II.1.A. "So God blessed the Sabbath day and hallowed it" (Gen. 2:3).

B.   R. Ishmael says, "He blessed it with mana and he hallowed it with mana.

C.   "He blessed it with mana, for on all the weekdays the mana would yield one *omer*-measure a day, but on the eve of the Sabbath there were two *omer*-measures.

D.   "He hallowed it [making it separate by a sign done] with mana, because on that day, mana did not come down at all."

E.   R. Nathan says, "He blessed it with mana, but he hallowed it with a blessing."

F.   R. Isaac said, "He blessed it with mana, but he hallowed it with the example of the man gathering wood [who was put to death for working on the Sabbath and this accomplished the perpetual sanctification of the Sabbath]."

2.*A.*   He blessed it [with the requirement to put on] fine clothing.

B.   R. Huna said, "One has to change [clothing for the Sabbath]."

C.   R. Hiyya in the name of R. Yohanan: "One has to mix [his garments, so that, if he cannot put on fresh clothing, he can at least use a given item of clothing for a different purpose on the occasion of the Sabbath]."

D.   Abin bar Hisdai said, "One has to let his garments hang out."

E.   R. Jeremiah and R. Zeira were walking together [on the Sabbath] and [Zeira] saw that the garment of R. Jeremiah was tucked up, and R. Zeira pulled it so that it hung down.

F.   That indicates that it is necessary to let one's garments hang loose on the Sabbath.

3.*A.*   R. Eliezer says, "He blessed it with the requirement that one kindle a lamp [in advance of the Sabbath, so as to have light in the home on the Sabbath].

B.   "And that involves a particular incident. One time I kindled the lamp on the eve of the Sabbath, and I came back at the end of the Sabbath and I found it burning, and it had not used up [any oil]."

4.   [God] blessed it with the shining face of man [which characterizes the person's appearance on the Sabbath].

B. The light of a man's face throughout the ordinary days of the week in no way compares to that of the Sabbath.

5.*A.* He blessed it with the lights.

B. [Referring to the view that there was a great light created at the time of creation, but, because Adam sinned, it was hidden away, said] R. Simeon bar Judah: "Even though the lights were spoiled on the eve of the Sabbath [the lights were in fact punished only after the Sabbath, so it was a special blessing of the Sabbath that that original light still illuminated the day]."

C. That view accords with the position of rabbis and not with that of R. Assi, who said, "The glory of the first man did not last through one night."

D. What is the scriptural evidence for that statement? "But man does not pass the night in glory" (Ps. 49:13).

E. Rabbis say, "The glory stayed the night, but at the end of the Sabbath [God] took the splendor from him and drove him out of the Garden of Eden. That is in line with this verse: 'You change his countenance and send him away' (Job 14:20).

F. "When the sun set on the night of the Sabbath, the Holy One, blessed be he, planned to hide away its light, but he paid respect to the Sabbath. That is in line with this verse: 'And God blessed the seventh day' (Gen. 2:3).

G. "With what, then, did God bless the seventh day? It was with light."

6.*A.* When the sun set on the night of the Sabbath, its glow hung on and it continued to give light. Everyone began to give praise, in line with this verse: "Under the whole heaven they give praise to him" (Job 37:3). On what account? Because: "His light is unto the ends of the earth" (Job 37:3).

B. R. Levi in the name of bar Nezirah: "For thirty-six hours that light continued to serve, twelve hours on the eve of the Sabbath [Friday], twelve on the night of the Sabbath, and twelve on the Sabbath day itself.

C. "When the sun began to set on the night following the Sabbath, darkness began to come on. The first man took fright: 'Surely indeed the darkness shall bruise me' (Ps. 139:11).

D. "Shall the one concerning whom it is written, 'He shall bruise your head' (Gen. 3:15) now come and confront me?

E. "What did the Holy One, blessed be he, do? He prepared for him two flints and had him strike them against one another, so that fire burst forth, and [man] said a blessing for [the fire]. That is in line with this verse: 'But the night was light about me' (Ps. 139:11)."

F. "The night was light about me" (Ps. 139:11): This view accords with the statement of Samuel, for Samuel said, "On what account do people say a blessing for a light at the end of the Sabbath? Because that was the point at which light originally was created. . . ."

XI:III.1.A. He blessed [the Sabbath day] by requiring additional expenses for the observance of that day.

B. R. Levi in the name of R. Yose bar Hanina: "With regard to every day of creation on which there is a diminution of what was created, a blessing in scripture is made explicit, so that what was created on that day in the end does not diminish.

C. "For example, on the fifth day, fowl and fish were created, but people slaughter fowl and eat them, catch fish and eat them. So scripture refers to a blessing in connection with that day, on which account what is created on that day never in the end will be diminished. [There will always be enough fowl and fish, because of God's blessing in that connection.]

D. "But with reference to the Sabbath, what can you say? [What diminishes on the Sabbath day, that is kept in good supply by God's blessing?]"

E. R. Levi in the name of R. Hama bar Hanina: "It is on account of the additional expenditure [involved in the keeping of the Sabbath]. [Even though Israelites have to lay out money for the additional enjoyments of the Sabbath, they will end up not losing at all.]"

F. R. Eleazar in the name of R. Yose: "It is because of the people who have delicate stomachs. [They can eat the extra food of the Sabbath without suffering on that account.]."

The first three answers to the question of what blessing God bestowed on the Sabbath take up Israel's Sabbath observances: food, clothing, light. From no. 4 onward we turn to issues of cosmological significance. No. 4 accomplishes the transition from the home to the cosmos. Then at no. 5 we introduce the issue of light in this deeper sense. No. 5 addresses the punishment of the first man and of the heavenly luminaries, because of man's rebellion, which, the coming chapter tells us, took place on the sixth day. The imperfections of nature accrue to the detriment of man. They do not testify to imperfections in the creator-God. Then no. 6 makes the stunning point that God was merciful, despite man's sin, and so gave him light, at the end of the Sabbath. So the framers of nos. 5–6 turn the Sabbath from an event in nature to a testimony to God's reconciliation with sinful man. The light then bears the symbolic meaning that God is merciful to man, even though man has sinned. So the blessing of the seventh day that God bestowed was the giving of light, and the light of the seventh day stands for God's forgiveness of man for the sin of the sixth day of creation. The message of the two parts—nos. 5–6—could not be more clearly stated.

The final passage makes its own point. Israelites make special efforts to keep the Sabbath not only holy, but also enjoyable. They spend extra money on food, wine, and the like. So the point is clear. The special blessing on the Sabbath is that the extra costs of the day—including not working on that day—will be made up.

Has the compositor of the whole given us a point of his own, in laying out matters in the order before us? He moves, we see, from the domestic life of Israel, which observes the Sabbath through this-worldly pleasures of food, clothing, and light, through the symbolism of light, to the cosmic dimension of the imperfection of nature, signified by the light's being punished for man's sin. This point allows the compositor to introduce the climactic theme, divine forgiveness of that sin on the sixth day, leaving the Sabbath as the mark of God's reconciliation with man. The net effect is to link the homely observance of the Sabbath to the most profound issues of human existence and divine love—all out of the simple statement that

God blessed the seventh day and hallowed it. To the Jewish people facing the despair of the hour, the message comes through with great force: if you need encouragement, find it in the very things that make Jews special and holy. The Sabbath is the most common, coming as it does every seventh day, so the Sabbath testifies more than anything else to Israel's special status. Specifically, the world of nature—light, cosmic illumination alike—come together with Israel's celebration of creation on the Sabbath. The distinctive life of Israel conforms to the deepest structure of the natural world. So the movement of the sun and the moon and the stars testify to the sanctification of Israel.

Israel's Sabbath and the Nations of the World

The Sabbath set Israel apart from all other peoples in ancient times, and sages drew a parallel between the singularity of the Sabbath among the days of the week and the singularity of Israel among the nations of the world. This once more they expressed in homely terms: the food tastes better.

XI:IV.1.A. "He blessed it" with tasty food.

B. Our Rabbi [Judah the Patriarch] on the Sabbath made a banquet for Antoninus. Rabbi set before [the Roman emperor] cold dishes, which he tasted and liked.

C. Rabbi made a banquet for him on a weekday and set before him boiling dishes [ordinarily to be preferred]. [The emperor] said to him, "The other ones please me more than these."

D. [The emperor] further said to him, "These lack a certain spice."

E. [The emperor] said to him, "Then does the king's pantry lack something [that your food should taste better cold than mine does hot]?"

F. [Rabbi] said to him, "What the food lacks is the Sabbath. Do you have the Sabbath [to add flavor to your food]?"

2.A. R. Ishmael b. R. Yose asked Rabbi, saying to him, "On account of what merit do the Babylonian Jews live so long?"

B. He said to him, "On account of the merit accruing to them for studying the Torah."

C. "And [on account of what merit do those who live] in the land of Israel live so long?"

D. "It is because of the merit accruing on account of the separation of tithes."

E. "And those who live abroad?"

F. "It is because of the merit of paying all due honor to the Sabbath and festival days." [We shall now have a case illustrating that fact.]

3.A. Said R. Hiyya bar Abba, "Once a man in Laodicea invited me [for a meal], and placed before us a table borne on sixteen poles, and on the table was everything that was created on the six days of creation. A child was sitting in the middle of the table, proclaiming, 'The earth is the Lord's and the fulness thereof, the world and all who dwell therein' (Ps. 24:1).

B. "Why so? So that the householder should not take pride in all this.

C. "I said to him, 'My son, on what account did you gain the merit to enjoy all this glory?'

D. "He said to me, 'I was a butcher, and I would set aside for the Sabbath every good beast that I saw.' "

4.A. Said R. Tanhuma, "There was a case in Rome that took place on the eve of the great fast [the Day of Atonement]. A certain tailor there went to buy himself a fish, and it happened that the governor's bondman was bidding for it too, and one bid for such and so, and the other bid for such and so, until the price reached twelve denars. And the tailor got it.

B. "At dinner the governor said to his servant, 'Why did you not serve fish?'

C. "He said to him, 'My lord, why should I keep from you what such and so, a certain Jew did to me. Do you want me to bring you a fish that cost twelve denars?'

D. "He said to him, 'Who is he?'

E. "He said to him, 'Such and so, a Jew.'

F. "He sent for him and summoned him, and he came. He said, 'Will a Jewish tailor eat a fish for twelve denars?'

G. "He said to him, 'My lord, we have a day which effects atonement for us for all of the sins of the year, and should we not treasure it?'

H. "He brought proof for his statement, and the governor let him go free."

XI:V.1.A. Tinneus Rufus, the wicked, asked R. Aqiba, saying to him, "Why is this day different from all other days?"

B. He said to him, "Why does one man differ from all other men?"

C. He said to him, "Look what I said to you and what you said to me!"

D. He said to him, "You said to me, what is the difference between the Sabbath and all other days, so I asked you what is the difference between Rufus and all other men."

E. He said to him, "It is because the king wanted to honor [Rufus that he is different from all other men]."

F. "So this day did the Holy One, blessed be he, wish to honor."

G. "How will you demonstrate that to me?"

H. He said to him, "The river Sabbatianus will prove the fact, for it carries rocks all week long, but on the Sabbath it rests."

I. He said to him, "You are carrying me far from the point [since I know no such river]."

J. He said to him, "And lo, let the [necromancer] prove the matter, for every day he can bring up the dead, but on the Sabbath he does not bring them up."

K. [Tinneus Rufus] went and tried the matter out with his deceased father, bringing him up every day, but on the Sabbath he did not come up. After the Sabbath he brought him up. He said to him, "Father, after you died, did you turn into a Jew? On what account did you come up every day of the week but not on the Sabbath?"

L. He said to him, "Whoever does not willingly keep the Sabbath when he is with you [the living] unwillingly is forced to keep it here."

M. He said to him, "What sort of labor do you have there [that you should have to rest on the seventh day]?"

N. He said to him, "Every day of the week we are put on trial, but on the Sabbath we are left alone."

O. He went back to R. Aqiba and said to him, "If it is true, as you say, that the Holy One, blessed be he, honors the Sabbath day, then he should not raise up winds on that day or bring down rain."

P. He said to him, "Woe to that man [you]! It is in the same category [for God to do these things] as for a human being to carry four cubits [which is permitted]. [God owns the whole world and is carrying in his own, private domain.]"

All four components of the opening paragraph present illustrations of how people honor the Sabbath by eating unusually fine meals. In a general way this paragraph carries forward the basic notion of XI:III about additional expenditures invested in keeping the Sabbath. The next paragraph contributes another entry to the catalogue of Sabbath stories. I see no detail particular to the present context. The story as a whole has been selected by the compositors for its illustrative value. But the closing detail, O-P, surely contributes an answer to the broader question of God's conduct on the seventh day.

The Sabbath and Salvation

The Sabbath, which crowns creation, also marks the occasion for Israel's salvation. This idea is expressed in a number of ways. The most important links the observance of the Sabbath to the full blessing received by Jacob.

XI:VII.1.A. R. Yohanan in the name of R. Yose: "Abraham, concerning whom Scripture makes no allusion as to his observing the Sabbath, inherited the world only in a limited measure. So it is written, 'Arise, traverse the land, length and breadth' (Gen. 13:17).

B. "But concerning Jacob, scripture provides evidence as to his observing the Sabbath, as it is written [in connection with his travels], 'And he observed a rest before the city' (Gen. 11:18). [Why did he observe a rest? Because he came in just at sunset and so established a Sabbath residence while it was still day. [Jacob] inherited the world not by limited measure. So it is stated, 'And you shall spread abroad to the west and to the east' (Gen. 28:14)."

The merit of the patriarchs, which Israel receives and of which Israel enjoys the benefit, is at issue here. The patriarchs were not required to observe the Sabbath, since the Torah had not yet been given. On that basis, the Christians argued that one did not have to keep the laws of the Torah in order to be saved. They pointed to Abraham, for example. Abraham did not keep the Sabbath, yet he was justified. The reply is to invoke the figure of Jacob, who, it is shown, did keep the Sabbath—as Israel, Jacob's namesake, now does—and the distinction between Jacob and Abraham, as specified, validates the Israelite view that the Sabbath is part of the requirements of the law that bring justification.

Why is the Sabbath Special?

With so vast a claim laid down for the Sabbath, one has to ask why the seventh day received the glory accorded to it. Underneath the surface is the question of why Israel, among all nations. But that question does not come to expression. In the context of creation, we speak of the Sabbath dwelling alone among days. That is like Israel, dwelling alone among nations. So the singularity of Israel, like the singularity of the Sabbath, constitutes a mark of special favor. Difference then adds up to destiny.

XI:VIII.1.A. And why did [God] bless [the seventh day]?

B. R. Berekhiah said, "It is because it has no mate. The first day of the week has the second, the third the fourth, the fifth the sixth. But the Sabbath has no mate."

C. R. Samuel bar Nahman said, "It is because it cannot be shifted about [by reference to the appearance of the moon]. A festival day may be shifted about [through citings of the moon, on the basis of which the festal calendar is determined], the Day of Atonement may be shifted about, but the Sabbath may not be shifted about."

2.A. R. Simeon b. Yohai taught on Tannaite authority, "The Sabbath said before the Holy One, blessed be he, 'Lord of the ages, everyone has a mate, but I have no mate.'

B. "The Holy One, blessed be he, said to her, 'The community of Israel, lo, that is your mate.'

C. "When Israel stood before Mount Sinai, the Holy One blessed be he, said to them, 'Remember what I said to the Sabbath: "The community of Israel is your mate." ' Now therefore: 'Remember the Sabbath day to keep it holy' (Ex. 20:8)."

The exegesis of the verse at no. 1, specifying that the Sabbath was given a blessing because it had no mate, then accounts for the inclusion of no. 2 in what is a cogent and harmonious composition. The powerful and continuing polemic that Israel's holy way of life corresponds to the order of creation reaches renewed expression here. Israel is the bride of the Sabbath, the fulfillment of creation.

God and the Sabbath

Israel follows God's way when Jews keep the Sabbath. Accordingly, we ask how God keeps the Sabbath. This leads us to the reconsideration of the order of creation.

XI:IX.1.A. "For on that day he rested from all of his work which he had created to make" (Gen. 2:3):

B. R. Levi in the name of R. Hama bar Hanina, "Three things did the Holy One, blessed be he, create each day: on the first, heaven, earth, and light; on the second, firmament, Gehenna, and angels; on the third, trees, grass, and the Garden of Eden; on the fourth, the sun, the moon, and the stars; on the fifth, fowl, fish, and Leviathan; on the sixth Adam, Eve, and the snake."

C. Said R. Phineas, "On the sixth he created six things: Adam, Eve, the snake, domesticated beasts, wild beasts, and demons."

2.A. Said R. Benaiah, " '. . . which God created and made . . .' (Gen. 2:3) is not what the text says, but rather, 'Which God created *to make*' [he was planning to make].

B. "The meaning is that everything that had been destined to be created on the seventh day, the Holy One, blessed
be he, went ahead and created on the sixth day [before the
Sabbath]. [So in fact it had been brought into being, and creation was perfected]."

XI:X.1.A. R. Phineas in the name of R. Oshaiah: "Even
though you read, 'Because in it he rested from all his work
which God created to make' (Gen. 2:3), it was from the work
of the world that he rested. But he did not rest from the work
involving the wicked or from the work involving the righteous.
But he continued to labor with these and with those.

B. "He shows these their essential character and he
shows those their essential character [Freedman]."

C. "And how do we know that punishing the wicked
falls into the category of work? As it is said, 'The Lord has
opened his armory and has brought forth the weapons of
his indignation, for it is a work that the Lord God has to
do' (Jer. 50:25).

D. "And how do we know that giving the just reward to
the righteous also falls into the category of work? As it is said,
'Oh how abundant is your goodness, which you have laid up
for those who fear you, which you have worked for those who
take refuge in you in the sight of the sons of men' (Ps. 31:20).
[Both activities therefore fall into the category of "work." This
sort of work nonetheless goes forward on the Sabbath day.]"

The concluding entry provides a limitation on the verse
subject to exegesis. The rest that God took was from creating
the world, but not from ruling it. The creator-God rules the
world, and there is no other dominion. The polemic once more
proves familiar.

4 The Garden of Eden

The First Commandment

What matters in the story of the garden of course is how woman and man lost the blessed life of Eden. They received one commandment. They did not keep it. Woman and man form the paradigm for humanity in general. God instructed humanity to observe a few fundamental rules. Humanity failed to keep those rules. But, our sages add, Israel received numerous instructions and faithfully tries to keep them all. So from our sages' viewpoint, the story of the fall of man and woman finds its counterpart in the story of Israel's sanctification. Eden ends at the flood, the flood leads to Abraham, and Abraham's heirs climb to Sinai. That tale tells the story of human history and informs Israel about the meaning of its life and destiny. All of this comes at the very beginning.

XVI:VI.1.A. "And the Lord God commanded the man, saying, 'You may freely eat of every tree of the garden [but of the tree of the knowledge of good and evil you shall not eat, for in the day that you eat of it you shall die]' " (Gen. 2:16).

B. R. Levi said, "He made him responsible to keep six commandments.

C. "He commanded him against idolatry, in line with this verse: 'Because he willingly walked after idols' (Hos. 5:11).

D. " 'The Lord' indicates a commandment against blasphemy, in line with this verse: 'And he who blasphemes the name of the Lord' (Lev. 24:16).

E. " 'God' indicates a commandment concerning setting up courts [and a judiciary]: 'You shall not revile the judges' [in the verse at hand, 'God'] (Ex. 22:27).

F. " '. . . the man' refers to the prohibition of murder: 'Whoever sheds man's blood' (Gen. 9:6).

G. " '. . . saying' refers to the prohibition of fornication: 'Saying, "If a man put away his wife" ' (Jer. 3:1).

H. " 'Of every tree you may eat' (Gen. 2:16) indicates that he commanded him concerning theft. [There are things one may take, and there are things one may not take.]"

2.A. Rabbis interpret the passage in this way: " 'And the Lord God commanded' (Gen. 2:16).

B. "He said to him, 'What am I? I am God. I wish to be treated like God, so he may not curse me.' [That proves only that Adam was commanded not to blaspheme.]

C. "How do we know that he was commanded not to fornicate? 'And cleave to *his* wife' (Gen. 2:24), and not to the wife of his neighbor, to a male, or to an animal." [So rabbis find in the verse only two prohibitions, against blasphemy and fornication.]

3.A. "Of every tree of the garden you may freely eat" (Gen. 2:16):

B. Said R. Jacob of Kefar Hanan, "When does [a beast] turn into food and become fit for eating? When it has been properly slaughtered. Accordingly, he gave man an indication that it is forbidden to eat a limb cut from a living beast." [Jacob here finds the commandment not to treat animals cruelly.]

4.A. "But of the tree of the knowledge of good and evil you shall not eat, for in the day that you eat of it you shall die" (Gen. 2:17):

B. [Since the verb, "you shall surely die," uses the root "die" more than once, what is indicated is] the death penalty for Adam, for Eve, and for coming generations.

At issue at nos. 1–3 is natural law, that is to say, the laws that apply to man in general. No. 1 presents six such laws, nos. 2, 3 then provide a different picture. So the condition of the first man prefigured the condition of all humanity, which is held liable to keep those commandments that were assigned to Adam. The secondary effect of the exegesis of the base verse is to develop links between the present passage and diverse verses elsewhere, so forming a single fabric. No. 4 moves on to the next matter.

The Tree of Knowledge, the Tree of Life

Since in today's world, people maintain that the sin of woman and man had something to do with sex, it is important to hear our sages on the matter.

XV:VII.1.A. ". . . the tree of knowledge . . ." (Gen. 2:9):

B. What was the tree from which Adam and Eve ate?

C. R. Meir says, "In fact it was wheat. When someone has no knowledge, people say, 'That man has never in his life eaten bread made out of wheat.' "

2.A. R. Samuel bar R. Isaac asked R. Zeira, saying to him, "Is it possible that it was wheat?"

B. He said to him, "Yes."

C. He said to him, "But lo, what is written is 'tree' [so how can it be wheat]!"

D. He said to him, "It was wheat that grew as high as cedars of Lebanon [and so fell into the classification of trees]."

3.A. Said R. Jacob bar Aha, "There was a dispute between R. Nehemiah and rabbis."

B. R. Nehemiah said, "[Before one eats bread, one says the blessing,] '. . . who has brought forth bread from the earth,' for [God] has already brought the bread forth from the earth."

C. Rabbis say, " '. . . who brings [forth bread from the earth]' for he will bring it forth in time to come, in line with this verse: 'There shall be a handful of grain in the land' (Ps. 72:16)." [Freedman explains the relevance of this passage as follows: They differ on the bringing forth of bread itself, not mere wheat which must be made into bread. Nehemiah holds that the phrase refers to the past, as God brought forth bread itself before Adam's sin, while the rabbis say that the word is said to refer to the messianic future, for it is then that God will cause bread to grow.]

4.A. As to the blessing one is to say for vegetables, between two Amoras there was a dispute on the word at hand, LPT. One of them said that the word LPT stands for "not bread" (L'PT).

B. The other said that the word stands for "it will not be bread in the future." [Freedman, p. 123, n. 2: "Not bread:" it was not food for man before he sinned, as bread fully seasoned grew out of the ground then.]

6.*A.* R. Judah bar Ilai said, "It was grapes [that Adam and Eve ate], as it is said, 'Their grapes are grapes of gall, they have clusters of bitterness' (Deut. 32:32).

B. "They were the grapes that brought bitterness into the world."

C. R. Abba of Acre said, "It was the *etrog,* in line with this verse: 'And the woman saw that the [wood of] the tree was good for food' (Gen. 3:6). Now go and find out what sort of tree produces wood that can be eaten just as much as its fruit can be eaten, and you will find only the *etrog.*"

7.*A.* R. Yose said, "It was figs."

B. [Yose] derives the meaning of what is not stated explicitly from the meaning of what is made explicit, and that very meaning he derives from its context. [How so?]

C. The matter may be compared to the case of a prince who misbehaved with one of his slave girls. When the king heard about it, he drove him out of the palace, and the prince went begging at the doors of slave girls, but they would not accept him. But the one with whom he had misbehaved opened her door to him and accepted him. So at the moment at which the first man ate from that tree, [God] drove him out of the Garden of Eden, and man went begging among all the trees, but none would accept him.

D. What did they say to him?

E. Said R. Berekhiah, " 'Here comes the thief who deceived his creator, here comes the thief who deceived his master.' That is in line with the following verse of scripture: 'Let not the foot of presumption come to me' (Ps. 36:12), meaning, 'the foot that presumed against its creator' [Freedman], 'and let not the hand of the wicked shake me' (Ps. 36:12), meaning, 'do not let it take a leaf from me.' "

F. [Reverting to E-F:] But it was the fig, of the fruit of which they had eaten, that opened its door and accepted him.

That is in line with this verse: "And they sewed fig leaves together" (Gen. 3:7).

8.A.   What kind of fig was it?

B.   R. Abin said, "It was a *bart sheba* fig, for it brought seven [*sheba*] days of mourning into the world."

C.   R. Joshua of Sikhnin in the name of R. Levi: "It was a *bart ali* fig, because it brought mourning and crying into the world. [Freedman: *ali* is connected with *eli*, lamentation.]"

9.A.   R. Azariah, R. Judah bar Simon in the name of R. Joshua b. Levi, "God forbid [that it was any of the types of trees just now listed]. In point of fact the Holy One, blessed be he, did not reveal the name of that particular tree to man, and it is not destined to be revealed."

B.   Note what is written, "And if a woman approach any beast and lie down with it, you shall kill the woman and the beast" (Lev. 20:16). Now if man has sinned, what sin did the beast commit [that it should be put to death too]? But it is so that that beast should not walk about in the marketplace, while people say, "It was because of that beast that so-and-so was stoned to death." Now if it is on account of the honor owing to [Adam's] descendants that God took account, on account of his own honor, how much the more so [M. San. 7:4]. [Freedman, p. 124, n. 6: Similarly, God did not reveal the nature of the tree that it might not be said, "Through this tree Adam brought death into the world."]

Nos. 1–4 present an anthology on the subject of wheat, in response to the question that provokes the composition at hand; no. 6 is devoted to grapes and the *etrog*; nos. 7–9, to figs. If Freedman's well-grounded exegesis at nos. 3–4 is sound, then the relevance to the present context is more than merely thematic; in his reading, the point once more serves to link the story of creation to the coming redemption. Nos. 7–8 do a better job of joining the identification of the tree to the present context, as is made explicit. No. 9 closes the discussion in an entirely appropriate way.

The Fall of Woman and Man

The biblical account of the sin and punishment of man and woman provokes our sages to set forth a broad set of themes. These encompass humanity's sin and God's forgiveness, humanity's betrayal and God's love and loyalty, above all, humanity's fall from grace and Israel's salvation. Our sages commonly read a biblical event to speak to a broad range of issues. Their entire worldview and way of life informs their vision of everything they see. If we were to read scripture in the same way, we should have to bring our entire existence to the judgment and solace of scripture.

XII:VI.1.A. "Generations" (Gen. 2:4):

B. Every reference in scripture to the word "generations" is written defectively [so that the first *vav* is omitted, thus, TLDWT rather than TWLDWT].

C. There are two exceptions: "These are the generations of Peretz" (Ruth 4:18), and "These are the generation of heaven" (Gen. 2:4).

D. And why are these two not written defectively?

E. R. Yudan in the name of R. Abun: "The [missing] six [that is, the numerical value of the *vav* correspond] to six things that were taken away from the first man, and these are they: his splendor, his immortal life, his stature, the fruit of the earth, the fruit of the tree, and the primordial lights.

F. "How do we know that that is the case for his splendor [Freedman: luster]? 'You change his countenance and send him away' (Job 14:20).

G. "His immortal life? 'For dust you are and to dust you shall return' (Gen. 3:19).

H. "His stature? 'And the man and his wife hid themselves' (Gen. 3:8)."

I. Said R. Aibu, "He was cut down in height and reduced to one hundred cubits."

J. [Resuming Abun's statement:] "The fruit of the earth and the fruit of the tree? 'Cursed is the earth on your account' (Gen. 3:17)."

K. As to the primordial lights:

L. R. Simeon bar Judah: "Even though the primordial lights were spoiled on the eve of the Sabbath, they were smitten only at the end of the Sabbath."

5.A. R. Berekhiah in the name of R. Samuel bar Nahman: "Even though the matters were stated in their fulness [Freedman, p. 92, n. 2: The fact that the word for generations is spelled here fully, with a *vav*, intimates that they were created with their full power], because the first man sinned, they were spoiled, and they will never return to their full perfection until the son of Peretz will come.

B. "[How so? Proof of that proposition derives from the verse:] 'These are the generations of Peretz' (Ruth 4:18), in which the word for generations is spelled out fully, with its *vav*."

6.A. [Since the word at Ruth 4:18 is spelled out with its *vav*, we ask about the six traits of Peretz which are encompassed by the full spelling of the word, hence:] What are the six [traits of the son of Peretz, the Messiah]?

B. [These six traits correspond to the ones lost by the first man, so that the redemption completes and perfects the defects of creation:] His splendor, his immortal life, his stature, the fruit of the land, the fruit of the tree, and the lights.

C. How do we know that that is the case for his splendor? "But they that love him shall be as the sun when he goes forth in his might" (Judges 5:31).

D. How do we know that that is the case for his immortal life? "For as the days of a tree shall be the days of my people" (Is. 65:22).

E. How do we know that that is the case for his stature? "And I will make you go upright" (Lev. 26:13).

F. R. Hiyya taught on Tannaite authority, "He will go about upright, afraid of no one."

7.A. [As to the stature of the messiah:] R. Yudan said, "He will be a hundred cubits tall."

B. R. Simeon said, "Two hundred."

C. R. Eleazar b. R. Simeon said, "Three hundred, as it is said, '. . . uprights [in the plural],' hence, one 'upright' would stand for a hundred cubits, and the plural adds two hundred more."

D. R. Abbahu said, "Nine hundred cubits."

E. R. Berekhiah in the name of R. Dosa: "The scriptural basis for the position of R. Abbahu is this: A sycamore tree goes on growing on the earth for six hundred years, and a baby comes forth from its mother's womb a cubit and a half in length. Now calculate growth of a cubit and a half a year, and you get nine hundred cubits. [Freedman: R. Abbahu refers to the verse, 'For as the days of a tree.' As no tree is specified, he assumes it to mean the longest lived one, that is, the sycamore, and holds that the point of similarity is not only the length of life, but also the manner of growth, the verse teaching that the height of men shall be as much as if they were to grow uniformly for six hundred years at one and a half cubits per annum, which is the average size of the newborn baby.]

8.A. [Reverting to the original proposition:] The fruit of the earth and the fruit of the tree?

B. "For as the seed of peace, the vine shall give her fruit" (Zech. 8:12).

C. The lights? "Moreover the light of the moon shall be as the light of the sun, and the light of the sun shall be sevenfold, as the light of the seven days" (Is. 30:26).

The main point begins at the beginning and concludes at the end. The exegete proposes once more to link the story of creation with the history of the salvation of Israel. The link proves powerful, namely, the common, and unusual, spelling of the word "generations"—that is, the historical genealogy—when it appears with reference to creation and to the Messiah. The clear and unmistakable polemic, then, is that what went wrong at the creation of the world, because of man's sin, will be righted, at the salvation of the world, by the Messiah. So there is a point-by-point correspondence between what went wrong and what will, in the end, be repaired and remedied. In any event the polemic proves consistent with the familiar one, linking the natural world of creation to the historical life of Israel.

The Fall of Man and Woman: The Sin Itself

We come to the story of the fall. Our sages represent the sin both in its own terms and as a pattern for the human condition. We begin with a general comment and proceed to attend to details of the larger story.

XVIII:VI.1.A. "And the man and his wife were both naked and were not ashamed" (Gen. 2:25):

B. Said R. Eleazar, "There were three who did not remain in their good fortune for six hours, and there are they: the first man, Israel, and Sisera.

C. "The first man: 'and were not ashamed' (Gen. 2:25). [Reading the consonants differently:] six hours had not passed.

D. "Israel: 'And the people saw that Moses tarried' (Ex. 32:1). Six hours had passed [again a play on the Hebrew consonants].

E. "Sisera: 'Why does his chariot tarry to come' (Judges 5:28)?: 'Every day he would routinely come home in three hours or in four hours, and today six hours have passed and he has not yet come.' "

2.A. "And they were not ashamed" (Gen. 2:25). "But the snake was more subtle [than any other wild creature that the Lord God had made]" (Gen. 3:1).

B. It would have been quite sufficient for scripture to say: "And the Lord God made for the man and his wife garments of skin" (Gen. 3:21) [since this was done prior to the sin, and not afterward, so that statement should have appeared right after Gen. 2:25, rather than the verse that comes as Gen. 3:1].

C. Said R. Joshua b. Qorha, "It serves to let you know the sin that that wicked [creature] had got them to do. When he saw that they were having sexual relations, and he lusted after the woman [he tried to kill Adam by getting him to sin]."

D. Said R. Jacob of Kefar Hanan, "[The presentation of that detail] was postponed to that latter passage so as not to conclude the story of the creation of man with the matter of the snake. [So that detail was introduced only at the end of the narrative.]"

XIX:III.1.A. "And the woman said to the snake. 'We may eat of the fruit of the trees [of the garden, but God said, "You shall not eat of the fruit of the tree which is in the midst of the garden, neither shall you touch it, lest you die"]" (Gen. 3:3):

B. Where was man when this conversation was going on?

C. Abba Halpun bar Qoriah said, "He had earlier had sexual relations, and now he was sleeping it off."

D. Rabbis say, "God had taken him and was showing him the whole world, saying to him, 'This is what an orchard looks like, this is an area suitable for sowing grain.' So it is written, 'Through a land that no man had passed through, and where Adam had not dwelt' (Jer. 2:6), that is, Adam had not lived there [but there were lands Adam had seen on his tour]."

2.A. ". . . of the fruit of the tree which is in the midst of the garden" (Gen. 3:3):

B. That is in line with this verse: "Add not to his words, lest he reprove you, and you be found a liar" (Prov. 30:6). [God had said nothing about not touching the tree, but the woman said they were not to eat of the fruit of the tree or even to touch it.]

C. R. Hiyya taught, "It is that one should not make the fence taller than the foundation, so that the fence will not fall down and wipe out the plants.

D. "So the Holy One, blessed be he, had said, 'For on the day on which you eat from it, you shall surely die' (Gen. 2:17). But that is not what she then said to the snake. Rather: 'God said, "You shall not eat from it *and you shall not touch it.*'" When the snake saw that she was lying to him, he took her and pushed her against the tree. He said to her, 'Have you now died? Just as you did not die for touching it, so you will not die from eating it.'

E. "Rather: 'For God knows that when you eat of it, your eyes will be opened and you will be like God' (Gen. 3:5)."

XIX:V.1.A. "[So when the woman saw] that the tree was good for food [and that it was a delight for the eyes, and that the tree was to be desired to make one wise]" (Gen. 3:6):

B. R. Eleazar in the name of R. Yose b. Zimra: "Three statements were made concerning the tree, that it was good to eat, a delight to the eyes, and that it added wisdom,

C. "and all of them were stated in a single verse:

D. " 'So when the woman saw that the tree was good for food,' on which basis we know that it was good to eat;

E. " 'and that it was a delight to the eyes,' on which basis we know that it was a delight for the eyes,

F. " 'and that the tree was to be desired to make one wise,' on which basis we know that it added to one's wisdom.

G. "That is in line with the following verse of scripture: 'A song of wisdom of Ethan the Ezrahite' (Ps. 89:1)" [and the root for "song of wisdom" and that for "to make one wise" are the same].

2.A. "She took of its fruit and ate" (Gen. 3:6):

B. Said R. Aibu, "She squeezed some grapes and gave him the juice."

C. R. Simlai said, "She approached him fully prepared [with strong arguments], saying to him, 'What do you think? Is it that I am going to die, and that another woman will be created for you?' [That is not possible:] 'There is nothing new under the sun' (Qoh. 1:9).

D. "Or perhaps you think that I shall die and you will live all by yourself? 'He did not create the world as a waste, he formed it to be inhabited' (Is. 45:18)."

E. Rabbis say, "She began to moan and weep to him."

3.A. The word "also" ['And she *also* gave some to her husband' (Gen. 3:6)] bears the force of a phrase of in-clusion, meaning to encompass domesticated beasts, wild beasts, and fowl.

B. Everyone obeyed her and ate of the fruit, except for one bird, which is called the phoenix.

C. For it is written, "Then I shall die with my nest and I shall multiply my days as the phoenix" (Job 29:18).

D. A member of the house of R. Yannai and R. Yudan bar Simeon [debated matters as follows]:

E. A member of the house of R. Yannai said, "It lives for a thousand years, and at the end of a thousand years a fire goes forth from its nest and burns it up and leaves an egg['s bulk of ash], which goes and grows limbs and lives on."

F.   R. Yudan bar Simeon said, "It lives for a thousand years and at the end of a thousand years its body dissolves and its wings drop off, but an egg['s bulk] is left and it goes and grows parts and lives on."

The exegesis of the encounter with the snake, Gen. 3:13, picks up the discrepancy between God's instruction not to eat the fruit of the tree and the woman's report that God had forbidden even touching the tree. No. 2 makes the general point that one should not add too much to the strict instructions of the law, and no. 3 then applies that general principle to the case at hand. The underlying motif is that it is arrogant for man to demand more than God has already laid down. The story is made to focus upon the dangers of human arrogance—here, even in a good cause. What follows is yet another such statement, at XIX:V, that man should not compete with God in ruling over creation. In that paragraph no. 1 provides an obvious exegesis of the base verse. No. 2 creates a colloquy explaining how the woman persuaded the man to follow her example. No. 3 then moves off in its own direction, beginning with the observation that a well-known hermeneutical principle now is to be invoked. Then we ask what was included, with the concomitant question of what was excluded, by the encompassing clause. The allusion to the myth of the phoenix follows.

The Result of the Sin of Man and Woman: Naked of What Garment?

What does it mean "to know," and what did man and woman find out that they had not known before? These are the questions answered now. The fall from innocence in the sages' view is marked by the discovery of one's nudity in a very specific context. Man and woman discovered they were naked of the garment formed of the doing of religious duties (*mitzvot*).

XIX:VI.1.A.   "Then the eyes of both of them were opened" (Gen. 3:7):

B. And had they been blind?

C. R. Yudan in the name of R. Yohanan b. Zakkai, R. Berekhiah in the name of R. Aqiba: "The matter may be compared to the case of a villager who was walking by a glass-maker's stall. In front of him was a basket full of fine goblets and cut glass. He swung his staff and broke them all. The glass-maker went and grabbed him.

D. "He said to him, 'I know full well that I am not going to get anything of value from you [since you are so poor that you cannot pay me back]. But come and let me at least show you how much property of worth you have destroyed.'

E. "So God showed them how many generations they had destroyed [and that is the manner in which their eyes were opened]."

2.A. "And they knew that they were naked" (Gen. 3:7):

B. Even of the single religious duty that they had in hand they were now denuded. [The word "naked" is associated with "being clothed by the merit accruing from the performance of religious duties."]

3.A. "And they sewed fig leaves together and made themselves aprons" (Gen. 3:7):

B. Said R. Abba bar Kahana, "What is not written is 'an apron,' but rather 'aprons.'

C. "The sense of the plural is this: a variety of clothing, such as shirts, robes, and linen cloaks.

D. "And just as these sorts of garments are made for a man, so for a woman they make girdles, hats, and hair nets. [So the plural of the word yields the sense that they clothed themselves in a variety of garments.]"

Considerations important to the sages' system, with special reference to "naked" of religious duties, guide sages' understanding here. That reading powerfully links the story at hand to the religious system of sanctification through religious duties. If we were to read the story as a living picture of our world, we would uncover new layers of meaning and possibilities none before us has dreamed of.

Adam and Eve in Eden, Israel in the Land of Israel: The Counterparts

At this point sages introduce the comparison and contrast of humanity, represented by the first man, and Israel, therefore of Eden and the land of Israel. This construction of the counterpart and opposite allows them to address Israel in its land and to make a powerful statement of the meaning of Israel's life in its land.

XIX:IX.1.A. "And the Lord God called to the man and said to him, 'Where are you?' " (Gen. 3:9):

B. [The word for "where are you" yields consonants that bear the meaning] "How has this happened to you?"

C. [God speaks:] "Yesterday it was in accord with my plan, and now it is in accord with the plan of the snake. Yesterday it was from one end of the world to the other [that you filled the earth], and now: 'Among the trees of the garden' (Gen. 3:8) [you hide out]."

2.A. R. Abbahu in the name of R. Yose bar Haninah: "It is written, 'But they are like a man [Adam], they have transgressed the covenant' (Hos. 6:7).

B. " 'They are like a man,' specifically, like the first man. [We shall now compare the story of the first man in Eden with the story of Israel in its land.]

C. "In the case of the first man, I brought him into the garden of Eden, I commanded him, he violated my commandment, I judged him to be sent away and driven out, but I mourned for him, saying 'How . . .' [which begins the book of Lamentations, hence stands for a lament, but which, as we just saw, also is written with the consonants that also yield, 'Where are you'].

D. " 'I brought him into the garden of Eden,' as it is written, 'And the Lord God took the man and put him into the garden of Eden' (Gen. 2:15).

E. " 'I commanded him,' as it is written, 'And the Lord God commanded' (Gen. 2:16).

103

F. " 'And he violated my commandment,' as it is written, 'Did you eat from the tree concerning which I commanded you?' (Gen. 3:11).

G. " 'I judged him to be sent away,' as it is written, 'And the Lord God sent him from the garden of Eden' (Gen. 3:23).

H. " 'And I judged him to be driven out.' 'And he drove out the man' (Gen. 3:24).

I. "But I mourned for him, saying, 'How. . . .' 'And he said to him, "Where are you" ' (Gen. 3:9), and the word for 'where are you' is written, 'How. . . .'

J. "So too in the case of his descendants [God continues to speak] I brought them into the land of Israel, I commanded them, they violated my commandment, I judged them to be sent out and driven away but I mourned for them, saying, 'How. . . .'

K. " 'I brought them into the land of Israel.' 'And I brought you into the land of Carmel' (Jer. 2:7).

L. " 'I commanded them.' 'And you, command the children of Israel' (Ex. 27:20). 'Command the children of Israel' (Lev. 24:2).

M. " 'They violated my commandment.' 'And all Israel have violated your Torah' (Dan. 9:11).

N. " 'I judged them to be sent out.' 'Send them away, out of my sight and let them go forth' (Jer 15:1).

O. " '. . . and driven away.' 'From my house I shall drive them' (Hos. 9:15).

P. "But I mourned for them, saying, 'How. . . .' 'How has the city sat solitary, that was full of people' (Lam. 1:1)."

I find deeply moving both treatments of Gen. 3:9. No. 1 simply contrasts one day with the next, a stunning and stark statement, lacking all decoration. No. 1 certainly sets the stage for no. 2. The other, no. 2, equally simply compares the story of man in the Garden of Eden with the tale of Israel in its land. Every detail is in place, the articulation is perfect, and the result, completely convincing as an essay in interpretation. All of this rests on the simple fact that the word for "where are you" may be expressed as "How," which, as is clear, invokes the opening words of the book of Lamentations. So Israel's history serves as a paradigm for human history, and vice versa. Then Israel stands at the center of humanity. To put matters in terms of the world we know, the sorrows of Israel show what it means to be human: to suffer, to despair, but also, to hope and to believe.

Israel and Humanity

Our sages see Adam and Israel as mirror images, opposite one another, so they find in the story of Adam's fall a promise of Israel's redemption. The story of Adam's fall because he could not keep the one religious duty assigned to him bears a profound message of hope for Israel. Why so? Because here and now, in the sages' view, Israel keeps the myriad of commandments entrusted to them. That fact promises Israel's coming redemption—whatever the near-term indications may forebode. So our sages read the crisis of man and woman in the garden as the assurance of Israel's future salvation.

XXI:VII.2.A. Said R. Joshua b. Levi, "When God created him, he created him in accord with the attribute of justice and also the attribute of mercy. When he drove him out, he drove him out in accord with the attribute of justice and also the attribute of mercy.

B. "Behold, the man: 'See, man, you could not abide in the commandment that applied to you for even a single hour!' " [In this way God expressed his pity for man.]

3.A. Judah b. Padaiah interpreted, "Who will remove the dust from between your eyes, O first man! For you could not abide in the commandment that applied to you for even a single hour, and lo, your children can wait for three years to observe the prohibition of the use of the fruit of a tree for the first three years after it is planted: 'Three years shall it be as forbidden to you, it shall not be eaten' (Lev. 19:23)."

B. Said R. Huna, "When Bar Qappara heard this, he said, 'Well have you expounded matters, Judah, son of my sister!' "

We now compare the character of Israel to the character of the first man, calling Israel "descendants of the first man" and pointing out that they can observe a commandment for a long time. The example is apt, since Israel observes the prohibition involving the fruit of a newly planted tree, and does so for three years, while the first man could not keep his hands off a fruit tree for even an hour. This of course states with enormous power the fact that Israel's history forms the counterpart to the history of humanity. But while the first man could not do what God demanded, Israel can and does do God's will. Israel, like Adam, is commanded, and Israel, like Adam, is weak, but Israel unlike Adam can overcome weakness and so gain a blessing.

5 From Adam to Noah

Adam and Moses:
Why the Torah was not Given to Adam

The continued contrast between Adam and Israel carries us to the question of why the first man did not receive the Torah. Sages held that the religious duties purify Israel, and the Torah is what makes Israel worthy of salvation. So they wonder why Adam did not enjoy the advantage and opportunity later on accorded to Israel. Here is the answer to that question, as it is spelled out by our sages' worldview and way of life.

XXIV:V.2.A. Said R. Yudah, "The first man [Adam] was worthy to have the Torah given through him. What is the verse of scripture that so indicates? 'This is the book of the generations of man' (Gen. 5:1). ["This book can be given over to man."]

B. "Said the Holy One, blessed be he, 'He is the creation of my hands, and should I not give it to him?' Then he reversed himself and said, 'I gave him no more than six commandments to follow, and he did not stand by them, so how can I now give him six hundred thirteen commandments, two hundred forty-eight commandments of things to do and three hundred sixty-five commandments of things not to do?'

C. " 'And he said to man,' meaning, 'not-to-man' [reading the L before the consonants for 'man,' read as 'to man,' as though it bore the negative]. 'To man I shall not give it. And to whom shall I give it? To his children.' 'This is the book that belongs to the children of man' (Gen. 5:1)."

3.A. Said R. Jacob of Kefar Hanan, "The first man was worthy to produce the twelve tribes. What is the verse of scripture that so indicates? 'This is the book of man.'

B. "The word 'this' in Hebrew has consonants with the numerical value of twelve (ZH).

C. "Said the Holy One, blessed be he, 'He is the creation of my hands, and should I not give it to him?' Then he reversed himself and said, 'Two sons I gave him, and one of them went and killed his fellow. How shall I then give him twelve?'

D. " 'And he said to man' (Job 28:27) meaning, 'not-to-man' [reading the L before the consonants for man as though it bore the negative]. To man I shall not give it. And to whom shall I give it? To his children: 'This is the book that belongs to the children of man' (Gen. 5:1)."

The selection of the first man for the role of Moses is presented as a choice that God considered and rejected, for the reason spelled out. The ongoing polemic now reaches a climax: what Adam could not accomplish, Moses did. Or, to state matters in more general terms, what man could not do, Israel, represented by Moses, can do. The contrast then between Adam and Moses bears a heavy weight of meaning.

Cain and Abel: The Nature of Sin

Why did God favor Abel over Cain? Here we consider the real story of the first murder, which carried forward the decline and fall of man. We start with the statement that sin couches by the door.

XXII:VI.1.A. "And the Lord had regard for Abel and his offering" (Gen. 4:3):

B. He was conciliated by it.

C. "But for Cain and his offering he had no regard" (Gen. 4:5):

D. He was not conciliated by it.

E. "So Cain was very angry and his countenance fell" (Gen. 4:5):

F. His face turned as red as a torch.

4.A. "Sin is couching at the door; its desire is for you, but you must master it" (Gen. 4:7):

B. The word for "couch" is written not in the feminine but in the masculine form. In the beginning sin is weak, like a woman, but afterward it grows strong, like a man.

C. Said R. Aqiba, "In the beginning it is as thin as a spider's thread, but later on it becomes as thick as a ship's rope. So it is written, 'Woe to them that draw iniquity with trifling cords, and sin with a cart rope' (Is. 5:18)."

D. Said R. Isaac, "At the beginning sin is like a drop-in, then it becomes like a regular guest, and at the end it becomes a member of the household.

E. "That is in line with this verse of scripture: 'And there came a traveler to the rich man' (2 Sam. 12:4). That is, as a traveler who goes right on by. 'And he spared to take of his own flock and of his own herd, to dress for the guest that had come to him' (2 Sam. 12:4). Now he is called a guest. 'And he dressed it for the man that had come to him' (2 Sam. 12:4). Now he has become the master. [Freedman, p. 185, n.1: He is no longer spoken of as a traveler or guest but simply man, the master of the house.]"

5.*A.* [Explaining the sense of the phrase, "Sin is couching at the door"] said R. Tanhum bar Merion, "There are dogs in Rome that know how to dissemble.

B. "A dog goes and sets down before a baker shop and pretends to doze. The owner of the shop dozes too, and then the dog knocks a loaf to the ground. While the people are collecting the bread, the dog snatches a loaf and makes its getaway. [Freedman, p. 185, n.3: Thus sin pretends to sleep until it catches its victim off guard.]"

C. [Explaining the same phrase] said R. Abba bar Yudan, "The matter may be compared to the case of a threatening but feeble thug, who sat at the crossroads. Whoever came by he ordered, 'Give me everything you've got.' But a smart fellow came by and realized that the thug was in fact decrepit. So he beat him up.

D. "So for many generations the impulse to do evil caused destruction. The generation of Enosh, the generation of the flood, and the generation of the dispersion [all were conquered by it]. When Abraham arose and saw that the impulse to do evil in fact amounted to nothing, he began to knock it about. That is in line with the following verse of scripture: 'And I will beat to pieces his impulse before him' (Ps. 89:24). [Freedman, p. 185, n.4: Thus 'sin couches at the door'—his strength being only simulated.]"

6.A.   Said R. Ammi, "The impulse to do evil does not walk along the sides of the path but right down the center. When it sees a man blinking his eyes, smoothing his hair, skipping along arrogantly [and generally preening himself about his good looks] he says, 'This one is mine.'

B.   "Why so? 'Do you see someone who considers himself wise? The fool [meaning, sin] has hope of seizing him' (Prov. 26:12)."

7.A.   Said R. Abin, "Whoever indulges his impulse to do evil in his youth in the end will be ruled by the evil impulse in his old age.

B.   "What verse of scripture so indicates? 'He who indulges his servant in youth shall have him as a master in the end' (Prov. 29:21)."

8.A.   R. Hanina said, "If your evil impulse comes to make you laugh, put it off with words of Torah: 'The evil impulse, when near you, you shall combat' (Is. 26:3).

B.   "And if you do so, I shall credit it to you as if you had created peace: 'You shall create peace' (Is. 26:3). What is written is not 'you shall keep,' but 'you shall create.'

C.   "And if you should say that the evil impulse does not lie within your domain, scripture says, 'Surely it is safe in you' (Is. 26:3), and I have already written for your attention in the Torah: 'And its desire is for you, but you must master it' (Gen. 4:7)."

D.   R. Simon said, "If your impulse to do evil comes to make you laugh, give it reason to rejoice in the Torah: 'Your impulse is gladdened' (Is. 26:3).

E.   "And if you do so, I shall credit it to you as if you had created two worlds. 'Peace' is not what is written here, but rather, 'Peace, peace' (Is. 26:3) [referring therefore to two whole worlds]."

The murder represents a sin, in the tradition of man. So we take the occasion to reflect on the nature of sin. We work out the meaning of Gen. 4:6–7, "if you do well. . . ." The explanation moves from the simple sense that if you do well, you get a blessing, and if not, you get a curse, to the somewhat more spiritual sense that, if you do well, you are forgiven, and if not, you are not forgiven. This leads to the long anthology on sin, nos. 4–8. The anthology, of course, links the story of humanity to the history of Israel. This is made explicit in two ways. First, we have the reference to the power of sin until the advent of Abraham. Then we find the message that the antidote to sin is study of Torah. In these two ways the deeper polemic of the document as a whole, concerning the role of Israel in the history of humanity, finds concrete expression. The sequence of propositions of the anthology follows a simple path. First, sin is weak but then becomes habitual and habits are hard to break; second, sin dissembles, and it is easy to overcome, as Abraham did. Third, the arrogant are the chief sinners. Fourth, the people who make sin a habit will find it hard to overcome. Finally, the Torah is the antidote. The compositor thus repeated his message and set the climax at the conclusion, to give the whole a clear point and purpose. The anthology represents a good piece of composition. The exegete-compositors thus register their point through what they select and how they make their arrangement.

The Murder Itself

What in fact was at issue between Cain and Abel? Where the scriptural tale falls short in telling all, our sages fill in the gap. At issue was jealousy and dissension. So the original sin now gains detail.

XXII:VII.1.A. "Cain said to Abel his brother, 'Let us go out to the field' " (Gen. 4:8):

B. [Treating the word "spoke" as meaning "had words with," or quarreled, we ask:] Concerning what did they quarrel?

C. They said, "Come and let us divide up the world. One will take the real estate, the other, the movables."

111

D. One said, "The land on which you are standing belongs to me."

E. The other said, "Even what you're wearing belongs to me."

F. The one said, "Strip."

G. The other said, "Move off."

H. And, as matters played themselves out: "[And when they were in the field], Cain rose up against his brother Abel and killed him" (Gen. 4:8).

2.A. R. Joshua of Sikhnin in the name of R. Levi: "Both of them took the real estate of the world, and both of them took the movables. Then what was the quarrel about? This one said, 'In my domain will the house of the sanctuary be built,' and that one said, 'In my domain.'

B. " 'And when they were in the field' (Gen. 4:8) [indicates it, for] the word 'field' can refer only to the house of the sanctuary, as it is said, 'Zion shall be ploughed as a field' (Micah 3:12).

C. "And, as matters played themselves out: 'Cain rose up against his brother Abel and killed him' (Gen. 4:8)."

3.A. Judah b. Rabbi said, "The quarrel was about the first woman."

B. Said R. Aibu, "The first woman had already returned to the dust, and what is it that they were quarreling about?"

C. Said R. Huna, "An additional baby, a twin, had been born with Abel. This one said, 'I shall take her,' and that one said, 'I shall take her.'

D. "This one said, 'I shall take her, for I am the first-born,' and that one said, 'I shall take her, for she was born with me.' "

The three related entries answer the same question, filling in an important gap in the narrative. But the basic conviction of the biblical story, that at issue was Cain's jealousy of Abel, because God had favored Abel, is curiously absent in all three explanations. The first theory of the dispute is that it concerned material things; the second, that it concerned the sacred service; the third, that it concerned who will possess the woman. If we substitute for the possession of the house of the sanctuary the prestige accruing to the one who holds possession of that domain, then at issue in the mind of the compositor of the whole is wealth, prestige, and sex. God's favor of one brother because of his superior offering, as against the other because of his niggardly one, then falls away from the story, which turns into an account of human greed, arrogance, and lust. No one, then, can blame God for what happened—namely, the first murder—and anyone who holds that God, the creator, is evil, is surely wrong. If this view is not farfetched, then the recasting of the story serves the polemic against those who condemn creation and the creator-God. In any event, whatever the target of the revision of the story, God ceases to be cause of the murder.

Cain Kills Abel: The Sin, The Punishment

We turn to the act itself. We recall how the tale of the fall of man and woman drew from sages comments meant to add detail and link the story to the worldview and way of life sages, among all Israel, cherished.

XXII:VIII.1.A. "Cain rose up against his brother Abel and killed him" (Gen. 4:8):

B. Said R. Yohanan, "Abel was stronger than Cain.

C. "For when scripture says, 'He rose up,' it teaches only that Cain had been located beneath him. [Freedman, p. 187, n.5: They had already quarreled and Abel had thrown Cain down.]

D. "He said to him, 'The two of us are the only ones in the world. What are you going to go and tell father?'

E. "So Abel was filled with pity for Cain. Then Cain overcame him and killed him.

F. "On the basis of this story people say, 'If you don't do good to a bad person, nothing bad will happen to you.'"

XXII:IX.1.A. R. Joshua in the name of R. Levi: "It is written, 'The wicked have drawn out their sword' (Ps. 37:14) refers to Cain.

B. " 'To cast down the poor and needy' (Ps. 37:14) refers to Abel.

C. " 'Their sword shall enter into their own hearts' (Ps. 37:14) and so it is written, 'A fugitive and a wanderer shall you be in the earth' (Gen. 4:12)."

2.A. "Then the Lord said to Cain, 'Where is Abel your brother?' " (Gen. 4:9):

B. The matter may be compared to the case of a local official, who was walking down the middle of the road. He found someone killed, with another standing over him. He said to him, "Who killed this one?"

C. The other said to him, "I ask you, and you ask me."

D. He said to him, "You have said nothing at all! [What kind of a claim is that? You obviously did it.]"

3.A. The matter may be compared to someone who went into a garden and picked berries and ate them. The farmer ran after him, saying to him, "What's in your hand?"

B. The other said to him, "Not a thing."

C. "But look at your hands, they're a mess!"

D. So: "The voice of your brother's blood is crying to me from the earth" (Gen. 4:10).

4.A. The matter may be compared to the case of someone who stole into a flock and grabbed a lamb, and he threw it over his shoulder. The herdsman ran after him and said to him, "What do you have in your hand?"

B. The other said to him, "Not a thing."

C. He said to him, "Lo, the thing is bleating on your backside."

D. So 'The voice of your brother's blood is crying to me from the earth' (Gen. 4:10).

6.A. Said R. Simeon b. Yohai, "The matter is not so easy to express, and it really is not possible to spell it all out. Still:

B. "The matter may be compared to the case of two gladiators who struggled with one another before the king. If the king had wanted, he could have separated them. But the king did not choose to pull them apart, and one of them outclassed the other and killed him. Before he was killed, the loser cried out, 'Let my cause be brought before the king.'

C. "So: 'The voice of your brother's blood is crying to me from the ground' (Gen. 4:10). [But God could have prevented the murder and did nothing, so the outcry came to the party responsible for the murder to begin with.]"

In each case the statement of God to Cain serves as a counterargument to a claim of innocence. The blood by itself gives testimony that Cain was guilty. No. 5 makes its own point, taking up the use of the plural, "bloods." No. 6 by contrast takes a breathtaking initiative, one that bears its own apology and then trails off into silence.

Rebellion: The Recurrent Sin of Man

Sages stress that Israel is saved through obedience to the commandments of God. The opposite—Israel falls from grace—through rebellion against God's will. To make that point, of course, sages turn to the story of the decline of humanity from Adam to the flood. So at each point they underline the issue of disobedience, rebellion, arrogance, and willfulness.

XXIII:VII.1.A. Said R. Simon, "In three passages the term at hand ['began'] bears the sense of 'rebel.'

B. " 'Then they rebelled to call upon the name of the Lord' (Gen. 4:26).

C. " 'And it came to pass when man rebelled in multiplying on the face of the earth' (Gen. 6:1).

D. " 'Nimrod rebelled when he was a mighty one in the earth' (Gen. 10:8)."

E. The objection was raised: "And lo, it is written, 'And this is what they have rebelled to do' (Gen. 11:6). [So there should be four examples, not three.]"

F. He said to them, "[The case of Nimrod should be removed from the catalogue, for God] hit Nimrod's head, saying, 'He is the one who incited them to rebel.' (Freedman, p. 197, n.5: Translating the last sentence, 'This man,

Nimrod, has incited them to revolt.' Hence it is not an additional instance.]"

2.A.   Said R. Levi, "The matter may be compared to the case of a woman who said to her husband, 'I dreamed that you divorced me.'

B.   "He said to her, 'Why in a dream? Here, let's make it the real thing.' [Freedman, p. 197, n.6: He derives the word 'began' from the word 'dream,' and translates: 'And this against which they dream, that is, the possibility of being scattered, will become an actuality, and they will be scattered.']"

3.A.   Said R. Aha, "'You made an idol and called upon your name.' [Freedman, p. 197, n.7: They had used names indicating that they themselves are gods. He translates: 'Then they rebelled by calling themselves by the name of the Lord.']

B.   "[God responded] 'So I too shall call the water of the ocean to act in my name, and I shall wipe out the wicked from the world.' "

"Beginning" now signifies "rebellion." The thrust of the exegesis remains the same, namely, to discredit the generations before the flood. Their "calling upon the name of the Lord" is revised. No. 3 and no. 4 then move to signal the coming flood, while no. 2 refers to the dispersion afterward. The net effect is to link one story to the next and to form all stories into a single proposition: human rebellion brought on the flood. Then human submission, that is, acceptance of God's will, will bring on redemption.

The Reason for the Flood

We proceed rapidly to the end of the story of Adam's seed. God lavished blessings on no-accounts. The story of creation tells the tale of God's disappointment at what God had made.

XXVII:I.1.A.   "The Lord saw that the wickedness of man was great [in the earth, and that every imagination of the thoughts of his heart was only evil continually]" (Gen. 6:5):

B. "For there is a man whose labor is with wisdom" (Qoh. 2:21).

C. Said R. Yudan, "The prophets' power is remarkable, since they compare the created to the creator: 'And I heard the voice of a man between the banks of the Ulai' (Dan. 8:16). [God was speaking, as is clear from the second half of the verse, yet he is referred to as a man's voice (Freedman, p. 220, n.1)]."

D. Said R. Yudan bar Simon, "We have another verse which provides still clearer evidence than that one: 'And upon the likeness of the throne was a likeness as the appearance of a man upon it above' (Ez. 12:36)."

E. [Reverting to Qoh. 2:21:] "With wisdom" as it is written, "The Lord by wisdom founded the earth" (Prov. 3:19).

F. "And with knowledge" (Qoh. 2:21), as it is written, "By his knowledge the depths were broken up" (Prov. 3:20).

G. "And with skill" (Qoh. 2:21):

H. R. Berekhiah in the name of R. Judah bar Simon, "Not with labor or with anguish did the Holy One, blessed be he, create his world, but 'By the word of the Lord the heavens were made' (Ps. 33:6)."

I. "Yet to a man that has not labored therein shall he leave it for his portion" (Qoh. 2:21) refers to the generation of the flood.

J. "This also is vanity and a great evil" (Qoh. 2:21). "The Lord saw that the wickedness of man was great" (Gen. 6:5).

XXVII:II.1.A. "The Lord saw that the wickedness of man was great [in the earth, and that every imagination of the thoughts of his heart was only evil continually]" (Gen. 6:5):

B. "For all his days are pains" (Qoh. 2:23), for they caused pains to the Holy One, blessed be he, through the wicked things that they did.

C. "And his occupation caused anger" (Qoh. 2:23), for they caused anger to the Holy One, blessed be he, through the wicked things that they did.

D. "Yes, even in the night his heart takes no rest" (Qoh. 2:23) from sin.

E. And how do we know that that also was the case by day? As it is written, "Only evil continually" (Gen. 6:5).

XXVII:III.1.A. "The Lord saw that the wickedness of man was great [in the earth, and that every imagination of the thoughts of his heart was only evil continually]" (Gen. 6:5):

B. R. Hinena said, "It continued to grew great."

C. R. Berekhiah in the name of R. Yohanan [said], "We know that the generation of the flood was judged and punished with water, and the Sodomites with fire. How do we know that we should assign what is stated here to the Sodomites, and what is stated in their regard to the generation of the flood?

D. "Scripture makes use of the word 'great' in both passages, providing for an analogy [between Gen. 6:5 and Gen. 18:29]."

2.A. "Only evil continually" (Gen. 6:5):

B. From the time that the sun came up until it set, there was nothing of redeeming value in them. That is in line with this verse: "The murderer rises with the light" (Job 24:14).

C. And lo it is written, "In the dark they dig through houses" (Job 24:16). [Why then emphasize that it is only at dawn that the murderer gets up?]

D. Why? Because "they make a sign for themselves in the daytime" (Job 24:16).

E. What did one do? He would bring balsam and smear it on a stone, then come by night and dig there [at the point at which entry would be easy].

F. When R. Hanina gave this interpretation in Sepphoris, on that night there were three hundred break-ins.

God created the world but handed it over to the generation that brought on the flood. This was a vanity and an evil. The wisdom, knowledge, and skill lavished on creating the world went for nothing. The point about what happened in Sepphoris requires no comment. The sages did not see much difference between the ancient day and their own time.

God Regrets Making Man

We come now to the terrible judgment: "And the Lord was sorry that he had made man on the earth, and it grieved him to his heart" (Gen. 6:6). Given our sages' hopeful view of humanity, their affirmation of creation and God's goodness, we realize how deep a thrust at the heart of their basic view of life they must have found in the verse at hand. These must be the most terrifying words of scripture.

XXVII:VI.1.A. "And the Lord was sorry that he had made [man on the earth, and it grieved him to his heart]" (Gen. 6:6):

B. R. Judah said, "[God said] 'It was a blunder before me that I created him below [out of earthly elements (Freedman)], for if I had made him of the elements of heaven, he would never have rebelled against me.' "

C. R. Nehemiah said, "[God said] 'I take comfort in the fact that I created him below, for if I had created him above, just as he brought rebellion against me from the creatures below, so he would have led a rebellion against me among the creatures above.' "

D. R. Aibu said, "It was a blunder that I created in him the impulse to do evil, for if I had not created the impulse to do evil in him, he would never have rebelled against me."

E. Said R. Levi, "I am comforted that I made him from the earth [mortal, so he will go back to the dust]."

2.A. "[And the Lord was sorry that he had made man on the earth] and it grieved him to his heart" (Gen. 6:6):

B. Said R. Berekhiah, "The matter may be compared to the case of a king who conducted his affairs through a trust officer and incurred a loss. To whom should he address his complaint? Is it not to the trust officer?

C. "Accordingly: 'And it grieved him in his heart' (Gen. 6:6). [He blamed himself, that is, his own heart, for its incorrect impulse.]"

3.A. A gentile asked R. Joshua b. Qorha, saying to him, "Do you not maintain that the Holy One, blessed be he, sees what is going to happen?"

B. He said to him, "Indeed so."

C. "But lo, it is written, 'And it grieved him in his heart' (Gen. 6:6)!"

D. He said to him, "Did you ever have a son?"

E. He said to him, "Yes."

F. He said to him, "And what did you do?"

G. He said to him, "I was happy, and I made everybody happy."

H. He said to him, "But did you not know that in the end he would die?"

I. He said to him, "Rejoice in the time of joy, mourn in the time of mourning."

J. He said to him, "And that is the way things are done before the Holy One, blessed be he."

K. For R., Joshua b. Levi said, "For seven days the Holy One, blessed be he, went into mourning for his world before he brought the flood, as it is said, 'And it grieved him in his heart' (Gen. 6:5), and further it says, 'For the king grieved for his son' (2 Sam. 19:3)."

No. 1 explains the meaning of the word used for "sorry," which sustains two quite different interpretations, the first and more obvious, God regretted what he had done, and, second, and less obvious, God took comfort in what he had done. This sequence repeats itself in a formally striking set of pairs. No. 2 presents a different approach to the base verse. No. 3 then raises the question that is necessary to remove the doubt that God, the creator, could not foresee what would happen later on.

The Sin of Humanity: Disobedience

Once more we revert to our sages' main polemic. To be saved, submit and obey. To sin, rebel and disobey. Israel will find salvation through submission to God. The tale of the fall of humanity makes that fact clear. Israel must trust in God. If Israel does not trust in God, it will not be saved. Here humanity serves as the pattern for Israel—not to follow.

XXVIII:II.1.A. ["So the Lord said, 'I will blot out man whom I have created from the face of the ground, man and beast and creeping things and birds of the air, for I am sorry that I have made them' " (Gen. 6:7)]:

120

A. R. Berekhiah in the name of R. Abba bar Yama:
"['Let the waters be gathered together into one place:'] 'Let there be a line set for the water,' in line with this verse of scripture: 'And a line shall be stretched forth over Jerusalem' (Zech. 1:1). [Freedman, p. 34, n.2: The radicals of the word for 'let . . . be gathered' thus derive from the word for a measuring line and are to be translated: 'let the waters be confined to a definite measure of quantity.']"

B. [Explaining the language for 'be gathered together' differently] R. Abba bar Kahana in the name of R. Levi:
" 'Let the water be gathered together *to me* [that is, in the sense of the dative, for my purpose, so that] I may do with them what I plan in the future.'

C. "The matter may be compared to the case of a king who built a palace and gave residences in it to people who lacked the power of speech. Lo, they would get up in the morning and greet the king by making appropriate gestures with their fingers and with flag-signals. The king thought to himself, 'Now if these, who lack the power of speech, get up in the morning and greet me by means of gestures, using their fingers and flag-signals, if they had full powers of speech, how much the more so [would they demonstrate their loyalty to me]!'

D. "So the king gave residences in the palace to people possessed of full powers of speech. They got up and took possession of the palace [and siezed it]. They said, 'This palace no longer belongs to the king. The palace now belongs to us!'

E. "Said the king, 'Let the palace revert to its original condition.'

F. "So too, from the very beginning of the creation of the world, praise for the Holy One, blessed be he, went upward only from water. That is in line with the verse of scripture which states, 'From the roar of many waters' (Ps. 93:4). And what praise did they proclaim? 'The Lord on high is mighty' (Ps. 93:4).

G. "Said the Holy One, blessed be he, 'Now if these [waters], which have neither mouth nor power of speech, so praise me, when mortals are created, how much the more so!'

121

H. "The generation of Enosh went and rebelled against him, the generation of the flood went and rebelled against him, the generation of the dispersion went and rebelled against him.

I. "The Holy One, blessed be he, said, 'Let these be taken away and let those [that were here before, namely, the waters] come back.'

J. "That is in line with the following verse of scripture: 'So the Lord said, "I will blot out man" ' (Gen. 6:7)." [The use of water in this connection therefore made sense, since God now would restore the primeval waters that he had earlier removed so as to make a place for man.]

2.A. "What are they thinking? Is it that I need armies? Did I not create the world by a mere word? I shall produce a word and destroy them."

B. Said R. Berekhiah, "Did I not create them from dirt? What blots out dirt? It is water. Let water come and blot out dirt."

The use of water in destroying humanity finds explanation in this elaborate account. In point of fact we have two explanations, as indicated, No. 1 works on the verse at hand by invoking the notion that the gathering of the waters was destined to serve God's particular purpose. The water had carried out God's will. Then man was created, but did not carry out God's will. Man made of dirt then was blotted out by the water. I find this a rather powerful exposition of the theme of water, both for its invocation of the affect of water on dirt and also for its explanation of the appropriateness of the means selected by God for blotting out man, that is, the obedient wipes out the disobedient.

Why Destroy the Beasts Too?

We proceed to a natural question: What had the beasts done to deserve their fate? The answer proves diverse. The question is what matters.

XXVIII:VI.1.A. "Man and beast and creeping things and birds of the air" (Gen. 6:7):

B. R. Yudan said, "The matter [of destroying the beasts and fowl] may be compared to the case of a king who handed his son over to a tutor, who misguided the boy and led him into bad ways. The king grew angry with his son and put him to death. Said the king, 'Is it not so that this one alone is responsible for leading my son into bad ways? My son has perished and should this one survive?' Therefore: 'Man *and beast*' (Gen. 6:7). [How the beasts are responsible for man's sin is not specified. This will come up shortly. The beasts contributed to an excess of prosperity, on which the sin is blamed. But the passage as a whole would better explain wiping out a generation accused of bestiality.]"

C. R. Phineas said, "The matter may be compared to the case of a king who was marrying his son off and made a marriage canopy for him, which he plastered, painted, and decorated. The king grew angry with his son and killed him. He went into the marriage canopy and began to break down the rods, destroy the partitions, and tear the hangings. He said, 'My son has perished and should these remain?' Therefore: 'Man *and beast*' (Gen. 6:7). [But here why the king killed the son is not specified at all. Following is an attempted explanation of the destruction of the beasts, but that does not help us with the killing of the son in the present parable.]

D. "That [verse, concerning destruction of the beasts and fowl too] is in line with this verse of Scripture: 'I will consume man and beast, and the stumbling blocks with the wicked' (Zeph. 1:3). [The beasts] were the ones that served as stumbling blocks for the wicked, for one would hunt a bird and say, 'Go, get fat, and then come back' which the bird did. [Freedman, p. 228, n.2: There was abundant prosperity, which led to evil.]"

Continuing the inquiry into the justice of God's decision to wipe out everything, the account now takes up the reason that the beasts and fowl also were destroyed, since they had done nothing. There are diverse explanations, as we see, the first and third maintaining that the animals and birds played a part in man's downfall, and the second treating their destruction as a merely appropriate gesture of respect for the victim of the destruction, man himself. If these, prepared for man, should survive man's fall, then it would serve to sadden God by reminding God of the humanity that God had made and destroyed. In all the main theme of theodicy continues, finding its appropriate expression in one detail after another. Each detail demands its explanation.

Noah Found Favor—Because of Israel

Thus far Israel has played a slight role in the story of the trail from Adam to the flood. At this point we explain why Noah was saved at all, and the explanation invokes the grace to be shown to Israel in the future.

XXIX:III.1.A. "And Noah found grace" (Gen. 6:8):

B. Said R. Simon, "There were three acts of finding on the part of the Holy One, blessed be he:

C. " 'And you found [Abraham's] heart faithful before you' (Neh. 9:8).

D. " 'I have found David my servant' (Ps. 89:21).

E. " 'I found Israel like grapes in the wilderness' (Hos. 9:10)."

F. His fellows said to R. Simon, "And is it not written, 'Noah found grace in the eyes of the Lord' (Gen. 6:8)?"

G. He said them, "Noah found it, but the Holy One, blessed be he, did not find it."

H. Said R. Simon, "'He found grace in the wilderness' (Jer. 31:1) on account of the merit of the generation of the wilderness."

The proposition draws on the verse at hand, but makes its own point. It is that the grace shown to Noah derived from Israel. Noah on his own—that is, humanity—enjoyed salvation only because of Israel's merit. The proposition is striking and daring. God "found"—that is, made an accidental discovery of a treasure—only three: Abraham, David, and Israel, that is, the beginning, the end, and the holy people that started with Abraham and found redemption through David. As if to underline this point, we refer, H, to the generation of the wilderness and its faith, which merited gaining the land. So once more, and in a stunning way, the story of creation reaches its fulfillment and resolution in the salvific history of Israel.

Part Two

NOAH:
Genesis Rabbah
Parashiyyot
XXX–XXXVIII

The Name of Noah: Comfort and Respite

Our sages paid attention to problems in scripture's explanation of meanings of words and phrases. They took note of obvious points of misinformation and even error. In the case of the name of Noah, as we shall now see, scripture assigns to the interpretation of Noah's name the meaning that would apply to a different name—namely, Nahman. Sages do not apologize for or explain away error. They draw meaning from it.

XXX:II.1.A. "[When Lamech had lived a hundred eighty-two years, he became the father of a son] and called his name Noah, saying ['Out of the ground which the Lord has cursed this one shall bring us relief from our work and from the toil of our hands']" (Gen. 5:29):

B. R. Yohanan said, "The name has no bearing on the interpretation that is given to it, and the interpretation has no bearing on the name. [The explanation does not fit the name that is explained.]

C. "Either the scripture should have said, 'This one will give us rest' [using the root NH, corresponding to the name Noah], or the text should have said, 'He called his name Nahman,' for 'this one will give us relief.' [The explanation given in the scripture is for the name Nahman, not the name Noah.] But is it possible that the name Noah corresponds to the explanation, 'give us relief'? [Surely not.]

D. "But when the Holy One, blessed be he, created man, he gave him rule over all things. The ploughing heifer obeyed the ploughman, the furrow obeyed the plough. But when man sinned, all things rebelled against him. The ploughing heifer would not obey the ploughman, and the furrow would not obey the plough. When Noah arose, they eased [their rebellion]. [How do we know it?]

E. "The word for 'ease' occurs here [in the name Noah], and the word for 'ease' occurs in the following: 'So that your ox and your ass may have ease' (Ex. 23:12). Just as the 'ease' that is stated later on refers to 'ease' for an ox, so the word for 'ease' that is used here also refers to the ease of the ox."

F. R. Simeon b. Laqish said, "The name has no bearing on the interpretation, and the interpretation has no bearing on the name.

G. "Either the scripture should have said, 'This one will give us rest' [using the root NH, corresponding to the name Noah], or the text should have said, 'He called his name Nahman,' for 'this one will give us relief.' [The explanation given in the scripture is for the name Nahman, not the name Noah.]

H. "But before Noah arose, the water would come up and flood the dead in their graves, for it is written two times in scripture: 'He calls forth the waters of the sea and pours them out upon the face of the earth' (Amos 5:8, 9:6), corresponding to the two times a day on which the water would come up and flood out the dead in their graves, once in the morning, once in the evening, in line with this verse: 'Like the slain that lie in the grave' (Ps. 88:6). Even those who were lying in the grave were as if they had been slain. But when Noah arose, they enjoyed rest.

I. "Here the word 'ease' is written, and elsewhere it is written, 'For he enters into peace, they rest in their beds' (Is. 57:2). Just as in that passage, the reference is to the rest of the grave, so here too the meaning is the rest of the grave."

J. R. Eleazar said, "He was named Noah on account of his offering: 'And the Lord smelled the sweet odor' (Gen. 8:21)."

H. R. Yose bar Hanina said, "It was on account of the fact that the ark rested: 'And the ark rested' (Gen. 8:4)."

I. Said R. Yohanan, "The planets did not function the entire twelve months [in which the flood took place] [and that means they had rest, in line with his name]."

J. Said R. Jonathan to him, "They served but they made no impression."

K. R. Eleazer said, " 'They shall not cease' (Gen. 8:22) indicates that they had never ceased."

L. R. Joshua said, "Since it says, 'They shall not cease' [in the future] it means they had ceased [in the past]."

The point of the several statements is to explain the name of Noah, taking note of the fact that the scriptural explanation of Noah's name does not correspond to the name itself. The stress throughout is on how Noah brought rest or respite to the world. The repertoire of cases involves every passage in which the consonantal root of Noah's name occurs in some credible form.

What Made Noah Special?

Noah comes forth as a herald of doom. He did something to merit God's favor, just as Israel has to carry out actions to please God. Noah did not gain favor for nought. He served God loyally, and God responded.

XXX:VII.1.A. "[Noah was a righteous] man" (Gen. 6:9):
B. Whenever scripture speaks of "man," it refers to a righteous man who admonished [his age].
C. For for the entire one hundred twenty years before the flood, Noah went about planting cedars and cutting them down. So people said to him, "Why are you doing this?"
D. He said to them, "The Master of the world told me that he is bringing a flood on the world."
E. They said to him, "If a flood is coming, it will come only on the house of the father of that man [on you alone]."
F. That is in line with the following verse of scripture: "A contemptible brand in the thought of him that is at ease, a thing ready for them whose foot slips" (Job. 12:5).

2.A. Said R. Abba, "Said the Holy One, blessed be he, 'A single herald stood up for me in the generation of the flood.' This is Noah.
B. "For hereabouts people say '[Freedman:] Arouse him, stir him up!' [Freedman, p. 235, n.5: The word is made up of the same consonants as the word in Job 12:5 translated brand, so the meaning is 'arouse, stir up.']

131

C. "[The cited verse refers to 'contemptible'] for people ridiculed him and called him a dirty old man.

D. " 'In the thought of him who is at ease' teaches that they were as hard as metal [Freedman: a play on the consonants of the word for 'in the thought of'].

E. " 'A thing ready for them whose foot slips' (Job. 12:5) for those people were indeed ready for their foot to sleep and break, breaking above and breaking below."

The exegetes single out Noah and underline that his contemporaries had their chance and threw it away. The exegetes thus fill in a noteworthy gap in the biblical narrative, which reports God's judgment on Noah's contemporaries, but does not tell us what those people actually did or indicate that they were warned. Since the biblical narrative is told from the viewpoint of God, the exegetes provide a second dimension to the account.

Was Noah Righteous only by Comparison to the Wicked, or was he Righteous in an Absolute Sense?

The framing of the verse at hand poses a problem. Was Noah blameless measured only by the standard of his own generation? In that case, in some more noble group he would have proved undistinguished. Or was he blameless even by the standard of any other generation as well? Underneath the issue is the question of whether we are measured by an absolute or a relative standard.

XXX:IX.1.A. "[Noah was a righteous man, blameless] in his generation" (Gen. 6:9):

B. R. Judah and R. Nehemiah:

C. R. Judah said, "By the standard of his generation, he was indeed righteous. But had he been in the generation of Moses or in the generation of Samuel, he would hardly have been regarded as righteous.

D. "In the market of the blind, they call a one-eyed man farsighted, and the baby is a scholar.

E. "The matter may be compared to the case of a man who had a wine cellar. He opened the first keg and found it vinegar, the second and found it vinegar. When he came to the third, he found it turning. They said to him, 'It is turning.' He said to them, 'Is there anything better here?' They told him. 'No.'

F. "So too by the standard of his generation, he was a righteous man. [But that is only by that standard.]"

G. R. Nehemiah said, "Now if in the generation in which he lived, he was righteous, in the generation of Moses, all the more so!

H. "The matter may be compared to the case of a vial of perfume lying tightly sealed in a cemetery, giving out a wonderful odor. If it were located outside the cemetery, how much the more so!"

The sense of the scripture's stress, "in his generation," is fully worked out, with the two possibilities made explicit.

The Violence of the Generation of the Flood

Precisely why was humanity wiped out? Sages draw on their own knowledge of wickedness to explain. In our own day we should have a more powerful case to make against humanity. Part of the work of response to scripture for us requires rewriting the record, just as our sages rewrote it, in light of today's tragic knowledge of the true nature of humanity. And we Jews know it better than anyone else.

XXXI:V.1.A. "And God said to Noah, 'The end of all flesh is come before me [RSV: I have determined to make an end to all flesh]' (Gen. 6:13).

B. The time has come for them to be chopped down, the time has come for them to be treated like unripe grapes, the time of their indictment has come.

C. All this why? "For the earth is filled with violence through them" (Gen. 6:13).

3.A. [We shall now have a case of the violence practiced by this generation.] This is what the men of the generation of the flood would do. Someone would bring out his basket full of beets [to the market]. One of them would come and snatch something of the value of less than a penny, and each one would come along and take something of similarly negligible value, so that the peddlar could not bring any one of them to court [since a matter of a value of less than a penny is not actionable].

B. Said the Holy One, blessed be he, "You have acted not quite on the up and up, so I too shall do something not quite on the up and up."

C. That is in line with this verse: "Is not their tent cord plucked up within them? They die, and that without wisdom" (Job 4:21), that is, because they lacked the wisdom of the Torah.

D. "Between morning and evening they are shattered, they perish forever without regarding it" (Job 4:20). The word for "regarding" refers only to judgment, in line with this verse: "These are the judgments which you shall set [using the same root] before them" (Ex. 21:1).

XXXI:VI.1.A. Another matter: "For the earth is filled with violence" (Gen. 6:13):

B. Said R. Levi, "The word for violence refers to idolatry, fornication, and murder.

C. "Idolatry: 'For the earth is filled with violence' (Gen. 6:13).

D. "Fornication: 'The violence done to me and to my flesh be upon Babylonia' (Jer. 51:35). [And the word for 'flesh' refers to incest, as at Lev. 18:6].

E. "Murder: 'For the violence against the children of Judah, because they have shed innocent blood' (Joel 4:19).

F. "Further, the word for 'violence' stands for its ordinary meaning as well."

The word for violence gains a broader range of meanings, within the repertoire of capital crimes. But the incongruity between everyday crimes and cosmic punishment did not strike the compositors of our document. They lived in a simpler age, a more civilized time and place.

God is Righteous and Loves the Righteous

Once more: Why Noah in particular? Because Noah was like God, doing the sorts of deeds God does. Then why test and try Noah in particular? Because Noah was strong and could show, through meeting the test, the full greatness inherent in humanity.

XXXII:II.1.A. "For the Lord is righteous, he loves righteousness, the upright shall behold his face" (Ps. 11:7).

B. R. Tanhuma in the name of R. Judah, R. Menahama in the name of R. Eleazar: "You have no case in which a person likes the competition [someone who practices the same trade]. But a sage likes the competition [someone who practices the same trade], for example, R. Hiyya [who has good will] for his colleagues, and R. Hoshaiah for his.

C. "And the Holy One, blessed be he, likes the competition [someone who practices the same trade]: 'For the Lord is righteous, he loves righteousness, the upright shall behold his face' (Ps. 11:7).

D. "This verse refers to Noah: 'And the Lord said to Noah, "Go into the ark" ' (Gen. 7:1)."

XXXII:III.1.A. "The Lord tries the righteous, but the wicked and him who loves violence his soul hates" (Ps. 11:5):

B. Said R. Jonathan, "A potter does not test a weak utensil, for if he hits it just once, he will break it. So the Holy One, blessed be he, does not try the wicked but the righteous: 'The Lord tries the righteous' (Ps. 11:5)."

C. Said R. Yose bar Haninah, "When a flax-maker knows that the flax is in good shape, then the more he beats it, the more it will improve and glisten. When it is not of good quality, if he beats it just once, he will split it. So the Holy One, blessed be he, does not try the wicked but the righteous: 'The Lord tries the righteous' (Ps. 11:5)."

D. Said R. Eleazar, "The matter may be compared to a householder who has two heifers, one strong, one weak. On whom does he place the yoke? It is on the one that is strong. So the Holy One, blessed be he, does not try the wicked but the righteous: 'The Lord tries the righteous' (Ps. 11:5).

2.A. Another interpretation: "The Lord tries the righteous" (Ps. 11:5) refers to Noah.

B. "Then the Lord said to Noah, 'Go into the ark, you and all your household, for I have seen that you are righteous before me in this generation' " (Gen. 7:1).

3.A. "For I have seen that you are righteous before me in this generation" (Gen. 7:1):

B. R. Eleazar b. Azariah said, "We find that people may express part of the praise owing to a person in that person's presence, and the whole of it only not in his presence. For lo, he says when speaking directly to Noah, 'For I have seen that you are righteous before me in this generation' (Gen. 7:1). But not in his presence: 'Noah was a righteous man, blameless in his generation' (Gen. 6:6).

B. R. Eliezer b. R. Yose the Galilean said, "We find that people may express only part of the praise owing to him who by an act of speech brought the world into being, as it is said, 'Say to God, how tremendous is your work' (Ps. 66:3), and, 'O give thanks to the Lord for he is good' (Ps. 118:1)."

The important side is the proof of Noah's righteousness. What follows is that God was just in saving Noah. God did not act in a peremptory or capricious manner. To our sages that is an important point. The world follows rules. God makes those rules, keeps them, and allows us through the Torah to know what they are. That proposition underlies much that we see only in detail. For their own day our sages' message brought assurance: God keeps the rules, so if Israel obeys them, God will save Israel. Because Noah was righteous, God was just too.

God Remembered Noah

God remembered Noah—and the beasts and cattle with him. The righteousness of God defines our sages' point of emphasis, as we have just seen. Now we take up the matter from a different perspective. Why did God remember and save the beasts? They had no acts of righteousness to serve as credit. The story of Noah is turned into a deep reflection on the nature of God's righteousness.

XXXIII.I.1.A. "But God remembered Noah and all the beasts and all the cattle that were with him in the ark" (Gen. 8:1):

B. "Your righteousness is like the mountains of God, your judgments are like the great deep, man and beast do you save, O Lord" (Ps. 36:7):

C. R. Ishmael says, "With the righteous, who received the Torah that was given on the mountains of God, you do righteousness up to the mountains of God. But with the wicked, who did not accept the Torah that was given on the mountains of God, you pursue every last detail, down to the great deep."

D. R. Aqiba says, "The same is the case for these and for those: 'you pursue every last detail, down to the great deep.' He follows up meticulously in every small matter involving the righteous, exacting a penalty from them for every last evil deed that they have done in this world, in order to give them abundant blessings to them and a great reward in the world to come. He gives an abundant blessing to the wicked and gives them a generous reward for the least of the religious duties that they have carried out in this world, in order to exact a full and just penalty from them in the world to come."

2.A. Said R. Levi, "There is an appropriate comparison for the righteous in their dwelling, and for the wicked in their dwelling.

B. "The righteous in their dwelling: 'I will feed them in a good pasture and upon the high mountains of Israel shall their fold be' (Ez. 34:14).

C. "The wicked in their dwelling: 'In the day when he went down to the netherworld I caused the deep to mourn and cover itself for him' (Ez. 32:15)."

D. Said R. Judah, "The word translated 'I caused to mourn' may be read 'I brought,' yielding the sense: 'People do not make a cover for a vat with silver or with gold, but with clay, the same material as the vat itself. So too the wicked are darkness, Gehenna is darkness, the great deep is darkness. So [God speaks] 'I brought the wicked to Gehenna, covered them with the deep, so that what is dark covers what is dark.' "

3.A. R. Jonathan in the name of R. Josiah reverses the elements of the cited verse, in this way: "Your righteousness is above your judgments, just as the mountains of God are above the great deep."

B. "The sense then is as follows: 'Just as mountains have no end, so [the reward coming to the] righteous has no end.'

C. "Just as mountains are forced down over the great deep so that the great deep should not open up and overflow the world, so the righteous are pressed down over punishment, so that it should not break forth and burn up the world.

D. "Just as mountains are down and produce crops, so the deeds of the righteous bring forth fruit.

E. "And just as the great deep is beyond all searching, so punishment of the wicked is beyond all searching.

F. "And just as the great deep may not be sown and yields no crops, so the deeds of the wicked produce no fruit, for if they could produce a crop of their own, they would wipe out the world."

4.A. When R. Joshua b. Levi went up to Rome, he saw that the columns were covered with tapestries so that, in cold weather, they would not contract, and in warm weather, they should not expand. Walking in the marketplace, he saw a poor old man covered up in a mat, and some say, in half of the pack saddle of an ass.

B. Concerning those protected columns he recited the verse: "'Your righteousness is like the mighty mountains' (Ps. 36:7). When you bestow blessing, you do it in a big way. And concerning the poor man: 'Your judgments are like the great deep' (Ps. 36:7). When you beat up on a man, you beat up in a big way."

5.A. Alexander of Macedonia paid a visit on the king of Kasia, who dwells on the other side of the mountains of darkness. The king came forth to receive him, offering gold bread on a gold tray. [Alexander] said to him, "Do you really think I need your money?"

B. He said to him, "And don't you have anything by way of food to eat in your country, that you have come to my country? [I assumed you came for gold, not for bread. Otherwise, why bother to make the trip?]"

C. He said to him, "I came only because I wanted to know how you people administer the public interest."

D. He took a seat when the other went into session. Someone came and complained about his fellow, saying, "This man sold me a manure pile and I found a stash in it." The one who bought it said, "I bought from him only a manure heap." The one who sold it said, "I sold him the manure pile and everything in it!" [So righteous were they that they would not accept what they did not think belonged to them. Each wanted to return to the other what he thought the other possessed.]

E. The king said to him, "Do you have a son?"

F. He said to him, "Yes."

G. He said to the other, "Do you have a daughter?"

H. He said to him, "Yes."

I. He said to them, "Get them married and give the stash to the two of them as a dowry."

J. The king saw Alexander looking on, amazed. He said to him, "Don't you think I made a good decision?"

K. He said to him, "Indeed so."

L. He said to him, "And if the case came to you in your country, how would you people have judged it?"

M. He said to him, "The court would have put both litigants to death and taken the treasure for the king."

N. [The king of Kasia] said to him, "Now tell me, does it rain in your country?"

O. He said to him, "Indeed so."

P. "Does the sun come out in your country?"

R. "Quite."

S. "Are there small cattle in your country?"

T. "There are."

U. "Well I tell you, it is not on account of any merit that you have attained [that there is rain and sun in your country] but only on account of the merit of the small animals, as it is written, 'Man and beast you save, O Lord' (Ps.

36:7). 'Man' you save 'on account of the merit accrued by the dumb animals' do you save, O Lord."

6.A. R. Judah b. R. Simon interpreted the cited verse to speak of Noah.

B. "Said the Holy One, blessed be he, The righteousness that I showed to Noah in the ark I carried out with him only on the mountains of God: 'And in the seventh month on the seventeenth day of the month, the ark came to rest on the mountains of Ararat' (Gen. 8:45).

C. " 'Your judgments are like the great deep' (Ps. 36:7): The suffering that I brought on his generation I brought on them only out of the great deep: 'On that day all the fountains of the great deep were broken up' (Gen. 7:11).

D. "And when I remembered him, I did not remember him alone, but I remembered him and everything that was with him in the ark. That is in line with this verse: 'But God remembered Noah and all the beasts and all the cattle that were with him in the ark' (Gen. 8:1)."

This is a strong and effective composition, beginning to end, because the intersecting verse, Ps. 36:7, demands that we pay attention, in particular, to the matter of God's preserving man *and beast*, and that is the point the exegete finds striking in the base verse: God remembered Noah *and all the beasts and cattle* in the ark. We work our way through the intersecting verse. But as we shall see, the intersecting verse leads us squarely into the center of the base verse. Ishmael and Aqiba produce an argument on suffering in this world and in the next, no. 1. No. 2 carries forward the same point of interest, in which the reward of the righteous and the punishment of the wicked are joined to the intersecting verse. The same theme—reward for righteousness, punishment for evil—defines the focus of the next compositions, nos. 3, 4, 5.

Only when we come to no. 6 do we shift back to the base verse, and at that point the center of interest moves from the established exegetical motif—reward and punishment—to the one of special, and surprising, interest, which is God's concern even for the dumb animals, who are neither righteous nor wicked. Yet no. 5 has prepared us for that shift, for as we look back, we see that the story provides precisely that point that serves to permit the exegete to accomplish his purpose, which is to shift the flow of discourse to a new and surprising point—namely, the theme that God rewards the wicked only because he takes care of dumb animals. That fact requires a second glance also at Joshua b. Levi's story, no. 4, and here too we notice that the suffering of the poor but righteous man forms the focus; the Romans care more for their columns than for people in their midst. And what about God?

If then we may ask the compositors of the entire composition to tell us their message, we should expect to hear something like this: God does reward the good and punish the wicked, but in this world the righteous suffer so that in the world to come they will enjoy a reward, while in the next world the righteous enjoy every sort of reward, and the wicked have nothing. The same picture derives from Ez. 34:13, 31:15. Whatever deeds the righteous do bear fruit, so their good deeds live on, but the wicked produce no crops after them; their deeds are ineffectual. The wicked enjoy this world so that they take care even of their possessions, putting coverings on marble columns but not on freezing human beings, ignoring the suffering of the poor. The wicked, moreover, know nothing of justice and murder and steal in the name of fair judgment. Then why does the world go on, with rain and sun? It is because of the merit of the dumb animals—for man has none.

This is quite a comment on Noah. In any event it would be hard to view the composition as random or episodic, because its polemical point is sustained and cogent—and urgent.

Noah Leaves the Ark

A mark of Noah's merit is his obedience to God. Now we find a new example of the same fact. God had to order him to leave the ark. Why?

XXXIV:IV.1.A. "If the spirit of the ruler rise up against you, do not leave your place" (Qoh. 10:4):

B. This verse speaks of Noah. Said Noah, "Just as I entered the ark only with permission, so I shall leave only with permission."

C. Said R. Judah bar Ilai, "If I were there, I should have broken down the door to get out. But Noah said, 'Just as I entered the ark only with permission, so I shall leave only with permission.'

D. " 'Come into the ark and Noah came in . . .' (Gen. 7:1). 'Go forth from the ark' (Gen. 8:15). 'So Noah went forth' (Gen. 8:18)."

XXXIV:VI.1.A. "To every thing there is a season and a time to every purpose" (Qoh. 3:1).

B. There was a season for Noah to enter the ark, "Come into the ark, with all your household" (Gen. 7:1),

C. And there was a time for him to leave the ark: "Go forth from the ark" (Gen. 8:15).

2.A. "Go forth from the ark" (Gen. 8:15): [Why did God have to order Noah to leave the ark?] This matter may be compared to the case of an administrator who went away and left someone else in his place. When he came back, he said to him, "Leave your office." But the replacement did not agree to leave. [Freedman, p. 270, n.2: Similarly, for twelve months Noah was in charge of the only creatures that were destined to live and thus acted, as it were, as God's regent. Now he was to leave this exalted position.] [That is why he had to be instructed to leave the ark.]

B. He said, "Should I go forth and procreate only for a curse [and produce children who will be subject to divine wrath]?"

C. Only when the Holy One, blessed be he, took an oath to him that he would never again bring a flood, as it is said, "For this is the waters of Noah to me, for as I have sworn that the waters of Noah should no more go over the earth" (Is. 54:9) [did Noah agree to leave the ark] and then he engaged in further acts of procreation.

Noah waited for God to tell him when the time had come to leave the ark, another mark of his obedience. In the opening paragraph the point is made twice, A-B, C-D. The proof-texts are entirely direct and apt. The intersecting text now is read to stress that one should wait for instructions from the ruler. In yet another way in the next paragraph, at no. 1, the correspondence between the entry and the exit is demonstrated. No. 2 contradicts the spirit of the foregoing by suggesting that God had to order Noah to leave the ark, thus suggesting that Noah did not wish to leave and had to be told to do so. It was now not a mark of obedience to God but of Noah's own independent judgment.

The Commandments that Apply to All Humanity, that is, to the Children of Noah

Noah stands for all of humanity. Only later, when Israel comes into being with the advent of Abraham, will scripture speak of Israel in particular. To our sages this means that when God gives commandments to Noah, they are commandments that all women and men, not only Jews, must keep. These commandments addressed to the children of Noah, hence the so-called Noachide commandments, state what the Torah demands of all humanity. In many ways what we now study is the view of Judaism about all God's creatures: What must everyone do to obey God's will?

XXXIV:VIII.1.A. "Bring forth with you every living thing that is with you of all flesh, birds and animals and every creeping thing that creeps on the earth" (Gen. 8:15):

B. Said R. Yudan, "What is written is, 'Go forth,' and what is read is, 'Put them out' [by force if necessary]."

C. "That they may breed abundantly on the earth" (Gen. 8:17) and not in the ark.

D. "And be fruitful and multiply on the earth" (Gen. 8:17) and not in the ark.

3.A. "By families" serves to forbid hybridization and serves to exclude emasculation.

4.A. The children of Noah received seven commandments, specifically those prohibiting idolatry, fornication, murder, blasphemy,

B. enjoining the establishment of good government,

C. prohibiting stealing and cruelty to animals ["cutting a limb off a living beast"].

D. R. Haninah said, "There also was a prohibition against eating blood drawn from a living beast."

E. R. Eleazar said, "They also were forbidden hybridization."

F. R. Simeon said, "They also were forbidden the practice of witchcraft."

G. R. Yohanan said, "They also were forbidden to emasculate males."

H. R. Issi said, "The children of Noah were forbidden to do any of the things that are written in the following section: 'There shall not be found among you anyone who makes his son or his daughter pass through the fire' (Deut. 18:10)."

XXXIV:XIII.1.A. "Every moving thing that lives shall be food for you, and as I gave you the green plants, I give you everything. Only you shall not eat flesh with its life, that is, its blood" (Gen. 9:3–4):

B. R. Yose b. R. Abin in the name of R. Yohanan: "The first man, who was not permitted to eat meat as a matter of mere appetite [and was permitted to eat only vegetables] was not admonished concerning not removing a limb from a living beast.

C. "But the children of Noah, who were permitted to eat meat as a matter of appetite, were admonished about not eating a limb cut from a living beast. [They were likely to want to cut a limb off a beast in order to eat the meat. They did not have to avoid all meat other than that produced by the sacrificial cult, but could eat meat whenever they wished. So the admonition was necessary.]"

2.A. "And surely your blood of your lives I will require" (Gen. 9:5):

B. The use of the word "and," which is understood to encompass an otherwise unstated category, serves to include one who hangs himself [so that a suicide is punishable]. [That is, God will not only punish someone for eating an animal's blood, Gen. 8:3–4, but also will punish someone who hangs himself.]

C. Is it possible that a suicide of someone in extremis such as Saul, would be encompassed?

D. Scripture accordingly uses the word "surely."

E. Is it possible that someone in the category of Hananiah, Mishael, and Azariah should be included in the prohibition of suicide [since they willingly gave up their lives for the sanctification of God's name]?

F. Scripture accordingly uses the word "surely." [The presence of that word serves to exclude those who willingly give their lives to sanctify God's name.]

3.A. "At the hand of every beast will I require it" (Gen. 9:5)

B. This refers to the four kingdoms [Babylonia, Media, Greece, and Rome, who are answerable for murders that they commit, as with Daniel, Hanaiah, Mishael, and Azariah.]

C. "At the hand of man" (Gen. 9:5):

D. Said R. Levi, "That means, from the hand of the Edomite."

E. "Even at the hand of every man's brother" (Gen. 9:5). "Deliver me, I pray you, from the hand of my brother, from the hand of Esau" (Gen. 32:12).

F. "Will I require the life of man" (Gen. 9:5). This refers to Israel. "And you my sheep, the sheep of my pasture, are men" (Ez. 34:31).

XXXIV:XIV.1.A. "Whoever sheds the blood of man, by man shall his blood be shed" (Gen. 9:6):

B. Said R. Haninah, "All of the following are laws that govern trials of children of Noah [as distinct from trials of Israelites accused of murder]:

C. "Such a person may be condemned on the testimony of a single witness, by the judgment of only one judge, without admonition in advance of the crime, for murder committed through an agent, and for murder of a foetus.

D. "[How do we know that such a trial may receive the testimony of] a single, unsubstantiated witness before a single judge? As it is said, 'Whoever sheds the blood of man, by man shall his blood be shed' (Gen. 9:6).

E. "Without admonition in advance of the crime: 'Whoever sheds the blood of man, by man shall his blood be shed' (Gen. 9:6).

F. "For murder committed through an agent: 'Whoever sheds the blood of man, by man shall his blood be shed' (Gen. 9:6)—meaning, 'by means of another person shall his blood be shed.'

G. "For the murder of a foetus: 'Whoever sheds the blood of man, by man shall his blood be shed' (Gen. 9:6)."

H. R. Yudah bar Simon said, "Also one who commits murder by strangling,

I. "and also one who strangles himself: 'Whoever sheds the blood of man, by man shall his blood be shed' (Gen. 9:6)."

3.A. R. Aqiba gave the following exposition: "Whoever sheds blood is regarded by scripture as if he had diminished the image of God. What is the scriptural basis for that statement?

B. " 'Whoever sheds the blood of man, by man shall his blood be shed' (Gen. 9:6).

C. "And on the basis of what further verse of scripture: 'For God made man in his own image' (Gen. 9:6)."

D. R. Eleazar b. Azariah gave the following exposition: "Whoever gives up procreating is regarded by scripture as if he had diminished the image of God.

E. "What is the scriptural basis for that statement? 'For God made man in his own image' (Gen. 9:6). And immediately thereafter it is written, 'And you, be fruitful and multiply, bring forth abundantly on the earth and multiply in it' (Gen. 9:7)."

F. Ben Azzai gave the following exposition: "Whoever gives up procreating is regarded by scripture as if he had shed blood and diminished the image of God.

G. "What is the scriptural basis for the statement that it is as if he shed blood? 'Whoever sheds the blood of man. . . .' On what account? 'For God made man in his own image' (Gen. 9:6). And immediately thereafter it is written, 'And you, be fruitful and multiply, bring forth abundantly on the earth and multiply in it' (Gen. 9:7)."

H. Said to him R. Eleazar, "Words are nice when they are spoken by people who really carry them out. Ben Azzai talks a good game but he doesn't do a thing." [Ben Azzai talks about procreation but never took a wife.]

I. He said to him, "It is because my soul lusts after the Torah. It is entirely possible for the world to be kept going by other people." [Ben Azzai wants to spend all his life studying Torah and does not want to take time off by marrying and raising a family. Other people, he says, can do that.]

The exegetes go over the verses, one by one, in each case imputing to a clause a meaning not visible to the untutored eye. Israel's history figures, both with regard to the sacrifice of one's life for God's sanctification and the role of the four kingdoms, with Esau/Edom/Rome at the climax. They are answerable for the blood that they shed. So even in what seems a neutral exposition, the fundamental polemic of the compositors makes its appearance. In the second paragraph, no. 1 links the passage at hand to laws governing the murder trial of a gentile, laws significantly more strict than those governing an Israelite's trial. That is to say, it is easier to convict a gentile than an Israelite. The exegesis links the rules to one word after another.

The Covenant with Noah

We move from the commandments that apply to all humanity to the covenant, the promise made by God to all humanity. It is that God will never again wipe out humanity. In an age of possible nuclear annihilation of everything alive on the face of the earth, we find in the covenant with Noah—hence with all humanity—a measure of comfort and hope. Sages find in the covenant renewed occasion to reflect on the nature of sin and salvation.

XXXIV:X.1.A. "The Lord said to his heart ['I will never again curse the ground because of man, for the imagination of man's heart is evil from his youth']" (Gen. 8:21):

B. [Reading the word "to his heart" to refer to someone in control of his heart, we interpret as follows:] The wicked act at the whim of their heart.

C. "The fool has said *in* his heart" (Ps. 14:1). "And Esau said *in* his heart" (Gen. 27:41). "And Jeroboam said *in* his heart" (1 Kgs. 12:25). "Now Haman said *in* his heart" (Est. 6:6).

D. But the righteous maintain their heart subject to their own control [speaking *to* their heart, as God does, and telling their heart what to do, rather than be governed by their heart's impulses, thus]:

E. "Now Hannah spoke upon her heart" (1 Sam. 1:13). "And David said to his heart" (1 Sam. 27:1). "But Daniel placed upon his heart" (Dan. 1:8).

F. "And the Lord said to his heart" (Gen. 8:21).

2.*A.* "I will not again curse the ground [and I shall never again destroy every living creature as I have done]" (Gen. 8:21):

B. Enough is enough.

C. And rabbis say, " 'I shall not again' do so with reference to the children of Noah in particular, 'and I shall never again' do so, for all generations."

3.*A.* "For the imagination of man's heart is evil from his youth" (Gen. 8:21):

B. Said R. Hiyya the elder, "Miserable is the dough concerning which the baker herself testifies that it is no good: 'For the imagination of man's heart is evil from his youth.' "

C. Abba Yose the potter said, "Miserable is the yeast concerning which the one who kneaded it testifies that it is no good: 'For he knows our evil passions, he remembers that we are dust' (Ps. 103:14)."

D. Rabbis say, "Miserable is the planting when the one who planted it testifies that it is no good: 'For the Lord of hosts, who planted you, has spoken ill of you' (Jer. 11:17)."

XXXIV:XI.1.A. "While the earth remains, seedtime and harvest, cold and heat, summer and winter, day and night shall not cease" (Gen. 8:22):

B. R. Yudan in the name of R. Aha: "What were the children of Noah thinking? Was it that the covenant with them ['neither will I again destroy every living creature,' (Gen. 8:21)] would last forever? Rather, only so long as heaven and earth lasted would the covenant with them endure. But when that day should come concerning which it is written, 'For the heavens shall vanish away like smoke, and the earth shall be worn out like a garment' (Is. 51:6), then: 'And [the covenant] will be broken in that day' (Zech. 11:11)."

2.A. Said R. Aha, "What is it that made them rebel against me? Was it not because they sowed but did not reap, produced offspring and did not have to bury them?

B. "Henceforward: 'Seedtime and harvest,' meaning that they will give birth and then have to bury their children.

C. " 'Cold and heat,' meaning they will have fever and ague.

D. " 'Summer and winter,' meaning: 'I shall give the birds the right to attack their summer crops,' in line with this verse, 'And the ravenous birds shall summer upon them and all the beasts of the earth shall winter upon them' (Is. 18:6)."

3.A. The story concerns one of the great authorities of the generation who had a headache. Some say it was R. Samuel b. Nahman.

B. He said, "What has the generation of the flood done to us!" ["Heat" referred to the high temperature behind his headache (Freedman, p. 276, n.6).]

4.A. Another interpretation: "While the earth remains [seedtime and harvest, cold and heat, summer and winter, day and night, shall not cease]" (Gen. 8:22):

B. R. Yudan in the name of R. Aha: "What were the children of Noah thinking? Was it that the covenant with them ['neither will I again destroy every living creature,' Gen. 8:21] would last forever? Rather, only so long as day and night endured, would the covenant with them endure.

C. "But when that day comes, concerning which it is written, 'And there shall be one day which shall be known as the Lord's, which is not day and not night' (Zech. 14:7), then: 'And it will be broken in that day' (Zech. 11:11)."

5.A. Said R. Isaac, " 'What is it that made them [he refers to the generation of the dispersion] rebel against me? Was it not because they sowed but did not reap?"

B. For R. Isaac said, "Once every forty years they would sow a crop, and as they made their trip they would travel from one end of the world to the other in a brief span and cut down the cedars of Lebanon. And the lions and leopards made no more of an impression on them than did a louse on their skin."

C. How so? The climate for them was like the climate from Passover to Pentecost.

In the first of the two paragraphs, nos. 1 and 2 interpret the language of the cited verses. The comment of no. 3 takes up the substance of the verse, the situation in which God, who made man, registers so negative a judgment of him. No. 4 is included because of its reference to the verse at hand, though, obviously, the issue is not the interpretation of the language or sense of the verse. In the second of the two paragraphs two distinct readings of the statement of Gen. 8:22 present themselves. The first emphasizes the limitations of the covenant made with humankind—that is, that covenant lasts up to the end-time but not beyond. The second reads the statement as essentially a curse—namely, humankind had rebelled under conditions of prosperity, so now they will have to endure "hot and cold," "seedtime and harvesttime," interpreted as misfortunes.

The Tower of Babel, the Generation of the Dispersion

We come to the story of the tower of Babel. Why did the people build it, and why did God take offense? The answer is that people built it as an act of rebellion, and God destroyed it to ridicule human pretention. In other words, humanity did not draw the lessons of the flood. God would not destroy humanity, but God also could not let things go on as they had before. In desperation, God would have to start a new humanity. The old one, even after the calamity of the flood, proved beyond hope.

XXXVIII:II.1.A. R. Abba bar Kahana commenced discourse by citing the following verse of scripture: "Though you should bray a fool in a mortar with a pestle among groats" (Prov. 27:22).

B. Said R. Abba b. Kahana, "To be compared to the case of a man who pounds barley in a frame, is the one who tries to improve a fool.

C. "Even as the pestle rises and falls: 'Yet will his foolishness not depart from him' (Prov. 27:22).

D. "So the generation of the flood [had perished] only two years prior to the generation of separation [that is, the generation of the tower of Babel], as it is written, 'Shem fathered Arpachshad two years after the flood' (Gen. 11:1).

E. "Yet: 'And the whole earth had one language' (Gen. 11:1.) [They had learned nothing:] 'Yet will his foolishness not depart from him' (Prov. 27:22)."

The intersecting verse now permits the point to be made that the generation of the tower of Babel learned nothing from the experience of the flood, which had been completed only two years earlier. The analogy then is apt.

One Language, Few Words

What indeed did the generation of the dispersion do wrong? We do well to explore that question, since, in a time of permanent war, we look back longingly on the age of one language and few words.

XXXVIII:VI.1.A. "Now the whole earth had one language and few words" (Gen. 11:1):

B. R. Eleazar said, " 'Few words' means that while the deeds of the generation of the flood were spelled out, the deeds of the generation of the dispersion were not spelled out [and hence were covered by only a few words]."

2.A. "Few words": That phrase means that they addressed words against the two who are singular [using the same word as is translated few], against the one of whom it is

151

said, "Abraham was one" (Ez. 33:24), and against, "The Lord, our God, the Lord is one" (Deut. 6:4).

B. [They thus spoke against Abraham and against God.] They said, "This man Abraham is a barren mule, who will never have offspring."

C. "Against 'The Lord our God, the Lord is one:' " "He does not have the power to select the heavenly spheres for himself and hand over to us merely the lower world. So come, let us make a tower for ourselves and put an idol on top of it, and put a sword in its hand, so that it will appear as if it carries on warfare with him."

4.A. Rabbis say, " 'One language' may be compared to the case of one who had a wine cellar. He opened the first jar and found it vinegar, the second and found it vinegar, the third and found it vinegar.

B. "He said, 'Thus I am satisfied that all the barrels are no good.' [Thus they convinced God that they were uniformly unfit (Freedman).]"

5.A. Said R. Eleazar, "Who is worse, one who says to the king, 'Either you or I shall live in the palace,' or the one who says to him, 'Neither you nor I shall live in the palace.' It is the one who says, 'Either you or I shall live in the palace.'

B. "So the generation of the flood said, 'What is the almighty, that we should serve him (Job 21:15)?'

C. "But the generation of the dispersion said [against 'The Lord our God, the Lord is one'], 'He does not have the power to select the heavenly spheres for himself and hand over to us merely the lower world. So come, let us make a tower for ourselves and put an idol on top of it, and put a sword in its hand, so that it will appear as if it carries on warfare with him.' [Thus: either you or I shall live in heaven.]

D. "Of the former not a remnant survived, while of the latter a remnant survived.

E. "Now as to the generation of the flood, because they were stuffed on the returns of thievery, 'They remove the landmarks, they violently take away flocks and feed them' (Job 24:2), not a remnant survived of them. But as to the others, because they [at least] loved one another, 'Now the whole earth had one language and few words' (Gen. 11:1), a remnant of them survived."

6.A. Rabbi said, "Great is peace, for even if Israel should worship idols, if there is peace among them, said the Holy One, blessed be he, it is as if I shall not exercise dominion over them [and punish them], as it is said, 'Ephraim is united in idol worship, let him alone' (Hos. 4:17).

B. "But if they are torn by dissension, what is written concerning them? 'Their heart is divided, now shall they bear their guilt' (Hos. 10:23)."

7.A. Another interpretation of "few words": They were sharp words that they spoke [using the same consonants as occur in 'few'].

B. They said, "One time in a thousand six hundred fifty-six years the firmament totters. Let us go and make supports, north, south, and west, while here we shall set its eastern support.

F. "['And the word of their lips' (Ps. 59:13)]: so it is written, 'Now the whole earth had one language and few words' (Gen. 11:1)."

The interpretation of "few words" covers a range of possible meanings. The first simply rests on the statement that few words were said about these people. No. 2 moves on to the sense of the same word as "one," hence those described as one, Abraham and God, are now at issue. No. 3 moves on to the word for "words," which can stand also for "things," and now the exegete has "few" stand for "unified," thus "property held in common." No. 4 presents a play on the word "language," connecting that word with the one for tranquilize or satisfy, so Freedman. No. 5 and no. 6 go on to contrast the generation of the flood with the generation of the dispersion, making the point that the latter proved superior in character to the former, for reasons that are worked out. This yields the emphasis on the harmony imputed to the generation at hand, which stands close to the simple sense of the verse of scripture with its stress on a single shared language. No. 7 draws us closer to the story that is to follow, since it brings up the matter of a war against God.

The Justice of God

Our sages work their way through the melancholy story of the decline of humanity, God's disappointment with God's own creation. At each point our sages introduce the question of divine justice and find good reason to justify what God did. So too now: Did God do right by Babel? Indeed so, they wanted to build a tower to the sky, God had to descend to look.

XXXVIII.IX.1.A. "And the Lord came down to see [the city and the tower which the sons of men had built]" (Gen. 11:5):

B. Said R. Simeon b. Yohai, "This is one of the ten passages in the Torah that refer to God's descending."

2.A. ". . . which the sons of men had built" (Gen. 11:5):

B. Said R. Berekhiah, "What could the passage have said? 'Sons of asses'? 'Sons of camels'? [Why specify these are the sons *of man* who built the city?]

C. "But [God said] 'They are the true heirs of the first man.' Just as in the case of the first man, after all that I lavished on him, he said, 'The woman whom *you* gave me [caused the sin, so you are responsible, not I]' (Gen. 3:21), so in the case of the generation of the dispersion [they learned nothing]."

D. "So the generation of the flood [had perished] only two years prior to the generation of separation, as it is written, 'Shem fathered Arpachshad two years after the flood' (Gen. 11:1).

E. "Yet: 'And the whole earth had one language' (Gen. 11:1)"

3.A. "And the Lord said, 'Behold they are one people' " (Gen. 11:6):

B. R. Judah said, "Since they are 'one people and they all have one language,' if they repent, I shall accept them back."

C. R. Nehemiah said, "What caused them to rebel against me? Is it not that 'they are one people and they all have one language'?"

4.A. "And now" (Gen. 11:6):

B. Said R. Abba bar Kahana, "This teaches that the Holy One, blessed be he, gave them an opening to repent. 'And now' means only to refer to repentance.

C. "That is in line with the following verse of scripture: 'And now, Israel, what does the Lord God require of you, but to fear the Lord your God' [an invitation to repentance] (Deut. 10:12)."

5.A. But they said, "No."

B. Said the Holy One, blessed be he, " 'And nothing that they propose to do will not succeed' (Gen. 11:6)."

C. When a vineyard does not produce a crop, what does the owner do to it? He uproots it.

Nos. 1 and 2 form links between the present story and others, creating as seamless a narrative as possible. Nos. 3, 4, and 5 all clarify the meaning of phrases at hand. The stress lies upon God's willingness to forgive and the unwillingness of the generation of the dispersion to be conciliated. So the underlying motif of the exegesis, the guilt of those who were punished, once more guides the interpretation of the passage before the exegetes.

Haran, Terah, Abraham

The descent of God from heaven finds its counterpart in the ascent of Abraham to belief in God. The way is now prepared to introduce the one man who overcame the human condition of rebellion, the human sin of arrogance toward God. Abraham through his own power of reason discovered God. He marked the end of the descent of humanity, the beginning of the creation as God had originally planned it.

XXXVIII:XIII.1.A. "Haran died in the presence of his father Terah in the land of his birth, in Ur of the Chaldaeans" (Gen. 11:28):

B. Said R. Hiyya [in explanation of how Haran died in his father's presence], "Terah was an idol manufacturer. Once he went off on a trip and put Abraham in charge of the store. Someone would come in and want to buy an idol. He would say to him, 'How old are you?'

C. "He said, 'Fifty years old.'

D. "He said, 'Woe to that man, who is fifty years old and is going to bow down to something a day old.' So the man would be ashamed and go his way.

E. "One time a woman came in with a bowl of flour, and said to him, 'Take this and offer it before them.'

F. "He went and took a stick, broke the idols, and put the stick in the hand of the biggest idol.

G. "When his father came back, he said to him, 'Why in the world have you been doing these things?'

H. "He said to him, 'How can I hide it from you? One time a woman came in with a bowl of flour, and said to me, "Take this and offer it before them." Then this idol said, "I'll eat first," and that idol said, "I'll eat first." One of them, the largest, got up and grabbed the stick and broke the others.'

I. "[Terah] said to him, 'Why are you making fun of me! Do those idols know anything [that such a thing could possibly happen]? [Obviously not!]'

J. "He said to him, 'And should your ears not hear what your mouth is saying?' He took him and handed him over to Nimrod.

K. "He said to him, 'Bow down to the fire.'

L. "He said to him, 'We really should bow down to water, which puts out fire.'

M. "He said to him, 'Bow down to water.'

N. "He said to him, 'We really should bow down to the clouds, which bear the water.'

O. "He said to him, 'Then let's bow down to the clouds.'

P. "He said to him, 'We really should bow down to the wind, which disperses the clouds.'

Q. "He said to him, 'Then let's bown down to the wind.'

R. "He said to him, 'We really should bow down to human beings, who can stand up to the wind.'

S. "He said to him, 'You're just playing word games with me. Let's bow down to the fire. So now, look, I am going to throw you into the fire, and let your God whom you worship come and save you from the fire.'

T. "Now Haran [Terah's son] was standing there undecided. He said, 'What's the choice? If Abram wins, I'll say I'm on Abram's side, and if Nimrod wins, I'll say I'm on Nimrod's side. [So how can I lose?]'

U. "When Abram went down into the burning furnace and was saved, Nimrod said to him, 'On whose side are you?'

V. "He said to him, 'Abram's.'

W. "They took him and threw him into the fire, and his guts burned up and came out, and he died in the presence of his father.

X. "That is in line with the verse of scripture: 'And Haran died in the presence of his father, Terah' (Gen. 11:28)."

The powerful story leads us back to the explanation of the verse at hand, but of course the story can stand alone and serve an other than exegetical purpose. In fact the point of the story is the polemic against idolatry as fetishism, to which the verse at hand is hardly critical. In the present context, the story links Abram to the story at hand. We are ready for Abram's outward voyage.

Part Three

LEKH
LEKHA:
Genesis Raffah
Parashiyyot
XXXIX–XLVII

God Calls, Abraham Responds

Why did Abram accept God's command and leave his home and family? It is because on his own he had so reasoned matters as to recognize the call when it came.

XXXIX:I.1.A. "Now the Lord said to Abram, 'Go [from your country and your kindred and your father's house to the land that I will show you']" (Gen. 12:1):

B. R. Isaac opened [discourse by citing the following verse of scripture:] "Hearken, O daughter, and consider and incline your ear; forget also your own people and your father's house" (Ps. 45:11).

C. Said R. Isaac, "The matter may be compared to the case of someone who was going from one place to another when he saw a great house on fire. He said, 'Is it possible to say that such a great house has no one in charge?'

D. "The owner of the house looked out and said to him, 'I am the one in charge of the house.'

E. "Thus since Abraham, our father [took the initiative and] said, 'Is it possible for the world to endure without someone in charge,' the Holy One, blessed be he, [responded and] looked out and said to him, 'I am the one in charge of the house, the lord of all the world.'

F. " 'So shall the king desire beauty' (Ps. 45:12), to show how splendid you are in this this world.'

G. " 'For he is your Lord and do homage to him' (Ps. 45:12): 'Now the Lord said to Abram, Go. . .' Gen. 12:1)."

The relevance of the intersecting verse, that the daughter is to leave her family, derives from the reference to leaving one's family, as Abram did. The metaphor deals with someone who reaches the conclusion, on his own, that, when there is trouble, someone must care about it. God responds to Abraham's remarkable insight.

From Noah to Abram

Abram takes his place in the line that began with Adam and led to Noah. He then has to be placed into that context, compared to his predecessors.

XXXIX:IV.1.A. "Wisdom makes a wise man stronger than ten rulers" (Qoh. 7:19):

B. The passage speaks of Abraham.

C. ". . . then ten . . ." [he was stronger] than the ten generations that lived from Noah to Abraham.

D. "Among all of them, I spoke only with you:"

E. "And the Lord said to Abram" (Gen. 12:1).

XXXIX:V.1.A. R. Azariah commenced discourse [by citing the following verse of scripture] "We would have healed Babylon, but she was not healed. Forsake her and let us go everyone to his own country (Jer. 51:9).

B. " 'We would have healed Babylon' refers to the generation of Enosh.

C. " 'But she was not healed' refers to the generation of the flood.

D. " 'Forsake her' refers to the generation of the dispersion.

E. ". . . and let us go every one to his own country":

F. "Thus: 'Now the Lord said to Abram, "Go from your country and your kindred . . . to the land that I will show you" ' (Gen. 12:1)."

In the opening paragraph the exegesis moves on from the general theme of leaving the fiery furnace of Nimrod to the next component of the base verse, which is the statement that the Lord spoke to Abram. Then, in the following paragraph, we reach the element, "from your country," and explain Abram's leaving Babylonia. Why did God not have him do his work there? God had worked with the generation of the flood and of the dispersion, and it had done no good. They returned to their own countries, so God had Abram leave Babylonia for the land of Israel. That is the basic view expressed here. Linking Abram's call to the generation of the dispersion not only ties the threads of the narrative. It also contrasts Israel's loyalty to the land with the cosmopolitan character of the generation of the dispersion, shown by its willingness to abandon its ancestral homeland. Whether or not there is a further judgment on the Jews of Babylonia I cannot say.

How Could Abram Leave his Family?

Our sages took for granted that Jews cherished their families. So a question urgent to them, if not necessarily to our own day, concerns the morality of Abram's leaving his father and mother.

XXXIX:VII.1.A. Now what is written prior to the passage at hand? It is this verse: "And Terah died in Haran" (Gen. 11:32). Then comes: "And the Lord said to Abram, 'Go [from your country and your kindred and your father's house to the land that I will show you']" (Gen. 12:1).

B. Said R. Isaac, "As to the chronology involved, another sixty-five years are needed [Freedman, p. 315, n. 3: to bring the narrative to the death of Terah. For Terah was seventy years old at Abram's birth, so Gen. 11:26, while Abram departed from Haran at the age of seventy-five, so Gen. 12:4, and so Terah, whose age at death was two hundred five, Gen. 11:32, died sixty-five years after this command, and yet it is narrated before].

C. "But to begin with, you must interpret the passage to indicate that wicked people are called dead while they are yet alive.

D. "For Abraham was concerned, reckoning, 'If I leave, through me people will curse the name of heaven, saying, "He abandoned his father in his old age and went away." '

E. "The Holy One, blessed be he, said to him, 'You in particular I shall free from the responsibility of paying honor to your father and your mother, but I shall never free anyone else from the responsibility of paying honor to his father and his mother. And not only so, but [in order to do so] I shall move up his death to before your departure.'

F. "Accordingly first comes: 'And Telah died in Haran' (Gen. 11:32). Then: 'And the Lord said to Abram, "Go [from your country and your kindred and your father's house to the land that I will show you"]' (Gen. 12:1).'"

The answer to our question proves somewhat technical, but it is solid. The exegete now asks about the interplay of the successive verses, in line with the chronology spelled out by Freedman. The result is a strong exegesis on how Abram found it possible to leave his family.

Why Abram in Particular?

We recall that our sages explain the justice of God's choice of Noah. So it is natural to expect them to spell out why Abram deserved God's favor.

XXXIX:X.1.A. R. Berekhiah b. R. Simon in the name of R. Nehemiah: "The matter may be compared to the case of a king who was traveling from place to place, and a pearl fell out of his crown. The king stopped there and held up his retinue there, collected sand in heaps and brought sieves. He had the first pile sifted and did not find the pearl. So he did with the second and did not find it. But in the third heap he found it. People said, 'The king has found his pearl.'

B. "So said the Holy One, blessed be he, to Abraham, 'Why did I have to spell out the descent of Shem, Arpachshad, Shelah, Eber, Peleg, Reu, Serug, Nahor, and Terah? Was it not entirely for you?'

C. " 'And he *found* his heart faithful before you' (Neh. 9:8). [Freedman, p. 319, n. 2: He was the pearl that God found.]

D. "So said the Holy One, blessed be he, to David, 'Why did I have to spell out the descent of Perez, Hezron, Ram, Aminadab, Nachshon, Shalomon, Boaz, Obed, and Jesse? Was it not entirely for you?'

E. "Thus: 'I have *found* David my servant, with my holy oil have I anointed him' (Ps. 89:21)."

Abraham and David compare to one another, one standing at the commencement of Israel's history, the other at the messianic end. The exegete is interested in the reason that Gen. 11 has preceded Gen. 12. Why has the scripture presented the genealogies at hand? It is to point to the treasure that God found by sifting the sand of the generations. That point, stated on its own, bears considerable power. The parable of the king bears the implication that Abraham and David had "fallen from God's head" and had to be recovered. The main point, so far as the exegete is concerned, lies in the sifting of the generations, on the one side, and the match at the start and finish, on the other.

Abram Made Converts to Faith in One God

Since today only Reform Judaism tries to win gentiles to the Judaic religion, we are reminded that Judaism began as a faith deeply interested in reaching humanity at large. That fact underscores the universalist conception of our sages. A person becomes Israel not because of the condition of birth or family alone, but because of conversion to the Torah. Gentiles have that power, and Israelites have the duty to confer it upon them. So nothing in our sages' conception of humanity presents a point of contact with racism. The stress on one's duty to spread the faith should prove the opposite.

XXXIX:XIV.1.A. "And Abram took Sarai his wife, and Lot his brother's son, and all their possessions which they had gathered, and the soul that they had made . . ." (Gen. 12:5):
B. R. Eleazar in the name of R. Yose b. Zimra: "If all the nations of the world should come together to try to create a single mosquito, they could not put a soul into it, and yet you say, 'And the soul that they had made'? [They could not have created souls.] But this refers to proselytes."
C. Then why should not the text say, "The proselytes whom they had converted." Why stress, "whom they had made"?

D. This serves to teach you that whoever brings a gentile close [to the worship of the true God] is as if he had created him anew.

E. And why not say, "That he had made"? Why, "That *they* had made"?

F. Said R. Huniah, "Abraham converted the men and Sarah the women."

The cited clause is subjected to a careful analysis. The activity of Abram and Sarai in creating converts to the one true God comes under repeated stress.

God Calls Abram to the Land but Abram Finds Famine There: What Sort of a Call Had He Received?

Our sages link one passage to the next. Accordingly, they find it surprising that when Abram reaches the land, what he finds is famine. Why did God do this to Abram?

XL:II.1.A. R. Phineas in the name of R. Hanan of Sepphoris commenced discourse [by citing the following verse]: " 'Happy is the man whom you chastise, O Lord' (Ps. 94.12).

B. "And if someone should come to complain [about God's chastisement], 'And teach out of your Torah' (Ps. 94:12). [The Torah provides the correct reply to those who complain against the justice of God's punishment.]

C. "What is written in regard to Abraham? 'And I shall bless you and make your name great' (Gen. 12:2).

D. "When [Abraham] went forth [from Ur], famine seized him, but he did not make a complaint or issue a condemnation, but [in all serenity,] 'Now there was a famine in the land, so Abram went down to Egypt' (Gen. 12:10)." [Abram did not complain but accepted the chastisement happily.]

2.A. R. Joshua b. Levi opened [discourse by citing the following verse of scripture]: "He has given what is torn [*teref*] to those who fear him, he will be ever mindful of his covenant (Ps. 111:5)."

B. Said R. Joshua b. Levi, "Being torn away [from home, that is, wandering] is what he has given to those who fear him in his world. But in the world to come, 'He will be ever mindful of his covenant' (Ps. 111:5).

C. "What is written with regard to Abraham? 'I shall bless you and make your name great' (Gen. 12:2).

D. "When [Abraham] went forth [from Ur], famine seized him, but he did not make a complaint or issue a condemnation, but [in all serenity,] 'Now there was a famine in the land, so Abram went down to Egypt' (Gen. 12:10)."

The intersecting verse now teaches a distinct lesson, at no. 1, which is that Abram, having been commanded to leave Ur and go to the land, made no complaint when he immediately had to leave the land. Once more the trust and faith of Abram call forth emphasis on the part of the exegetes. The underlying polemic against those who ask how God can both promise the land and also hinder Israelite access to it certainly is to be noted. But I should not be inclined to see that polemic in the center of the passage. The point of no. 2 is the same, but now the chosen verse yields not the rather general theological observation. Rather, the specific issue, Abram's having to wander after having been told to seek a home in the land, finds full symbolization in the key word, "tearing up," which is exploited for its several meanings. The composite of no. 1 and no. 2 certainly forms a fine piece of unitary composition. The fundamental message is clear: Abram was saved by his faith, which was unquestioning and uncomplaining. So too will his children be saved by their trust in God, despite present suffering.

Israel Relives the Life of Abraham

What has the story of Abram to do with the life of Israel? The Torah appears to tell us domestic tales about private persons, not truth about the condition of Israel. Given the insistence of our sages upon reading the story of creation as an account of the salvation of Israel, we are not surprised at what is now before us. It is a systematic account of how Abram in his biography lives out the future history of Israel. Each of the patriarchs and matriarchs will be asked to testify to what is coming, much as, at the end of their lives, Jacob and Moses tell the future. The point is simple: the deeds of the patriarchs and matriarchs signal the life of Israel in time to come.

XL:VI.1.A. "And for her sake he dealt well with Abram" (Gen. 12:16):

B. "And pharaoh gave men orders concerning him [and they set him on the way, with his wife and all that he had]" (Gen. 12:20).

C: R. Phineas in the name of R. Hoshaiah said, "The Holy One, blessed be he, said to our father, Abraham, 'Go and pave a way before your children.' [Set an example for them, so that whatever you do now, they will do later on.] [We shall now see how each statement about Abram at Gen. 12:10–20 finds a counterpart in the later history of Israel, whether Jacob or the children of Jacob.]

C. "You find that whatever is written in regard to our father, Abraham, is written also with regard to his children.

D. "With regard to Abraham it is written, 'And there was a famine in the land' (Gen. 12:10). In connection with Israel: 'For these two years has the famine been in the land' (Gen. 45:6).

E. "With regard to Abraham: 'And Abram went down into Egypt' (Gen. 12:10).

F. "With regard to Israel: 'And our father went down into Egypt' (Num. 20:15).

G. "With regard to Abraham: 'To sojourn there' (Gen. 12:10).

H. "With regard to Israel: 'To sojourn in the land we have come' (Gen. 47:4).

I. "With regard to Abraham: 'For the famine is heavy in the land' (Gen. 12:10).

J. "With regard to Israel: 'And the famine was heavy in the land' (Gen. 43:1).

K. "With regard to Abraham: 'And it came to pass, when he drew near to enter into Egypt' (Gen. 12:11: 'When he was about to enter Egypt').

L. "With regard to Israel: 'And when pharaoh drew near' (Ex. 14:10).

M. "With regard to Abraham: 'And they will kill me but you will they keep alive' (Gen. 12:12).

N. "With regard to Israel: 'Every son that is born you shall cast into the river, and every daughter you shall save alive' (Ex. 1:22).

O. "With regard to Abraham: 'Say you are my sister, that it may go well with me because of you' (Gen. 12:13).

P. "With regard to Israel: 'And God dealt well with the midwives' (Ex. 1:20).

Q. "With regard to Abraham: 'And when Abram had entered Egypt' (Gen. 12:14).

R. "Israel: 'Now these are the names of the sons of Israel, who came into Egypt' (Ex. 1:1).

S. "With regard to Abraham: 'And Abram was very rich in cattle, in silver, and in gold' (Gen. 13:23).

T. "With regard to Israel: 'And he brought them forth with silver and gold' (Ps. 105:37).

U. "With regard to Abraham: 'And pharoah gave men orders concerning him and they set him on the way' (Gen. 12:20).

V. "Israel: 'And the Egyptians were urgent upon the people to send them out' (Ex. 12:33).

W. "With regard to Abraham: 'And he went on his journeys' (Gen. 13:3).

X. "With regard to Israel: 'These are the journeys of the children of Israel' (Num. 33:1)."

This powerful litany carefully links the story of Abram to the history of Israel, showing how the Israelites later on point by point relived the life of Abram. Any claim, therefore, that there were children of Abraham other than Israel ("after the flesh") finds refutation in this statement. Since Christians maintained that there was an Israel "after the spirit" too, the matter is made explicit here. Only by joining Israel after the flesh, through birth or conversion, does one gain a place in the seed of Abraham. The passage forms a striking conclusion to Gen. 12:10–20, because it treats the whole and not merely its segments, one by one, and the cogent statement draws out a message that relates to the entire composition. It would be hard to find a more careful effort to conclude a sustained discussion (whether what has gone before in fact was or was not a sustained discussion).

Lot Chooses Sodom

No less than Abram, Lot in his way prefigures Israel's history. But Lot appears not as a model but as a bad example. Lot, after all, chose to live in Sodom.

XLI:VII.1.A. "And Lot lifted up his eyes [and saw that the Jordan valley was well watered everywhere, like the garden of the Lord, like the land of Egypt, in the direction of Zoar; this was before the Lord destroyed Sodom and Gomorrah]" (Gen. 13:10):

B. Said R. Nahman bar Hanan, "Whoever lusts after fornication in the end will be fed with his own flesh [committing incest]." [The word for lust contains letters which form the name of Lot.]

C. Said R. Yose bar Haninah, "This entire verse speaks of fornication."

D. "And Lot lifted up his eyes" (Gen. 13:10): "And his master's wife lifted up her eyes to Joseph" (Gen. 39:76).

E. "And saw all the plain of the Jordan" (Gen. 13:10): "For on account of a harlot a man is brought to a loaf of bread" (Prov. 6:26) [the word for "loaf" and that for "plain" being the same]. [Freedman, p. 337, n. 4: Translation: "and beheld all the loaf, the immorality, of the Jordan."]

F. "That it was well watered everywhere" (Gen. 13:10: "And he shall make the woman drink" (Num. 5:24) [using the same root].

G. "Before the Lord destroyed Sodom and Gomorrah" (Gen. 13:10): "And it came to pass, when he went in unto his

brother's wife, that he spilled on the ground" (Gen. 38:9).
[The word for "destroyed" and "spilled" being the same.]

2.A. "And saw that the Jordan valley was well watered
everywhere like the garden of the Lord" (Gen. 13:10) in
trees,
B. "like the land of Egypt" (Gen. 13:10) in grain.

3.A. "So Lot chose for himself all the Jordan valley"
(Gen. 13:11):
B. Said R. Yose b. Zimra, "It is like a man who covets
his mother's dowry."

4.A. "And Lot journeyed east" (Gen. 13:11):
B. He removed himself from the ancient of the world
[with the word for "ancient" and "east" using the same root]:
C. "I want no part of Abraham or of his God."

5.A. "Thus they separated from each other" (Gen.
13:11):
B. Rabbi said, "You have no more evil city than Sodom.
When a man is evil, they call him a Sodomite.
C. "And you have no more harsh people than the
Amorites. When a man is harsh, they call him an Amorite."
D. R. Issi said, "You have no more beautiful city than
Sodom. When Lot traveled among all the cities of the plain,
he found none like Sodom.
E. "And those people were the most impressive among
them."

6.A. "The men of Sodom were wicked and sinners
against the Lord" (Gen. 13:31):
B. "Wicked" to one another.
C. "Sinners" in fornication.
D. "Against the Lord" through idolatry.
E. "Greatly" in committing murder.

Lot sinned because he was wicked. He settled in Sodom
with every reason to acknowledge its true character. The sexual
character of the city's sin is now underlined by showing that the
description of the area in fact alluded to its immoral character.

Nos. 3, 4, and 5 pursue the same point, each making it in its own way. No. 3 portrays Lot as covetous, No. 4 has Lot abandon God by leaving Abram, no. 5 as progenitor of mean and wicked people, no. 6 sums it all up. Only no. 2 seems a neutral point of exposition. So once more God's ways are just. Lot will later on show us his true character.

What it Means to be the Children of Abraham

God blesses Abram's descendants by comparing them to dirt. That analogy demands explanation, for it is hardly a very honorable one. Who wants to be like the dust of the earth? But Israel is dirt. And that marks the foundation for Israel's eternity.

XLI:IX.1.A. "I will make your descendants as the dust of the earth" (Gen. 13:16):

B. Just as the dust of the earth is from one end of the world to the other, so your children will be from one end of the world to the other.

C. Just as the dust of the earth is blessed only with water, so your children will be blessed only through the merit attained by study of the Torah, which is compared to water [hence: through water].

D. Just as the dust of the earth wears out metal utensils and yet endures forever, so Israel endures while the nations of the world come to an end.

E. Just as the dust of the world is treated as something on which to trample, so your children are treated as something to be trampled upon by the government.

F. That is in line with this verse: "And I will put it into the hand of them that afflict you" (Is. 51:23), that is to say, those who make your wounds flow [Freedman].

G. Nonetheless, it is for your good that they do so, for they cleanse you of guilt, in line with this verse: "You make her soft with showers" (Ps. 65:11). [Freedman, p. 339, n. 33: "Words of the same root are used for 'make soft' and 'who afflict you.' The passage understands the former in the sense of making the rain flow and hence the latter too—to make the wounds flow."]

172

H. "That have said to your soul, 'Bow down, that we may go over' " (Is. 51:23):

I. What did they do to them? They made them lie down in the streets and drew ploughs over them.

J. R. Azariah in the name of R. Aha: "That is a good sign. Just as the street wears out those who pass over it and endures forever, so your children will wear out all the nations of the world and will live forever."

The metaphor of "dust of the earth" yields quite a fresh meaning for the exegetes. Now it is not a mark that Israel will be numerous, but that Israel will survive the rule of the nations of the world. However humble its condition, Israel in the end will outlast its enemies. Israel's humility therefore testifies to its ultimate triumph. All of this emerges from the lesson of God to the patriarch, once more prefiguring Israel's life later on.

Abraham's Life and Israel's History

We revert once more to the main point of insistence by our sages: deeds of the fathers, examples for the children.

XLII:II.2. Said R. Abin, "Just as [Israel's history] began with the encounter with four kingdoms, so [Israel's history] will conclude with the encouter with the four kingdoms.

B. " 'Chedorlaomer, king of Elam, Tidal, king of Goiim, Amraphel, king of Shinar, and Arioch, king of Ellasar, four kings against five' (Gen. 14:9).

C. "So [Israel's history] will conclude with the encounter with the four kingdoms: the kingdom of Babylonia, the kingdom of Medea, the kingdom of Greece, and the kingdom of Edom."

3.A. R. Phineas said in the name of R. Abun, " 'But they do not know the thoughts of the Lord, nor do they understand his counsel, for he has gathered them as sheaves to the threshing floor' (Mic. 4:12).

B. "Why did 'all these join forces' (Gen 14:3)? So that they might come and fall by the hand of Abraham: 'And it came to pass in the days of Amraphel' (Gen. 14:1)."

We draw the analogy between the beginning and the ending (just as Samuel has done for the life of the private person). Just as Israel's history began with Abraham's encounter with the four kings, so it will end with a similar encounter. Accordingly, the fourth monarchy, namely Rome, marks the end. No. 3 presents a distinct and fresh point, that people do not know why God does things, or why they do them at God's initiative. But there is a solid reason. The message of the reading, all together, is that Israel may not know the meaning of its history, but God does know and have a plan, and things will work out in the end. The upshot is that Israel's later history finds its counterpart in the initial event in the public life of Abram, so, once more, the powerful motif of finding a counterpart between the life of Israel and the lives of the patriarchs makes its impact. Abraham at the beginning, the Messiah at the end—that is the balance.

The Merit of Abraham, the Model of the Patriarchs and Matriarchs, and Israel

The point becomes more specific. Why do the deeds of the patriarchs and matriarchs matter? Because the founders of Israel laid up a treasury of merit, through the great deeds they did, and it is that merit that protects and sustains Israel now. This point proves particularly important in an age, such as the fourth century, when Christianity held it now formed the true Israel, and Israel after the flesh had lost its opportunity. Our sages reply that Israel after the flesh carries forward the founders' way and inherits their merit: a direct and explicit refutation of the polemic at hand.

XLIII:VIII.1.A. "And blessed be God Most High, who has delivered your enemies into your hand" (Gen. 14:20):

B. [Since the word for "deliver" yields the letters that serve for the word for plans or schemes] R. Huna said, "It is that he turned your plans against your enemies."

C. R. Yudan said, "How many schemes did I work out to place them under your hand? They were friendly with one

another, sending one another dry dates and other gifts. But I
made them rebel against one another so that they would fall
into your hand."

2.A. "And Abram gave him a tenth of everything"
(Gen. 14:20):

B. R. Judah in the name of R. Nehorai: "On the
strength of that blessing the three great pegs on which the
world depends—Abraham, Isaac, and Jacob—derived suste-
nance.

C. "Abraham: 'And the Lord blessed Abraham in *all*
things' (Gen. 24:1) on account of the merit that 'he gave him
a tenth of *all* things' (Gen. 14:20).

D. "Isaac: 'And I have eaten of *all*' (Gen. 27:33), on
account of the merit that 'he gave him a tenth of *all* things'
(Gen. 14:20).

E. "Jacob: 'Because God has dealt graciously with me
and because I have all' (Gen. 33:11) on account of the merit
that 'he gave him a tenth of *all* things' (Gen. 14:20).

3.A. Whence did Israel gain the merit of receiving the
blessing of the priests?

B. R. Judah said, "It was from Abraham: '*So* shall your
seed be' (Gen. 15:5), while it is written in connection with
the priestly blessing: '*So* shall you bless the children of Israel'
(Num. 6:23)."

C. R. Nehemiah said, "It was from Isaac: 'And I and
the lad will go *so* far' (Gen. 22:5), therefore said the Holy
One, blessed be he, '*So* shall you bless the children of Israel'
(Num. 6:23)."

D. And rabbis say, "It was from Jacob: '*So* shall you say
to the house of Jacob' (Ex. 19:3) (in line with the statement,
'*So* shall you bless the children of Israel' (Num. 6:23)."

4.A. When shall "I magnify your children like the stars?"

B. R. Eleazar and R. Yose bar Hanina:

C. One of them said, "When I shall be revealed to
them with the word '*so*': 'So shall you say to the house of Jacob' (Ex. 19:3).

D. The other said, "When I shall be revealed to them through their leaders and give a message invoking the word '*so*': 'So says the Lord, Israel is my son, my firstborn' (Ex. 4:22)."

No. 1 works out a play on the root for "deliver," thereby explaining exactly what God contributed to the salvation of Abram. No. 2 once more links the blessing at hand with the history of Israel. Now the reference is to the word "all," which joins the tithe of Abram to the blessing of his descendants. Since the blessing of the priest is at hand, no. 3 treats the origins of the blessing.

Why was Abraham Afraid?

Our passage says that God tells Abraham not to fear. But to begin with, what reason did Abram have to be fearful?

XLIV:IV.1.A. [As to the statement, "Do not fear, Abram" (Gen. 15:1)], R. Levi made two statements concerning the matter, while rabbis stated only one.

B. R. Levi said, "It was because Abraham feared, saying, 'Perhaps it is the case that among those troops whom I killed, there was a righteous man or a God-fearer.'

C. "The matter may be compared to the case of a straw dealer who was passing by the king's orchards. He saw bundles of thorns and dismounted and collected them. The king looked out and saw him. The man began to hide from him. The king said to him, 'Why are you trying to hide? I needed workers to collect them, but now that you have collected them for me, come and take your fee.' So the Holy One, blessed be he, said to Abraham, Among those troops whom you killed were only 'thorns that already had been cut down:' 'And the peoples shall be as the burnings of lime, as thorns cut down that are burned in the fire' (Is. 33:12)."

D. R. Levi made yet a second statement, "It was because Abraham feared, saying, 'Perhaps it is the case that the children of those kings whom I killed will collect troops and come and make war against me.' Said the Holy One, blessed be he, to him, 'Do not fear, Abram, I am your shield' (Gen. 15:1).

E. "Just as a shield takes all sorts of spears and stands up against them, so shall I stand by you."

F. Rabbis say, "It was because Abraham was afraid, saying, 'I went down into the fiery furnace and was saved, underwent famine and war and was saved. Perhaps now I already have received my reward in this world and will have nothing in the age to come'

G. "Said to him the Holy One, blessed be he, 'Do not fear, Abram, I am your shield' (Gen. 15:1).

H. " 'I am a gift of grace to you' [using the same letters as those for the word for shield]. Everything that I did for you in this world adds up to nothing. In the world to come, 'Your reward shall be very great' (Gen. 15:1). That is in line with this verse: 'Oh how abundant is your goodness, which you have laid up for those who fear you' (Ps. 31:20)."

XLIV:VII.1.A. "Fear not, Abram" (Gen. 15:1):

B. On what account was he afraid?

C. R. Berekhiah said, "He was afraid of Shem [for he had killed his descendants, Chedorlaomer and his sons], as it is said, 'The isles saw and feared' (Is. 41:5).

D. "Just as islands are distinct in the sea, so Abraham and Shem were distinguished in the world.

E. " '. . . and were afraid:' This one [Abraham] feared that one [Shem], and that one feared this one.

F. "This one [Abraham] feared that one, thinking, 'Perhaps he has a gripe against me, because I killed his descendants.'

G. "That one [Shem] feared this one, thinking, 'Perhaps he has a gripe against me, because I produced wicked descendants.'

H. " 'The ends of the earth' (Is. 41:5): This one lived at one end of the world, and that one lived at the other end of the world.

I. " 'They drew near and came' (Is. 41:5): this one drew near that one, and that one drew near this one.

J. " 'They helped each one his neighbor' (Is. 41:6): this one helped that one, and that one helped this one.

K. "This one helped that one by means of bless-ings: 'And he blessed him and said, "Blessed be Abram" ' (Gen. 14:19).

L. "And that one helped this one by means of gifts: 'And he gave him a tenth of all' (Gen. 14:20).

M. " 'So the carpenter encouraged' (Is. 41:7) refers to Shem, who made the ark.

N. " 'The refiner' refers to Abraham, whom the Holy One, blessed be he, refined in the fiery furnace.

O. " 'And he that smoothes with the hammer him that smites the anvil' (Is. 41:7): he smoothed with the hammer and beat all of those who pass through the world into a single path.

P. " 'Saying of the joint, it is good' (Is. 41:7) refers to the nations of the world, who say, 'It is better to cleave to the God of Abraham and not to the idolatry of Nimrod.'

Q. " 'And he strengthens it with nails' (Is. 41:7): Abra-ham strengthened Shem through the practice of religious du-ties and good deeds, so that 'he shall not be moved' (Is. 41:7), meaning, Abraham."

The exegesis in the first of the two paragraphs remains close to the verse at hand, answering the obvious question of why Abram was afraid. The answer is that Abram recognized how much had already been done for him, so he feared that he had used up in this world the merit he had attained. Or he feared that those he had killed might have been worthy. Or he feared that those whom he had killed would be avenged. In all, the exegete-compositors link one story to the next and do so in a powerful and complex way.

In the second of the two paragraphs, no. 1 introduces the exegesis of Is. 41:5f. in terms of the relationship between Abram and Shem, represented by Melchizedek. Then the events of Gen. 14 are linked to the beginning of Gen. 15, as is clear. Once the exegesis of Is. 41:5 in line with Shem is intro-duced, the matter is carried forward rather effectively. This is a masterpiece of sustained reading of a verse in line with a com-pletely independent theme. It furthermore succeeds in tying together the elements of the narrative into a sustained story.

Sarah's Complaint with Abraham

Our sages cannot claim the honorable title of feminists. But, within their context and the limits of their age, they time and again prove sensitive to the viewpoint of women characters in scripture. They take seriously Sarah's complaint with Abram and spell it out.

XLV:V.1.A. "And Sarai said to Abram, 'May the wrong [done to me be on you. I gave my maid to your embrace, and when she saw that she had conceived, she looked on me with contempt. May the Lord judge between you and me!]' " (Gen. 16:5):

B. R. Yudan in the name of R. Judah: "You wrong me with words. Why so? Because you hear me humiliated and say nothing."

2.A. R. Berekhiah in the name of R. Abba: " 'I have a case against you.'

B. "The matter may be compared to the case of two men who were in prison. The king went by. One of them said, 'Do justice for me.' The king said to let him go. The other said to him, 'I have a case against you. If you had said, "Do justice for *us*," just as he let you out, so he would have let me out.'

C. "Similarly [Sarai speaks,] 'If you had said, "*We* go childless," then, just as [God] gave you a child, so he would have given me one. And what you said was, "And I go childless" (Gen. 15:2), so he gave you a child, but to me he gave no child.'

D. "The matter may further be compared to the case of two men who were going to borrow seed from the king. One of them said, 'Let me borrow seed.' The king gave orders to give it to him. His fellow said to him, 'I have a case against you. If you had said, "Let us borrow some seed from you," just as he gave seed to you, so he would have given it to me. But since you said, "Let *me* borrow some seed," to you he gave, but to me he did not give.'

E. "Along these same lines [Sarai speaks], 'If you had said, "Behold to us you have given no seed," then, just as he

gave to you so he would have given to me. But what you said
was, "Behold, to *me* you have given no seed" ' (Gen. 15:3)."

No. 1 extends the statement of Sarai. No. 2 supplies Sarai
with a persuasive case against Abram, thus explaining why she
accused him of wronging her. This makes a better case than
Yudan at no. 1.

Circumcision

The passage before us introduces God's command to
Abram to circumcise himself. Our sages explain why the foreskin is deemed a flaw and how Abram knew what he was to do.

XLVI:IV.1.A. "Walk before me and be blameless"
(Gen. 17:1):
B. Said R. Levi, "The matter may be compared to the
case of the matron to whom the king said, 'Pass before me.'
She passed before him and she grew white with apprehension.
She said, 'It may be that some sort of flaw is found in me.'
Said the king to her, 'There is only one flaw in you, that the
nail of your little finger is a bit long. Cut it off and the blemish will be removed.'
C. "So did the Holy One, blessed be he, say to Abraham, 'You have no refuse in you except for the foreskin. Remove it and the blemish will go away: 'Walk before me and
be blameless' (Gen. 17:1)."

2.A. "And I will make my covenant between me and
you, and will multiply you exceedingly" (Gen. 17:2):
B. R. Huna in the name of Bar Qappara: "Abraham
went and argued by analogy. 'Here it is said "foreskin," and
"foreskin" is said with reference to a tree. Just as in the case
of the tree, when the word "foreskin" is used, it refers to the
place which produces fruit, so here too "foreskin" with reference to man speaks of a place which produces fruit.' "
C. Said to him R. Haninah, "But was the mode of argument through analogy available to Abraham? [Surely not.]

Rather: 'And I will make my covenant between me and you, and will multiply you exceedingly.'

D. "From the place from which 'I will multiply you exceedingly,' at that place: 'I will make my covenant between me and you.' "

The exposition of the relationship between circumcision and perfection, no. 1 yields, at no. 2, the explanation of how Abraham knew that it was through the circumcision of the penis in particular that the covenant would be effected.

The Covenant of Circumcision

The covenant of circumcision marks the imprint, in the Israelite male's flesh, of his relationship to God. The covenant is now spelled out, item by item.

XLVI:IX.1.A. "And I will give to you and to your descendants after you [the land of your sojournings, all the land of Canaan, for an everlasting possession; and I will be their God]" (Gen. 17:8):

B. In this connection R. Yudan made five statements [imputing to God five propositions, which are now spelled out].

C. R. Yudan said, "[God said] 'If your descendants accept my divinity, I shall be their patron-God, and if not, I shall not be their patron-God.'

D. " 'If your children enter the land, they will receive my divinity, and if they do not enter the land, they will not receive my divinity.'

E. " 'If your descendants accept circumcision, they will receive my divinity, and if not, they will not receive my divinity.'

F. " 'If your descendants accept circumcision, they will enter the land, and if not, they will not enter the land.' [So the cited verse yields a number of distinct conditions.]"

G. [As a further example of the association of circumcision to receiving the land] R. Berekhiah and R. Helbo in the name of R. Abin bar Yose: "It is written, 'And this is the cause that Joshua circumcised' (Joshua 5:4). Joshua spoke a word [using the same letters as 'cause'] to them, then he circumcised them [Freedman, p. 394, n. 5: "And by this word did Joshua circumcise them."]

H. "Joshua said to them, 'Now do you really imagine that you will enter the land uncircumcised?' So did the Holy One, blessed be he, say to Abraham: 'And I will give to you and to your descendants after you the land of your sojournings, all the land of Canaan, for an everlasting possession; and I will be their God' (Gen. 17:8). And that is on this stipulation: 'As for you, you shall keep my covenant, you and your descendants after you throughout their generations' (Gen. 17:9)."

The base verses, given at H, are read at no. 1 as interdependent conditions, both by Yudan and by the authorities cited thereafter. In this way the exegesis of the base verses yields an important lesson.

The Blessing of Sarah

Alongside the commandment to Abram to circumcise himself, scripture reports a blessing to Sarah. So women, as much as men, fall within the covenanted relationship between God and Israel. An account of man's relationship to God finds its match in a picture of woman's.

XLVII:I.1.A. "And God said to Abraham, 'As for Sarai, your wife, you shall not call her name Sarai, but Sarah shall be her name' " (Gen. 17:15):

B. "A virtuous woman is a crown to her husband" (Prov. 12:4).

C. Said R. Aha, "Her husband was crowned through her, but she was not crowned through her husband. [Freedman, p. 399, n. 1: He refers this verse to Sarah. Her original name was Sarai, spelled with a Y. The numerical value of Y is 10, while that of H, her new name being spelled with an H rather than a Y, is 5. Thus God took the Y from her name and split it up into two Hs, one for her name, which became Sarah, with an H, and one to be added to Abraham's name, which thus received an H and was changed from Abram to Abraham. Hence Abraham was "crowned" through Sarah, but Sarah was not crowned through him.]

D. Rabbis say, "She was master of her husband. In every other context the man gives the orders, but here: 'In all that Sarah says to you, listen to her voice' (Gen. 21:12)."

2.A. "You shall not call her name Sarai, but Sarah shall be her name" (Gen. 17:15):

B. Said R. Joshua b. Qorha, "The Y that the Holy One, blessed be he, took away from the name of Sarai went fluttering above, before the Holy One, blessed be he, saying, 'Lord of all ages, because I am the smallest of all the letters you took me out of the name of that righteous woman!'

C. "Said the Holy One, blessed be he, to it, 'In the past you were in the name of a woman and at the end of the letters of the name. Now I shall put you in the name of a male, and as the first of the letters of his name: "And Moses called Hoshea ben Nun Yehoshua" ' (Num. 13:16)."

D. Said R. Mana, "In the past she was princess for her own people, now she shall be princess for all humankind." [Freedman, p. 400, n. 1: He holds that both Sarai and Sarah denote princess, but that the latter is more comprehensive.]

XLVII:II.1.A. "I will bless her and moreover I will give you a son by her [I will bless her and she shall be a mother of nations; kings of peoples shall come from her]" (Gen. 17:16):

B. R. Judah says, " 'I will bless her' by giving her a son, 'and moreover I will give you a son by her;' 'I will bless her' by giving her the blessing of milk."

C. Said to him R. Nehemiah, "And had she already been informed about the matter of milk? But this teaches that the Holy One, blessed be he, restoreth her youth to her."

2.A. R. Abbahu in the name of R. Yose b. R. Hanina: "I shall place fear of her over all the nations of the world, so that they will not abuse her by calling her barren."

B. R. Yudan in the name of R. Simeon b. Laqish: "She had no ovary, so the Holy One, blessed be he, formed an ovary for her."

3.*A.*   ". . . and she shall be a mother of nations; kings of peoples shall come from her" (Gen. 17:16):

B.   Said R. Hama bar Haninah, "From the statement at hand Abraham so reasoned that he took Kenturah back. [Kenturah is the same as Hagar. 'From her,' namely from Sarah he would produce kings, so he might have children from another wife, and those children would not be kings (Freedman, p. 400, n. 3).]"

Sarah, no less than Abram, serves as the founder of nations. The blessing reaches both, and—again within the limits of their time and circumstance—our sages show themselves deeply interested in the place and position of women in the sacred economy of Israel. True, we cannot represent them as feminists. We can, however, claim a place for them in the camp of those who honor women and accord them every dignity. More important, in the tasks of serving God, women find a full and ample share. More than that, in the present setting, none can have expected.

Part Four

Genesis Rabbah
Parashiyyot XLVIII–LVII

The Merit of Abraham and
the Salvation of his Children

Israel endures on the merit of the patriarchs and matriarchs. Consequently, each act of the patriarch Abraham must be carefully matched with a response, on God's part, in the history of Israel later on.

XLVIII:X.2.A. "Let a little water be brought" (Gen. 18:4):

B. Said to him the Holy One, blessed be he, "You have said, 'Let a little water be brought' (Gen. 18:4). By your life, I shall pay your descendants back for this: 'Then sang Israel this song, "spring up O well, sing you to it' " (Numb. 21:7).

C. That recompense took place in the wilderness. Where do we find that it took place in the Land of Israel as well?

D. "A land of brooks of water" (Deut. 8:7).

E. And where do we find that it will take place in the age to come?

F. "And it shall come to pass in that day that living waters shall go out of Jerusalem" (Zech. 14:8).

G. ["And wash your feet" (Gen. 18:4)]: [Said to him the Holy One, blessed be he] "You have said, 'And wash your feet.' By your life, I shall pay your descendants back for this: 'Then I washed you in water' (Ez. 16:9)."

H. That recompense took place in the wilderness. Where do we find that it took place in the Land of Israel as well?

I. "Wash you, make you clean" (Is. 1:16).

J. And where do we find that it will take place in the age to come?

K. "When the Lord will have washed away the filth of the daughters of Zion" (Is. 4:4).

L. [Said to him the Holy One, blessed be he] "You have said, 'And rest yourselves under the tree' (Gen. 18:4). By your life, I shall pay your descendants back for this: 'He spread a cloud for a screen' (Ps. 105:39)."

M. That recompense took place in the wilderness. Where do we find that it took place in the land of Israel as well?

N. "You shall dwell in booths for seven days" (Lev. 23:42).

O. And where do we find that it will take place in the age to come?

P. "And there shall be a pavilion for a shadow in the daytime from the heat" (Is. 4:6).

Q. [Said to him the Holy One, blessed be he] "You have said, 'While I fetch a morsel of bread that you may refresh yourself' (Gen. 18:5). By your life, I shall pay your descendants back for this: 'Behold I will cause to rain bread from heaven for you' (Ex. 16:45)"

R. That recompense took place in the wilderness. Where do we find that it took place in the land of Israel as well?

S. "A land of wheat and barley" (Deut. 8:8).

T. And where do we find that it will take place in the age to come?

U. "He will be as a rich cornfield in the land" (Ps. 82:16).

V. [Said to him the Holy One, blessed be he] "You ran after the herd ['And Abraham ran to the herd' (Gen. 18:7)]. By your life, I shall pay your descendants back for this: 'And there went forth a wind from the Lord and brought across quails from the sea' (Num. 11:27)."

W. That recompense took place in the wilderness. Where do we find that it took place in the land of Israel as well?

X. "Now the children of Reuben and the children of Gad had a very great multitude of cattle" (Num. 32:1).

Y. And where do we find that it will take place in the age to come?

Z. "And it will come to pass in that day that a man shall rear a young cow and two sheep" (Is. 7:21).

AA. [Said to him the Holy One, blessed be he] "You stood by them: 'And he stood by them under the tree while they ate' (Gen. 18:8). By your life, I shall pay your descendants back for this: 'And the Lord went before them' (Ex. 13:21)."

BB. That recompense took place in the wilderness. Where do we find that it took place in the land of Israel as well?

CC. "God stands in the congregation of God" (Ps. 82:1).

DD. And where do we find that it will take place in the age to come?

EE. "The breaker is gone up before them . . . and the Lord at the head of them" (Mic. 2:13).

Our passage presents a sizable and beautifully disciplined construction, making one point again and again. Everything that Abraham did brought a reward to his descendants. The enormous emphasis on the way in which Abraham's deeds prefigured the history of Israel, both in the wilderness and in the land, and, finally, in the age to come, provokes us to wonder who held that there were children of Abraham beside Israel. The answer then is clear. We note that there are five statements of the same proposition, each drawing upon a clause in the base verse. The extended statement moreover serves as a sustained introduction to the treatment of the individual clauses that now follow, item by item.

Sarah Laughed

Our tale of domestic relations yields lessons for Israel in more than one way. The narrator tells us that Sarah laughed. What do we learn from that laughter—ringing downward through the ages? No less than the merit of the founders, their deeds teach lessons.

XLVIII:XVII.2.A. "So Sarah laughed to herself, saying, 'After I have grown old and my husband is old, shall I have pleasure?'" (Gen. 18:12):

B. She said, "While a woman is young, she has orna-ments. After I have grown old and my husband is old, shall I have ornaments?"

C. For the word for "pleasure" also means "ornaments," as in the verse: "I have decked you also with ornaments" (Ez. 16:11).

D. "While a woman is young, she has her regular pe-riod. After I have grown old and my husband is old, I none-theless shall have my regular period. But [the real problem is]: '. . . my husband is old.' "

E. R. Judah said, "He grinds but does not produce [se-men]."

F. Said R. Judah b. R. Simon, "[God said to them] 'You treat yourselves as young, and treat your Associate [me] as old. But "Am I too old" (Gen. 18:13) to do miracles?' " [We read Gen. 18:13 and 18:14 together. Thus God says both clauses, but the former is treated as a wry observation. "Am I too old to do it? Is anything too hard for the Lord?"]

XLVIII:XVIII.1.A. "The Lord said to Abraham, 'Why did Sarah laugh [and say, "Shall I indeed bear a child now that I am old?"]' " (Gen. 18:13):

B. Bar Qappara said, "The greatness of peace is shown in the fact that even scripture told a lie so as to bring peace between Abraham and Sarah.

C. "Why did Sarah laugh [and say, "Shall I indeed bear a child *and my lord has grown old*'" is not what it says here, but rather, *"now that I am old."* [But that is not the language that Sarah had originally used.]"

What lesson we learn derives from a close reading of the passage. The exegete deals with a discrepancy between two verses of the same conversation. The discrepancy is deliberate and shows that God wanted to keep peace.

God Tells Abraham about the Coming Overthrow of Sodom and Gomorrah

The tale now breaks off, while Abraham receives a weighty statement of praise from God. Why just here and just now? And why does God tell Abraham what God is going to do? The answers to these questions lead to deep reflection on the honor owing to the patriarchs.

XLIX:1.1.A. "The Lord said, 'Shall I hide from Abraham [what I am about to do, seeing that Abraham shall become a great and mighty nation and all the nations of the earth shall bless themselves by him? No, for I have chosen him that he may charge his children and his household after him to keep the way of the Lord by doing righteousness and justice . . .']" (Gen. 17:17–19):

B. R. Isaac opened discussion by citing this verse: "The memory of the righteous shall be for a blessing" (Prov. 10:7).

C. Said R. Isaac, "Whoever mentions the name of a righteous man and does not say a blessing for him violates a religious duty of commission. What is the biblical text that indicates it? 'The memory of the righteous shall be for a blessing' (Prov. 10:7). [Hence when one mentions the name of a righteous person, a blessing of that name must be recited.]

D. "And whoever mentions the name of a wicked person and does not curse him violates a religious duty of commission. What is the biblical text that indicates it? 'But the name of the wicked shall rot' (Prov. 10:7)."

2.A. Said R. Samuel bar Nahman, "The names of the wicked are like weaver's webs. Just as a web, so as you use it, remains taut, but if you leave it, it becomes slack, so have you ever heard a man call his son 'Pharaoh'? 'Sisera'? 'Senacherib'?

B. "But [people commonly call their children] Abraham, Isaac, Jacob, Reuben, Simeon, Levi, and Judah."

3.A. Rab said, "Cursed is Haman and his sons."

B. Said R. Phineas, " 'Harmboa—of blessed memory' [is how one should express things]."

4.A. Said R. Samuel bar Nahman, "We have found that the Holy One, blessed be he, mentions the name of Israel and says a blessing for them, as it is said, 'May the Lord bless the mention of our name' (Ps. 115:12)."

B. R. Huna in the name of R. Aha, "I know that that is the case only for the six hundred thousand [mentioned all at once, that is, the nation as a whole is blessed when God mentions their name]. How do I know that when the Holy One, blessed be he, mentions the name of each and every Israelite, he mentions the name and says a blessing for it?

C. "As it is said, 'The Lord said, "Shall I hide from Abraham what I am about to do, seeing that Abraham shall become a great and mighty nation [and all the nations of the earth shall bless themselves by him]?" ' (Gen. 18:17). Now it was necessary for him to say only, 'Because the outcry against Sodom and Gomorrah is great [and their sin is very grave, I will go down to see whether they have done altogether according to the outcry which has come to me, and if not, I will know].'

D. "Said the Holy One, blessed be he, 'I have made mention of the name of that righteous man, and shall I not [interrupt my thought only to] say a blessing for him? "Abraham shall become a great and mighty nation [and all the nations of the earth shall bless themselves by him]" ' (Gen. 18:17)."

XLIX:II.1.A. [Referring to God's telling Abraham what he is about to do:] "The secret of the Lord is with them who fear him and his covenant to make them know it" (Ps. 25:14).

B. To begin with "The secret of the Lord is with them who fear him" but in the end it was with the upright: "But his secret is with the upright" (Ps. 3:32).

C. Then it is with the prophets: "For the Lord God will do nothing without revealing his secret to his servants the prophets" (Amos 3:7).

D. Said the Holy One, blessed be he, "This Abraham fears God: 'Now I know that you are a God-fearing man' (Gen. 22:12).

E. "This Abraham is upright: 'The upright love you' (Song 1:4).

F. "This Abraham is a prophet: 'Now therefore restore the man's wife, for he is a prophet' (Gen. 20:7).

G. "Shall I not reveal it to him?"

H. "The Lord said, 'Shall I hide from Abraham [what I am about to do, seeing that Abraham shall become a great and mighty nation and all the nations of the earth shall bless themselves by him? No, for I have chosen him that he may charge his children and his household after him to keep the way of the Lord by doing righteousness and justice']" (Gen. 17:17–19).

2.A. "The Lord said, 'Shall I hide from Abraham [what I am about to do, seeing that Abraham shall become a great and mighty nation and all the nations of the earth shall bless themselves by him? No, for I have chosen him that he may charge his children and his household after him to keep the way of the Lord by doing righteousness and justice']" (Gen. 17:17–19).

B. Said R. Joshua b. Levi, "The matter may be compared to the case of a king who gave an estate to his ally and then later on the king wanted to cut down from the property five barren trees [for use as wood]. The king said, 'If I had wanted to cut down trees from his inherited property [and not from the property I gave him], he would not stop me. So what difference does it make?' He nonetheless [paid him respect and so] took counsel with him.

C. "So said the Holy One, blessed be he, 'Now I have already given the land as a gift to Abraham: "To your seed have I given this land" (Gen. 15:18). These towns fall within my property. But if they belonged to his inheritance, he would not object. So what difference does it make to me if I ask his permission?' "

3.A. Said R. Judah bar Simon, "The matter may be compared to the case of a king who had three allies and who would do nothing without their knowledge and consent. One time, however, the king wanted to do something without their knowledge and consent. He took the first and drove him out and put him away from the palace. He took the second and put him in prison. He put his seal on the prison door. As to the third, who was a special favorite, he said, 'I simply shall do nothing without his knowledge and consent.'

B. "So in the case of the first man [Adam]: 'So he drove out the man' (Gen. 3:23).

C. "As to Noah: 'The Lord shut him in' (Gen. 7:5).

D. "But when it came to Abraham, who was the special favorite, he said, 'I simply shall do nothing without his knowledge and consent.' "

4.A. Said R. Samuel b. Nahman, "The matter may be compared to the case of a king who had an adviser, without whose knowledge and consent he would do absolutely nothing. One time he considered doing something without his knowledge and consent. Said the king, 'Did I not make my counselor only so as not to do anything without his knowledge and consent?' "

B. Said R. Yudan, "So said the Holy One, blessed be he, 'Did I not call him a man of my own counsel only so as not to do anything outside his knowledge and consent? Lot, his brother's son is with [the Sodomites], and should I not let him know?' "

5.A. Rabbis say, "I have already called him their father: 'For the father of a multitude of nations have I made you' (Gen. 17:5).

B. "Do they judge a son without the knowledge and consent of the father?

C. "I have already revealed to him Gehenna, the revelation of the Torah, and should I not reveal to him the judgment against Sodom?"

6.A. R. Aha in the name of R. Alexandri, R. Samuel b. Nahman in the name of R. Jonathan: "Even the laws governing the commingling of domain in courtyards [for purposes of creating a single domain for carrying on the Sabbath] did Abraham know."

B. R. Phineas, R. Hilqiah, R. Simon in the name of R. Samuel: "Even the new name that the Holy One, blessed be he, is destined to assign to Jerusalem: 'On that day they will call Jerusalem "the throne of God" ' (Jer. 3:17) Abraham knew."

C. R. Berekhiah, R. Hiyya, the rabbis of the other place [Babylonia] in the name of R. Judah: "There is not a single day on which the Holy One, blessed be he, does not create a new law in the court above. What is the scriptural verse that shows it? 'Hear attentively the noise of his voice and the med-

itation that goes out of his mouth' (Job 37:2). The word medi-
tation speaks only of the Torah, as it is said, 'But you shall
meditate therein day and night' (Joshua 1:8). Even those new
laws Abraham knew."

In the opening paragraph, nos. 1–3 work out the exegesis of
Prov. 10:7. But the intersecting verse is well chosen and leads
us naturally back to the base verse. The exegete has asked the
question of why the text goes into such fulsome praise of Abraham, which breaks up the flow of the narrative with its reference
to the nations of the earth blessing themselves by Abraham's
name. So the exegete provides a suitable explanation of the
matter, drawing on the lesson of Prov. 10:7 to do so. This does
represent a case in which the intersecting verse answers an important question in the base verse and the materials in exegesis
of the former furthermore illuminate the latter.

When we reach the second of the two paragraphs, we note
that No. 1 sets the stage for the articulation of God's thinking
in the base verse by proving that God reveals his secret to persons of Abraham's category. That explains the self-evidence of
God's question, cited at the end. It is a persuasive exercise.
No. 2 is equally effective in expanding the account of God's
reasoning in the rhetorical question in hand. No. 3 presents a
powerful explanation for the special favor shown to Abraham,
underlining how different was his relationship to God from that
of Adam and Noah. No. 4 makes the same point in a different
way. No. 5 shifts the ground of argument, reverting to Abraham
in particular. No. 6 then expands on the theme of how much
God revealed to Abraham. This is the point at which the narrative crosses the distinctive history of Israel. Abraham now
knows the name of Jerusalem, the new laws of the heavenly
academy, and the rules of the commingling of courtyards—that
is, a matter quite distinctive to the rabbis and their tradition, at
least, as they portray that particular matter. So in all the climax
has Abraham know particularly Israelite matters.

Will not the Judge of All the World Do Justice?

Abraham's appeal to God to keep the rules by which God
made the world draws us deep into our sages' understanding of

God's life of feeling, God's attitudes toward humanity. To our sages humanity is in God's image. So how we feel tells us how God feels about things. Then we hope that God will surpass us, forgiving where we would seek vengeance, supressing anger, and yielding to feelings of compassion. Our sages read the encounter between Abraham and God in the matter of Sodom as the model for humanity's relationship with God. People can appeal to God in accord with the rules that govern humanity.

XLIX:VIII.1.A. "Then Abraham drew near and said . . ." (Gen. 18:23):

B. R. Judah, R. Nehemiah, and Rabbis:

C. R. Judah said, "This was a drawing near as for battle, as it says, 'So Joab and the people who were with him drew near to battle' (2 Sam. 10:13). [Abraham drew near to fight with God.]"

D. R. Nehemiah said, "It was a drawing near for conciliation, in line with the usage in this verse: 'Then the children of Judah drew near to Joshua' (Joshua 14:6). The purpose was to conciliate him."

E. Rabbis say, "It was a drawing near for prayer, in line with the usage in this verse: 'And it came to pass at the time of the offering of the evening offering, that Elijah the prophet came near and said, "O Lord, God of Abraham, Isaac, and Israel, this day let it be known that you are God in Israel" ' (1 Kgs. 18:36)."

F. Said R. Eleazar, "Interpret the verse to bear this encompassing meaning: 'If it is for war, I am coming. If it is for conciliation, I am coming. If it is for prayer, I am coming.' "

2.A. R. Phineas, R. Levi, and R. Yohanan in the name of Menahem of Gallia: "As to one who goes down before the ark [to lead worship service], people do not say to him, 'Come and do the job,' but, 'Come and draw near,' which is to say, 'Come and carry out our war, come and prepare the offering for the community.' "

B. Said R. Tanhuma, "Why is it in particular in the fifteenth blessing [of the Eighteen Blessings] that the reference to God's hearing prayer, that is, '. . . who hears prayer,' is located? That corresponds to the fact that the name of God appears fifteen times in the Psalm, 'Ascribe to the Lord, O you sons of might . . . ,' to, '. . . the Lord sat enthroned at the flood' (Ps. 29), for that is what keeps punishment from visiting the world."

3.A. "Will you indeed destroy the righteous with the wicked?" (Gen. 18:23):

B. R. Huna in the name of R. Aha: " 'Will you indeed destroy [the righteous with the wicked]?' (Gen. 18:23): [Since the word 'indeed' uses the consonants which produce the meaning 'anger'] the sense of the passage is, 'You place limits around anger, and anger does not fence you in.' "

C. Said R. Joshua bar Nehemiah, "[This is the sense of Abraham's statement:] 'With the anger which you bring onto your world will you destroy the righteous along with the wicked? It is not enough that you should not suspend the punishment coming to the wicked on account of the righteous, but you wipe out the righteous with the wicked!' "

4.A. Rabbi and R. Jonathan:

B. Rabbi said, "In the case of a mortal, anger conquers him, but the Holy One, blessed be he, conquers anger: 'The Lord avenges and masters wrath' (Nahum 1:11)."

C. R. Jonathan said, "In the case of mortal man, envy conquers him, but the Holy One, blessed be he, conquers envy: 'The Lord is God over envy and vengeance' (Nahum 1:1)."

5.A. R. Simlai asked R. Jonathan, saying to him, "What is the meaning of the verse: 'But there is one who is swept away without judgment' (Prov. 13:23)?"

B. He said to him, "Without being affected by the judgment coming to his own town."

C. There is the case of one who was sent to collect fines owed by people of Tiberias and Sepphoris. When he was collecting in Tiberias, he saw someone from Sepphoris and went and arrested him.

D. The man said to him, "I am from Sepphoris."

E. He said to him, "I have warrants against Sepphoris people to make my collection there too."

F. Before he completed collecting what was owing from the people of Tiberias, a remission of the fine was issued for the people of Sepphoris.

G. So the Sepphorean in Tiberias was "swept away" without being subject to the "judgment affecting his own town."

6.A. R. Levi and R. Simon:

B. R. Levi said, "[Abraham's plea was to ask God, 'Is your anger like that of a] bear, who, not finding prey, eats its own?' "

C. R. Simon said, "[Abraham's plea was to ask God, 'Is your anger like] a scythe, which cuts down thorns, then goes on to the roses?' "

XLIX:IX.1.A. "Far be it from you [to do such a thing, to slay the righteous with the wicked, so that the righteous fare as the wicked. Far be that from you. Shall not the Judge of all the earth do justly?]" (Gen. 18:25):

B. [Interpreting the consonants for the word "far be it from you," in diverse ways] said R. Yudan, "It is a profanation for you, it is alien from you."

C. Said R. Aha, "The word 'far be it' [yielding the sense of 'profanation'] is used two times, meaning, 'It is a profanation of the name of heaven, it is a profanation of the name of heaven.' "

2.A. Said R. Abba, "What is written is not 'from doing the thing,' but rather, 'from doing *such* a thing' [that is, 'an act like this act'] [Abraham's meaning is] 'Not this act, and not an act like this act, and not an act of even less severe consequences.' "

3.A. R. Levi said, "Two men said the same thing, Abraham and Job.

B. "Abraham said, 'Far be it from you to do such a thing, to slay the righteous with the wicked [so that the righteous fare as the wicked. Far be that from you. Shall not the Judge of all the earth do justly?]' (Gen. 18:25).

C. "Job said, 'It is all one, therefore I say, "He destroys the innocent and the wicked' " (Job 9:22).

D. "Abraham received a reward on account of making that statement, while Job was punished on that account.

E. "The difference is that Abraham said it with confidence [that God would never do such a thing], while Job said it as a complaint: 'Is it all one?' "

4.A. R. Hiyya bar Abba said, "What we have here is a collection of answers.

B. "Abraham said, 'Far be it from you,' and the Holy One, blessed be he, answered, 'So shall the wicked be as the righteous' [The sense of this reply of God's is as follows:] 'Should the punishment coming to the wicked be suspended on account of the righteous? But the righteous themselves are fakers.' "

C. That judgment is in line with the observation that R. Yohanan made, "Every time the word 'righteous' is stated in connection with Sodom, it is written as though it were to be read 'Their righteousness,' that is, defectively [hence the righteousness was fake]."

D. This is further in line with the approach of R. Yohanan, for R. Yohanan said, " 'And our elders and all the inhabitants of our country spoke to us' (Joshua 9:11). The word for 'elders' is written defectively, which indicates that these were elders who gave leadership for doing wrong, elders for giving counsel in doing wickedness [Freedman, p. 429, n. 2: In wickedness and evil too they were elders.]"

5.A. Said R. Joshua b. Levi, "[Abraham made this plea:] 'Combine the various good deeds and you will get up to the number of fifty.' " [Freedman, p. 429, n. 2: If you combine the good of all, it will be equivalent to that of fifty righteous men.]"

B. Said R. Judan, "Are you not the righteous one of the world? Join yourself with them and you will get up to the number fifty."

C. Said R. Judah bar Simon, "In the case of mortals, one can make an appeal from the commander to the regional governor, and from the regional governor to the head of state. But as to you, since there is no appeal from your judgment, will you [the judge of all the world] not do justly?"

199

D. Said R. Judan, "When you wanted to judge your world, you handed it over to two such as Romulus and Remus [that is, the mythic founders of Rome]. The upshot was that if one of them wanted to do something, his colleague could hold him back. [So there is a balance of power in worldly government.] But as to you, since there is no one who can hold back anything you want to do, 'will you not do justice?' "

6.A. [R. Azariah in the name of R. Aha interpreted the verse to speak of our father, Abraham: "When our father, Abraham, stood to seek mercy for the Sodomites, what is written there? 'Far be it from you to do such a thing' (Gen. 18:25)."] Said R. Aha, "[Abraham said to God] 'You bound yourself by an oath not to bring a flood upon the world. Are you now going to act deceitfully against the clear intent of that oath?'

B. "True enough, you are not going to bring a flood of water, but you are going to bring a flood of fire.

C. "If so, you will not faithfully carry out the oath!"

D. Said R. Levi, " 'Will not the judge of all the earth do justly?' (Gen. 18:25). 'If you want to have a world, there can be no justice, and if justice is what you want, there can be no world. You are holding the rope at both ends, you want a world and you want justice. If you don't give in a bit, the world can never stand.'

E. "Said the Holy One, blessed be he, to him 'Abraham, "You have loved righteousness and hated wickedness. Therefore God, your God, has anointed you with the oil of gladness above your fellows' " (Ps. 45:8).

F. "From Noah to you there are ten generations [that is, that lived from Noah to Abraham].

G. "Among all of them, I spoke only with you."

XLIX:X.1.A. "And the Lord said, 'If I find at Sodom [fifty righteous in the city, I will spare the whole place for their sake]" (Gen. 18:26):

B. R. Judah bar Simon in the name of R. Joshua b. Levi: "For it is for God to have said, 'I have forgiven' " (Job 34:31).

C. "So: 'I will spare the whole place for their sake' (Gen. 18:26)."

D. "I shall not take a pledge" (Job 34:31) means, "I shall not exact a surety," in line with the use of the same root in this verse: "If you take your neighbor's garment as a pledge" (Ex. 22:25).

E. [Speaking in the name of God:] "Yet people complain [using the consonants for the word for 'exact a surety'] against me, claiming that I do not judge rightly."

F. "Apart from me, I will see" (Job 34:32): [God speaks:] "Even without me, you go and examine my judgment. If I have made a mistake, 'You teach me' (Job 34:32), and 'if I have committed an injustice' to the earlier generation, 'I will not do it again' to the later generations."

2.A. "To him will I keep silence, and to his branches" (Job 41:4): [God further speaks to Abraham:] "For you I shall keep silent, and for the branches that come forth from you."

B. This is addressed to Abraham, who said, "Far be it from you to do such a thing" (Gen. 18:25).

C. It is further addressed to Moses, who said, "Lord, why are you angry against your people?" (Ex. 32:11).

D. . . . to Joshua, who said, "Why have you brought this people over the Jordan?" (Joshua 7:7).

E. . . . to David, who said, "Why do you stand afar off, O Lord?" (Ps. 10:1).

3.A. "Or his proud talk, or his fair array of words" (Job 41:4):

B. Grace infused [Abraham's] extended speech when he sought mercy for the Sodomites.

In the opening paragraph, no. 1. presents three meanings imputed to the word "draw near," with the satisfying conclusion that Abraham was ready for all purposes. The composite at no. 2 selects the meaning of prayer and by putting together two discrete items makes the important point for our context. It is that Abraham's intent in drawing near was to pray, as we know from no. 1, and the purpose of the prayer was to keep divine punishment from affecting the world, as 2.B indicates. So here

201

is a case in which the topic at hand finds amplification through set-piece insertion of materials on other topics entirely. No. 3 revises the meaning imputed to the word translated "anger." This yields the amplifications of nos. 3, 4, 5, and 6. The net effect is to emphasize that God did not act with wrath but only after reflection and deliberation. So Abraham is not the only party to the coming discourse who has a commitment to justice.

In the second of the three paragraphs, no. 1 explains the sense of the word "far be it," reading the consonants to mean "it is a profanation." Then Abraham's meaning is reconstructed. No. 2 again concentrates on interpreting the language at hand. No. 3 broadens the matter to compare the cases of Abraham and Job, both of whom took up the same proposition. But the upshot still is to remain within the limits of the verse at hand and to point up a dimension of its meaning. No. 4 falls into the same category, in which several verses are illuminated by the same principle. The compositor of no. 5 has presented a series of strong pleas to God, and, we now realize, the purpose of the bulk of the composition is to present a range of pleas that Abraham made to God. No. 6, familiar from its own context, then produces the climactic statement that God honored Abraham for making his plea.

This brings us to the third paragraph. The two interesting verses, Job 34:31 and 41:4, cast fresh light on Abraham's statement at hand. No. 1 assigns a long response to God, in which he accepts Abraham's plea. No. 2 assembles a range of examples of Abraham's descendants' following his example, and no. 3 reverts to the case at hand. This is a striking and successful amplification of a base verse and its case through the invoking intersecting verses. The upshot is to introduce into Abraham's discourse the entire history of Israel.

Why was Lot Saved?

Since God acts justly, we want to know what justice motivated God to save Lot.

LI:VI.1.A. "So it was that, when God destroyed the cities of the valley, God remembered Abraham and sent Lot out of the midst of the overthrow, when he overthrew the cities in which Lot dwelt" (Gen. 19:29):

B. What was it about [what Lot had done for] Abraham that God remembered?

C. It was the silence that [Lot] kept when Abraham said concerning Sarah, "She is my sister." He knew the truth but said nothing.

2.A. ". . . and sent Lot out of the midst of the overthrow, when he overthrew the cities in which Lot dwelt" (Gen. 19:29):

B. R. Samuel bar. Nahman said, "The sense is that Lot had lived in all those cities."

C. Rabbis say, "It is because he lent money on interest in all of them."

No. 1 interprets the verse to refer to something Lot had done in connection with Abraham. The exegete cannot imagine that there is any other merit associated with Lot. No. 2 spells out why the verse refers to Lot's dwelling in more than one city. He is tied up with all the wicked cities, explaining why not only Sodom but the others were overturned.

The Sin of Ishmael

Since Sarah insisted that Hagar and Ishmael go, we wonder what sin they had committed. For our sages cannot imagine that Sarah would commit an injustice, any more than God would. We understand the hidden agenda here when we realize that Ishmael stands for Rome.

LIII:XI.1.A. "But Sarah saw the son of Hagar the Egyptian, whom she had borne to Abraham, making sport" (Gen. 21:9):

B. Said R. Simeon, "R. Aqiba would explain this matter [of making sport] in a way that deprecated Ishamel."

C. R. Aqiba interpreted the matter in this way: " 'But Sarah saw the son of Hagar the Egyptian, whom she had borne to Abraham, making sport' (Gen. 21:9). The word 'making sport' bears only one meaning—namely, fornicating—in line with this verse: 'The Hebrew servant whom you brought me came in to me to make sport of me' (Gen. 39:17).

D. "This teaches, then, that Sarah saw Ishmael seducing 'gardens [virgins],' making love to married women and dishonoring them."

2.A. R. Ishmael taught on Tannaite authority, "The word 'making sport' refers only to idolatry, as it is said, 'And rose up to make sport' (Ex. 32:6).

B. "This teaches, then, that Sarah saw Ishmael building little altars, hunting locusts, and offering them up [on the altars, as a game]."

3.A. R. Eleazar says, "The word 'make sport' refers only to murder: 'Let the young men, I pray you, arise and make sport before us' (2 Sam. 2:15)."

B. [Showing just what murder is in mind] R. Azariah in the name of R. Levi: "They said, 'Come and let's go see our portion of the fields. Then Ishmael took a bow and arrows and shot at Isaac and pretended to be making sport. That is in line with this verse: 'As a madman who casts firebrands, arrows, and death, so is the man who deceives his neighbor and says, Am I not making sport?' (Prov. 22:18)."

4.A. [Reverting to Simeon, 1.B:]"But I say that the word 'making sport' refers only to inheritance.

B. "For when our father, Isaac, was born, everybody rejoiced. Ishmael said to them, 'You really are fools. I am the firstborn, and I shall take a double portion.'

C. "For from the answer that Sarah gave to Abraham, you learn what is at issue: '. . . for the son of this slave woman shall not be heir with my son Isaac.'

D. " '. . . with my son' even if it were not Isaac, '. . . with Isaac' even if it were not my son. All the more so: '. . . with my son, Isaac.' "

The composition is unitary and powerful. It rings the changes on the conventional trilogy of mortal sins—fornication, idolatry, and murder—and then comes back to the main point.

It is thoroughly persuasive. The deeper message is that Rome commits the mortal sins and will be punished, and Israel will enjoy the standing of Isaac. The two are siblings—but with what a difference! This foreshadows the still more explicit contrast of Esau/Rome and Jacob/Israel. So there is a series of generations, first Isaac/Ishmael, then Jacob/Esau, in which the future salvation of Israel finds its original expression.

God Tests Abraham: The Justice of God

We move from Noah to Abraham in our search for the rules that govern how and why God puts people to the test. The interest is not only specific to the story at hand. We search for rules that will tell us why others, even now, find themselves tried.

LV:I.1.A. "And it came to pass after these things God tested Abraham" (Gen. 22:1):

B. "You have given a banner to those that fear you, that it may be displayed because of the truth, *selah*" (Ps. 60:6).

C. [Since the word for "banner" shares the consonants of the word for "test," we interpret:] test after test, one attainment of greatness after another, so as to test them in the world and so as to endow them with greatness in the world, like the ensign of a ship.

D. And all this why? ". . . because of the truth, *selah*" (Ps. 60:6).

E. [Since the word for "truth" and the word for "validate" share the same consonants, we interpret:] it is so that the attribute of justice may be validated in the world.

F. For if someone should say, "He gives riches to whomever he wishes, and he impoverishes whomever he wishes, and whomever he wishes he makes king [all this without justice], and so too as to Abraham, when he wanted, he made him rich, and when he wanted, he made him king [and all this without justice], you may reply to him, saying, "Can you do what Abraham did?"

G. "Abraham was a hundred years old when Isaac, his son, was born to him" (Gen. 21:5). And after all that anguish, it was stated to him, "Take your son" (Gen. 22:2).

H. And he did not demur.

I. Accordingly: "You have given a banner to those that fear you, that it may be displayed because of the truth, *selah*" (Ps. 60:6).

J. "And it came to pass after these things God tested Abraham" (Gen. 22:1)

LV:II.1.A. "The Lord tries the righteous, but the wicked and him who loves violence his soul hates" (Ps. 11:5):

B. Said R. Jonathan, "A potter does not test a weak utensil, for it he hits it just once, he will break it. So the Holy One, blessed be he, does not try the wicked but the righteous: 'The Lord tries the righteous' (Ps. 11:5)."

C. Said R. Yose bar Haninah, "When a flax maker knows that the flax is in good shape, then the more he beats it, the more it will improve and glisten. When it is not of good quality, if he beats it just once, he will split it. So the Holy One, blessed be he, does not try the wicked but the righteous: 'The Lord tries the righteous' (Ps. 11:5)."

D. Said R. Eleazar, "The matter may be compared to a householder who has two heifers, one strong, one weak. On whom does he place the yoke? It is on the one that is strong. So the Holy One, blessed be he, does not try the wicked but the righteous: 'The Lord tries the righteous' (Ps. 11:5).

In the opening paragraph, the intersecting verse serves because it highlights the key word of the base verse, "try" or "test." The power of the intersecting verse is to demonstrate that what God did in favoring Abraham rested on justice, not capriciousness. The two plays on words are secondary, since the main point flows from the sense of the intersecting verse. The insistence that what man does matters constitutes the main point of the exegesis. In the second paragraph, sages maintain that what God did for Abraham was just, and we now are told that Abraham was chosen for the test because of his strength. The sequence of statements produces a coherent message, that of the compositors. Abraham was the right choice for the test.

God Tries Abraham: The Nature of the Test
The True Temptation of Abraham and Isaac

What in fact had Abraham achieved, and why do we derive so rich a treasury of merit from his strength? The answer lies in our discovery of the true temptation which Abraham resisted and Isaac suffered. Only when the story reaches us in all its humanity do we understand what Abraham accomplished and Isaac endured.

LVI:IV.1.A. "And Isaac said to his father Abraham, 'My father' " (Gen. 22:7):

B. Samuel [the tempter] came to our father, Abraham. He said to him, "What sort of nonsense is troubling your heart? The son that was given to you at the age of a hundred are you going to slaughter?"

C. He said to him, "Indeed so."

D. He said to him, "And if he tests you still further than this, can you stand the test? 'If a thing be put to you as a trial, will you be wearied' (Job 4:2)?"

E. He said to him, "And still more."

F. He said to him, "Tomorrow he will [reverse himself and] tell you that you are a murderer, and you are liable."

G. He said to him, "Indeed so."

H. When he saw that he could accomplish nothing with him, he came to Isaac. He said to him, "Oh son of a miserable mother. He is going to slaughter you."

I. He said to him, "Indeed so."

J. He said to him, "If so, all those lovely cloaks which your mother made will be the inheritance of Ishmael, the hated one of her house."

K. [This statement made its mark, for] if a word does not make its way entirely, it makes its way in part. That is in line with this verse: "And Isaac said to his father Abraham, 'My father' " (Gen. 22:7).

L. Why does the verse state, "And Isaac said to Abraham *his* father and said, '*My* father' "? Why thus: "his father . . . my father"?

M. It was so that he should be filled with mercy for him.

N. And he said, "Behold the fire and the wood, but where is the lamb for a burnt offering?"

O. Abraham said, "May that man who incited you drown."

P. In any event: " 'God will provide himself the lamb for a burnt offering,' and if not, then: 'the lamb for the burnt offering will be my son' " (Gen. 21:8).

Q. "So they went both of them together" (Gen. 22:6):

R. This one went to tie up and the other to be tied up, this one went to slaughter and the other to be slaughtered.

The sustained narrative turns the laconic description of the event into a dialogue, in which Isaac engages Abraham in a difficult conversation. I am inclined to see the whole as a unity. The main point recurs: Isaac, though troubled, accepted the decision. Israel, tried in the difficult days at hand, is like Isaac. That is, Israel too asks the question, How can these things be? But Israel responds like Isaac, obediently accepting God's will. So Isaac stands for Israel in the narrative at hand: bound on the altar, saved by God through the blood of the ram.

The True Merit of Abraham: His Perfect Faith

What did Abraham achieve? It was a gesture that required perfect faith, complete trust, confidence, and submission. These he gave. His descendants live on the merit thereby gained.

LVI:VII.1.A. "But the angel of the Lord called to him from heaven and said, 'Abraham, Abraham!' [And he said, 'Here am I']" (Gen. 22:11).

B. R. Hiyya repeated on Tannaite authority, "The repeated name represents an expression of affection and eagerness."

C. R. Eliezer said, "It means that he spoke both to him and to coming generations.

D. "You have not got a single generation lacking someone of the standing of Abraham, and you have not got a single generation lacking someone of the standing of Jacob, Moses, and Samuel."

2.*A.*   "He said, 'Do not lay your hand on the lad or do anything to him, for now I know that you fear God, seeing you have not withheld your son, your only son, from me' " (Gen. 22:12):

B.   Where was the knife ["Do not lay your *hand*"]?

C.   Tears from the ministering angels had fallen on it and dissolved it.

D.   Then he said, "So I shall strangle him."

E.   He said to him, "Do not lay your hand on the lad."

F.   Then he said, "Then let us at least draw a drop of blood [symbolic of the offering]."

G.   He said to him, ". . . or do anything to him."

H.   ". . . for now I know [that you fear God]:"

I.   "Now I am telling everybody that you love me: 'seeing you have not withheld your son, your only son, from me' (Gen. 22:12).

J.   "And do not claim, 'Whatever sickness does not affect one's own body is no sickness,' for I credit the merit to you for this action as though I had said to you, 'Offer me yourself,' and you did not hold back."

LVI:VIII.1.A.   Said R. Aha, "[Abraham said to God] 'Are there jokes even before you? Yesterday you said to me, "For in Isaac shall seed be called to you" (Gen. 21:12). And then you went back on your word and said, "Take your son" (Gen. 22:2). And now: "Do not lay your hand on the lad or do anything to him." [What's next?]

B.   "Said the Holy One, blessed be he, to him, "Abraham, my covenant I will not profane" (Ps. 89:35). "And I *will* establish my covenant with Isaac" (Gen. 17:21).

C.   "True, I commanded you, 'Take now your son' (Gen. 33:2). "I will not alter what has gone out of my lips" (Ps. 89:35). Did I ever tell you to kill him? No, I told you, 'Bring him up.'

D.   "Well and good! You did indeed bring him up. Now take him down."

In the opening paragraph, no. 1 allows the exegete to make the important point that each generation lives out the lives of the patriarchs. No. 2 constructs a dialogue for God and Abraham. Out of the angel's statement Abraham's answers are worked out.

In the second paragraph, no. 1 raises the obvious question of how God can have changed his mind and given so many conflicting promises and instructions to Abraham. The exegete shows that he did not contradict himself. The underlying polemic favors God's faithfulness and reliability.

The Binding of Isaac and its Meaning for Israel

For our sages the principal event in Isaac's life was being bound on the altar, and a key to the merit bestowed by Abraham upon Israel is found in the same event. Accordingly, we dwell upon the story of the binding of Isaac. We search out each detail of the merit attained by Abraham and Isaac, and then we turn to the history of Israel to see how that merit sustains the children of Abraham and Isaac.

LV:VII.1.A. "And he said, 'Take, I pray you, your son, your only son, Isaac, whom you love, and go to the land of Moriah, and offer him there as a burnt offering upon one of the mountains of which I shall tell you' " (Gen. 22:3):

B. He said to him, "Take, I pray you," meaning, "By your leave."

C. ". . . your son."

D. He said to him, "Which son?"

E. He said to him, ". . . your only son."

F. "This one is the only son of his mother, and that one is the only son of his mother."

G. ". . . whom you love."

H. "Where are the dividing walls within the womb? [I love them both.]"

I. "Isaac."

J. Why did he not tell him to begin with? It was so as to make Isaac still more precious in his view and so to give him a reward for each exchange.

K. This accords with the view of R. Yohanan, for R. Yohanan said, " 'Go from your country' (Gen. 12:1), refers to your country [hyparchy].

L. " 'From your birthplace' refers to your neighborhood.

M. " 'From your father's house' refers literally to the house of your father.

N. "To the land that I will show you": but why did he not inform him [in advance where that would be]?

O. "It was so as to make it still more precious in his view and to give him a reward for each step that he took [in perfect faith and reliance on God]."

P. Said R. Levi bar Haytah, " 'Go, go' (Gen. 12:1) is repeated twice [once in the present context, the other at Gen. 22:1, in going to offer up Isaac at Mount Moriah].

Q. "We do not know which of them is more precious, the first or second. On the basis of that which is written, 'And take yourself to the land of Moriah' (Gen. 22:2), I know that the second was more precious than the first. [Mount Moriah is the holiest place in the land of Israel because that is the mountain on which the temple was built, the same as Mount Zion.]"

2.A. "And take yourself to the land of Moriah" (Gen. 22:2):

B. R. Hiyya the Elder and R. Yannai:

C. One of them said, "[The meaning of the name, Moriah, which shares the consonants of the word for instruction] is, 'to the place from which instruction goes forth to the world [namely, the temple].' "

D. The other said, "It is the place from which awe goes forth to the world [since the word 'Moriah' and the word for 'awe' likewise share the same consonants]."

E. Along these same lines we deal with the matter of the word for sanctuary [DBYR]:

F. R. Hiyya and R. Yannai:

G. One of them said, "It is the place from which divine speech (*dibbur*) goes forth to the world."

H. The other one said, "It is the place from which pestilence [as retribution] [*deber*] goes forth to the world."

I. Said R. Joshua b. Levi, "Moriah is so called because that is the place from which the Holy One, blessed be he, shoots [using the same consonants as appear in the word "Moriah"] at the nations of the world and brings them down to Gehenna."

J. R. Simeon b. Yohai says, "To the place that matches [using the same letters as Moriah] the house of the sanctuary that is above."

K. R. Yudan b. Palya said, "It is the place that he will show you [the consonants of the word for "show" and of "Moriah" being common]."

L. R. Phineas said, "It is to the seat of the domination of the world."

M. Rabbis said, "It is the place at which the incense will be offered: 'I will get me to the mountain of myrrh' (that is, *mor*) (Song 4:6)."

3.A. ". . . and offer him there as a burnt offering" (Gen. 22:2):

B. Said R. Yudan, "He said before him, 'Lord of all ages, is it possible to make an offering without a priest?'

C. "He said to him, I have already appointed you as priest: 'The Lord has sworn and will not repent, you are a priest forever after the manner of Melchizedek' (Ps. 110:4)."

4.A. ". . . on one of the mountains of which I shall tell you" (Gen. 22:2):

B. That is in line with what R. Huna said in the name of R. Eliezer, "He whom the Holy One, blessed be he, puts in doubt and holds in suspense, namely, the righteous, he then informs, explaining the meaning of the matter.

C. "Thus: 'To the land that I will show you' (Gen. 12:1). 'On one of the mountains which I shall tell you' (Gen. 22:2). 'And make to it the proclamation that I shall tell you' (Jonah 3:2). 'Arise, go forth to the plain, and there I will speak with you' (Ez. 3:22)."

In the opening paragraph, the phrase-by-phrase exegesis of the verse, at no. 1, produces an important syllogism. No. 2 provides a series of plays on the word Moriah. The point is to identify Moriah with the temple, Abraham's binding of Isaac with the consecration of the temple, and the temple with the place whence his sanctification, instruction, and authority radiate to the world. No. 3 supplies a missing detail and obviates an objection. No. 4 draws the present discourse in line with others.

LV:VIII.1.A. "And Abraham rose early in the morning [saddled his ass, and took two of his young men with him, and his son Isaac, and he cut the wood for the burnt offering and arose and went to the place which God had told him]" (Gen. 22:3):

B. Said R. Simeon b. Yohai, "Love disrupts the natural order of things, and hatred disrupts the natural order of things.

C. "Love disrupts the natural order of things we learn from the case of Abraham: '. . . he saddled his ass.' But did he not have any number of servants? But that proves love disrupts the natural order of things.

D. "Hatred disrupts the natural order of things we learn from the case of Balaam: 'And Balaam rose up early in the morning and saddled his ass' (Num. 22:21). But did he not have any number of servants? But that proves hatred disrupts the natural order of things.

E. "Love disrupts the natural order of things we learn from the case of Joseph: 'And Joseph made his chariot ready' (Gen. 46:29). But did he not have any number of servants? But that proves love disrupts the natural order of things.

F. "Hatred disrupts the natural order of things we learn from the case of the pharaoh: 'And he made his chariot ready' (Ex. 14:6). But did he not have any number of servants? But that proves hatred disrupts the natural order of things."

2.A. Said R. Simeon b. Yohai, "Let one act of saddling an ass come and counteract another act of saddling an ass. May the act of saddling the ass done by our father Abraham, so as to go and carry out the will of him who spoke and brought the world into being [that is, God] counteract the act of saddling that was carried out by Balaam when he went to curse Israel.

B. "Let one act of preparing counteract another act of preparing. Let Joseph's act of preparing his chariot so as to meet his father serve to counteract the pharaoh's act of preparing to go and pursue Israel."

C. R. Ishmael taught on Tannaite authority, "Let the sword held in the hand serve to counteract the sword held in the hand.

D. "Let the sword held in the hand of Abraham, as it is said, 'Then Abraham put forth his hand and took the knife to slay his son' (Gen. 22:10) serve to counteract the sword taken by the pharaoh in hand: 'I will draw my sword, my hand shall destroy them' (Ex. 15:9)."

3. ". . . and took two of his young men with him, and his son Isaac" (Gen. 22:3):

B. Said R. Abbahu "Two men behaved most appropriately, Abraham and Saul.

C. "Abraham: '. . . and took two of his young men with him.'

D. "And Saul: 'And Saul . . . went, he and two men with him' (1 Sam. 28:8)."

4. ". . . and he cut the wood for the burnt offering [and arose and went to the place which God had told him]" (Gen. 22:3):

B. R. Hiyya bar Yose said the following in the name of R. Miasha, while it has been taught on Tannaite authority in the name of R. Benaiah, "[Since the word for wood is written in the plural, we know that Abraham cut up two logs. Hence] on account of the reward of the two acts of wood-cutting that our father, Abraham, carried out in preparing wood for the burnt offering, he received the merit that the Holy One, blessed be he, would cut the sea in half before his children, as it is said: 'And the waters were divided' (Ex. 14:21)."

C. Said R. Levi, "Enough for you. This is as far [as we can go]. In point of fact, Abraham did what he could do, and the Holy One, blessed be he, did what he could do. [The comparison of Abraham's chopping wood to God's chopping the sea in half is not appropriate.]"

5.A. ". . . and arose and went to the place which God had told him" (Gen. 22:3):

B. To him was given a reward for the act of rising and a reward for the act of going [which is why both acts are stated explicitly].

The second of the two paragraphs turns to the matter of Israel. Abraham's action prefigured the salvation of Israel. In

214

response to each gesture of Abraham, God produced a counterpart in saving Israel from its enemies. No. 1 executes a striking syllogism, with a beautifully balanced articulation. No. 2 goes over the ground of no. 1, giving a somewhat different statement of the same idea. No. 3 has its own syllogism. The contribution of nos. 2–3 is to link Israel's history to Abraham's biography, a familiar notion. It is proper to go with companions when making such a trip. No. 4 reverts to the polemic of nos. 1–2. No. 5 makes a minor observation.

The Merit of the Binding of Isaac and the Future History of Israel

The salvation attained by the binding of Isaac again is made explicit. Moriah is Jerusalem. The temple with its sacrificial service will serve Israel the way Isaac served Abraham.

LVI:II.2.A. Said R. Isaac, "Will this place [the temple mount] ever be distant from its owner [God]? Never, for scripture says, 'This is my resting place forever; here I will dwell, for I have desired it' (Ps. 132:14).

B. "It will be when the one comes concerning whom it is written, 'Lowly and riding upon an ass' (Zech. 1:9)."

3.A. "I and the lad will go thus far [and worship and come again to you]" (Gen. 22:5):

B. Said R. Joshua b. Levi, "[He said] 'We shall go and see what will be the end of "thus."' " [Freedman: God had said, "Thus shall your seed be" (Gen. 15:5). So the sense is, "We will see how that can be fulfilled, now that I am to lose my son."]

4.A. ". . . and we will worship [through an act of prostration] and come again to you" (Gen. 22:5):

B. He thereby told him that he would come back from Mount Moriah whole and in peace [for he said that *we* shall come back].

5.A. Said R. Isaac, "And all was on account of the merit attained by the act of prostration.

B. "Abraham returned in peace from Mount Moriah only on account of the merit owing to the act of prostration: '. . . and we will worship [through an act of prostration] and come [then, on that account] again to you' (Gen. 22:5).

C. "The Israelites were redeemed only on account of the merit owing to the act of prostration: And the people believed . . . then they bowed their heads and prostrated themselves' (Ex. 4:31).

D. "The Torah was given only on account of the merit owing to the act of prostration: 'And worship [prostrate themselves] you afar off' (Ex. 24:1).

E. "Hannah was remembered only on account of the merit owing to the act of prostration: 'And they worshipped before the Lord' (1 Sam. 1:19).

F. "The exiles will be brought back only on account of the merit owing to the act of prostration: 'And it shall come to pass in that day that a great horn shall be blown and they shall come that were lost . . . and that were dispersed . . . and they shall worship the Lord in the holy mountain at Jerusalem' (Is. 27:13).

G. "The temple was built only on account of the merit owing to the act of prostration: 'Exalt you the Lord our God and worship at his holy hill' (Ps. 99:9).

H. "The dead will live only on account of the merit owing to the act of prostration: 'Come let us worship and bend the knee, let us kneel before the Lord our maker' (Ps. 95:6)."

No. 2 takes up the language of "seeing the place from afar," and by a play on the words, asks whether this place will ever be made far from its owner, that is, God. The answer is that it will not. No. 3 draws a lesson from the use of "thus" in the cited verses. No. 4 then signals that Abraham really enjoyed God's advance indication of what would happen. No. 5 then links Israel's mode of worship on the New Year—prostration at certain points in the liturgy for that day—to the entire history of Israel, parallel to the worship through use of the ram's horn on the New Year. Here again the sages find reason to assure Israel of its future salvation.

Part Five

HAYYE
SARAH:
Genesis Rabbah
Parashiyyot LVIII–LXII

When the Righteous Die

We deal with the death of Sarah, and that leads us to reflect on the rhythm of life in the setting of the history of Israel. God does not leave Israel without leaders. When one dies, another arises.

LVIII:II.1.A. "The sun rises and the sun goes down" (Qoh. 1:5):

B. Said R. Abba, "Now do we not know that the sun rises and the sun sets? But the sense is this: before the Holy One, blessed be he, makes the sun of one righteous man set, he brings up into the sky the sun of another righteous man.

C. "On the day that R. Aqiba died, our rabbi [Judah the Patriarch] was born. In his regard, they recited the following verse: 'The sun rises and the sun goes down' (Qoh. 1:5).

D. "On the day on which our rabbi died, R. Adda bar Ahbah was born. In his regard, they recited the following verse: 'The sun rises and the sun goes down' (Qoh. 1:5).

E. "On the day on which R. Ada died, R. Abin was born. In his regard, they recited the following verse: 'The sun rises and the sun goes down' (Qoh. 1:5).

F. "On the day on which R. Abin died, R. Abin his son was born. In his regard, they recited the following verse: 'The sun rises and the sun goes down' (Qoh. 1:5).

G. "On the day on which R. Abin died, Abba Hoshaiah of Taraya was born. In his regard, they recited the following verse: 'The sun rises and the sun goes down' (Qoh. 1:5).

H. "On the day on which Abba Hoshaiah of Taraya died, R. Hoshaiah was born. In his regard, they recited the following verse: 'The sun rises and the sun goes down' (Qoh. 1:5).

I. "Before the Holy One, blessed be he, made the sun of Moses set, he brought up into the sky the sun of Joshua:

219

'And the Lord said to Moses, Take you Joshua, the son of Nun' (Num. 27:18).

J. "Before the Holy One, blessed be he, made the sun of Joshua set, he brought up into the sky the sun of Othniel, son of Kenaz: 'And Othniel the son of Kenaz took it' (Joshua 15:17).

K. "Before the Holy One, blessed be he, made the sun of Eli set, he brought up into the sky the sun of Samuel: 'And the lamp of God was not yet gone out, and Samuel was laid down to sleep in the temple of the Lord' (1 Sam. 3:3)."

L. Said R. Yohanan, "He was like an unblemished calf."

M. [Reverting to K:]"Before the Holy One, blessed be he, made the sun of Sarah set, he brought up into the sky the sun of Rebecca: 'Behold Milcah also has borne children' (Gen. 22:20). 'Sarah lived a hundred twenty-seven years. These were the years of the life of Sarah' (Gen. 23:1)."

One rule of Israel's history is yielded by the facts at hand. Israel is never left without an appropriate hero or heroine. The relevance of the long discourse becomes clear at the end. We in point of fact take up exactly where the preceding *Parashah* has left off, and the bridge from one passage to the next has been constructed.

What it Means to be in God's Image: The Case of Abraham

We recall the emphasis our sages lay on humanity in God's image. They unpack that idea by explaining that to be like God is to do deeds that God does. An important statement of that view links Abraham's act of burying Sarah to those acts of loving kindness that God does. So this is how Abraham is like God—and so are we all.

LVIII:IX.1.A. "After this, Abraham buried [Sarah his wife in the cave of the field of Machpelah east of Mamre, that is Hebron, in the land of Canaan]" (Gen. 23:19):

B. "He who follows after righteousness and love finds life, prosperity, and honor" (Prov. 21:21).

C. "He who follows after righteousness" refers to Abraham, as it is said, "That they may keep the way of the Lord, to do righteousness and justice" (Gen. 18:19).

D. ". . . and love": for he dealt lovingly with Sarah [in burying her].

E. ". . . finds life [prosperity, and honor]" (Prov. 21:21): "And these are the days of the years of Abraham's life, which he lived, a hundred seventy-five years" (Gen. 25:7).

F. ". . . prosperity, and honor":

G. Said R. Samuel bar R. Isaac, "Said the Holy One, blessed be he, to him, 'My profession is to practice acts of love. Since you have taken over my profession, put on my cloak as well' [as a fellow craftsman, wearing the same signifying clothing]: 'And Abraham was old, well advanced in age' (Gen. 24:1)." [God dresses in the garment of old age, so Dan. 7:13 (Freedman, p. 515, n. 1)]."

The intersecting verse leads to a stunning climax at G. The framer has built a bridge from story to story, joining the burial of Sarah to the beginning of the next account, Gen. 24:1. In theological terms he has linked Abraham to God. In moral terms he has made the principal trait of God, hence of the human being like God, the practice of acts of loving kindness, that is, those acts of *hesed,* translation here "love," that God does as the divine profession.

The Life of Abraham, the History of Israel

We reflect now on the virtues of Abraham and on how Israel carries forward the lessons of Abraham's life. The occasion? It is the reflective statement that Abraham had gotten old. So what had he achieved, for himself and for Israel? That is the question our sages answer here.

LIX:V.1.A. "You are fairer than the children of men" (Ps. 45:3):

B. You have found praise among the beings of the upper world,

221

C.   as it says, "Behold, their valiant ones cry without" (Is. 33:7).

D.   You have been praised among the beings of the lower world,

E.   as it says, "You are a mighty prince among us" (Gen. 23:6).

F.   "Therefore God has blessed you forever" (Ps. 45:3).

G.   "Now Abraham was old, well advanced in years; and the Lord had blessed Abraham in all things" (Gen. 24:1).

2.A.   "Who shall ascend into the mountain of the Lord, and who shall stand in his holy place? [He who has clean hands and a pure heart, who has not taken his life without cause, and who has not sworn deceitfully. He shall receive a blessing from the Lord]" (Ps. 24:3–5):

B.   "Who shall ascend into the mountain of the Lord" speaks of Abraham, as it is said, "For now I know that you fear God" (Gen. 22:12).

C.   ". . . and who shall stand in his holy place" speaks of Abraham, as it is said, "And Abraham got up early in the morning, to the place where he had stood before the Lord" (Gen. 19:27).

D.   "He who has clean hands," as it is said, "I will not take a thread or a shoe latchet" (Gen. 14.23).

E.   ". . . and a pure heart." "Far be it from you to do such a thing" (Gen. 18:25).

F.   ". . . who has not taken his life without cause," the life of Nimrod.

G.   ". . . who has not sworn deceitfully." "I have lifted up my hand to the Lord, God most high, maker of heaven and earth" (Gen. 14:22).

H.   "He shall receive a blessing from the Lord." "Now Abraham was old, well advanced in years; and the Lord had blessed Abraham in all things" (Gen. 24:1).

3.A.   Abraham blessed everyone, as it is said, "And through you will all the families of the earth be blessed" (Gen. 12:3). But who blesses Abraham? The Holy One, blessed be he, blesses him, as it is said, ". . . and the Lord had blessed Abraham in all things" (Gen. 24:1).

B. Moses was the ensign of Israel, as it is said, "Why strive you with me? Why do you make me the ensign before the Lord" (Ex. 17:2). But who was the ensign of Moses? It was God: "And Moses built an altar and called the name of it, 'The Lord is my ensign' " (Ex. 17:14).

C. David was the shepherd of Israel, as it says, "You shall shepherd my people, Israel" (1 Chr. 11:2). But who was the shepherd of David? It was the Holy One, blessed be he, as it is said, "The Lord is *my* shepherd, I shall not want" (Ps. 23:1).

D. Jerusalem is the light of the world, as it is said, "And nations shall walk in your light" (Is. 60:3). But who is the light of Jerusalem? It is God, as it is written, "But the Lord shall be for you an everlasting light" (Is. 60:3).

What we are given is summaries of the life and virtues of Abraham, as these illustrate passages of Psalms and are illustrated by them. No. 3 goes along its own way, making one point through three examples. It is included because it makes use of our base verse. Its basic point is that the lives of the patriarchs prefigure the entire history of Israel. That point brings us no surprises, but it cannot be stated enough. Once more we see that the method of our sages in reading Genesis is to bring to the sacred scripture their deepest convictions, their highest hopes.

Asking in the Proper Way

When we pray, we may not set up conditions that God—in our minds—is required to meet. We ask in the right way and not in the wrong way. Eliezer now shows the difference: he set up a stupid condition, but God forgave him.

LX:III.1.A. "Behold, I am standing by the spring of water, and the daughters of the men of the city are coming out to draw water. Let the maiden to whom I shall say, 'Pray let down your jar that I may drink,' and who shall say, 'Drink, and I will water your camels'—let her be the one whom you have appointed for your servant Isaac. By this I shall know that you have shown steadfast love to my master" (Gen. 24:13–14):

B. Four asked for what they wanted in an improper way. To three what they asked was given in a proper way, and to the fourth what was asked was not given in the proper way.

C. These are they: Eliezer, Caleb, Saul, and Jephthah.

D. Eliezer: "Let the maiden to whom I shall say, 'Pray let down your jar that I may drink,' and who shall say, 'Drink, and I will water your camels'—let her be the one whom you have appointed for your servant Isaac. By this I shall know that you have shown steadfast love to my master" (Gen. 24:13–14).

E. [What made this statement improper?] Would that apply even to a serving girl?

F. But the Holy One, blessed be he, designated Rebecca for him, so in a proper way he gave him what he had asked.

G. Caleb: "And Caleb said, 'Whoever smites Kiriath Sepher and takes it, to him will I give Achsah, my daughter, as wife' " (Joshua 15:16).

H. Is it possible that he would give her even to a slave? The Holy One, blessed be he, designated Othniel for him.

I. Saul: "And the men of Israel said, 'Have you seen this man who has come up? Surely he has come up to defy Israel, and the man who kills him the king will enrich with great riches and will give him his daughter' " (1 Sam. 17:25).

J. Is it possible that he would give her even to a slave? The Holy One, blessed be he, designated David for him.

K. Jephthah asked not in a proper way, and it was not in a proper way that the Holy One, blessed be he, responded to him.

L. He asked not in a proper way, as it is said, "And Jephthah made a vow to the Lord and said, 'If you will give the Ammonites into my hand, then whoever comes forth from the doors of my house to meet me when I return victorious from the Ammonites shall be the Lord's, and I will offer him up for a burnt offering' " (Judges 11:30–31).

M. Said to him the Holy One, blessed be he, "If a camel or an ass or a dog should come forth from your house, would you then offer him up as a burnt offering before me?"

N. What did the Holy One, blessed be he, do to him?

O. He responded to him not in a proper way and designated his daughter, as it is said, "Then Jephthah came to his home at Mizpah, and behold, his daughter came out to meet him with timbrels and with dances; she was his only child; beside her he had neither son nor daughter. And when he saw her, he tore his clothes and said, 'Alas my daughter, you have brought me very low and you have become the cause of great trouble to me' " (Judges 11:34–35).

P. R. Yohanan and R. Simeon b. Laqish:

Q. R. Yohanan said, "He was liable to pay off his statement of sanctification by paying the monetary worth involved."

R. R. Simeon b. Laquish said, "He was not even liable to pay off his statement of sanctification by paying the monetary worth involved."

S. "For we have learned in the Mishnah: "If one has made a statement concerning an unclean beast or a beast that was blemished and unfit for the altar, 'Lo, this one is in the status of a burnt offering,' he has said nothing, 'Lo, this is for the purpose of a burnt offering,' then the thing is to be sold and a burnt offering purchased with the proceeds" [M. Temurah 5:6]."

T. But was Phineas not there, who could have released him from his vow?

U. Phineas said, "Lo, he needs me, and should I go to him? And not only so, but I am high priest and the son of a high priest, and should I go to an ordinary person?"

V. Jephthah said, "I am the head of the rulers of Israel, and should I go to Phineas?"

W. Between this one and that one, the girl perished.

X. In a proverb people say, "Between the midwife and the woman in travail, the poor woman's baby is going to die."

Y. Both of them, therefore, were punished on account of her blood.

Z. Jephthah's limbs fell off of him limb by limb, and he therefore was buried in many places. That is in line with the following verse of scripture: "And Jephthah died and was buried in the cities of Gilead" (Judges 12:7). What is written is not, "in a city of Gilead" but rather "in the cities of Gilead."

This teaches that a limb would fall off from him here and was buried where it fell, and a limb would fall off of him in another place and was buried where it fell.

AA. From Phineas the Holy Spirit was taken away, as it is said, "Phineas, the son of Eleazar, was ruler over them; in times past the Lord was with him" (I Chr. 9:20). He had been with him in times past, but not now.

We have an extended illustration of how not to ask, and of God's mode of answering. If Israel will ask in the proper way and condition, God will answer. The message, repeated in diverse ways, is single and cogent: Israel has in its power the possibility of gaining salvation.

Abraham Married after the Death of Sarah

A mark of the vitality of Abraham derives from his remarriage. Our sages view long life, with many children, as a mark of blessing. Particular favor is shown by the capacity to continue to function even in old age.

LXI:II.1.A. "They shall still bring forth fruit in old age [they shall be full of sap and richness]" (Ps. 92:15):

B. This refers to Abraham.

C. ". . . they shall be full of sap and richness:"

D. "Abraham took another wife, and her name was Kenturah [and she bore him Zimran, Jokshan, Medan, Midian, Ishbak, and Shuah]" (Gen. 25:1).

2.A. "For there is hope of a tree. [If it be cut down, that it will sprout again. And that his tender branch will not cease. Though his root wax old in the earth, and his stock die in the ground, yet through the scent of water he will blossom, and put forth boughs like a plant]" (Job 14:7-9):

B. "For there is hope of a tree" refers to Abraham, who has hope.

C. "If it be cut down, that it will sprout again." If concerning him it is said that he has entered the covenant [using the same verb as serves to mean "cut down"] "it will sprout

226

again." He shall produce more actions in conformity with religious requirements as well as good deeds.

D. "And that his tender branch will not cease." That is, his semen.

E. "Though his root wax old in the earth . . ." "And Abraham was old" (Gen. 24:1).

F. ". . . and his stock die in the ground . . ." "And Sarah died" (Gen. 23:2).

G. ". . . yet through the scent of water he will blossom." That is, from the scent of religious duties and good deeds, he will blossom.

H. ". . . and put forth boughs like a plant."

I. What is said is not, ". . . put forth a plant like boughs," but rather, "boughs like a plant," in that the further growth was more than the original.

J. "Abraham took another wife, and her name was Kenturah and she bore him Zimran, Jokshan, Medan, Midian, Ishbak, and Shuah" (Gen. 25:1).

Abraham even in old age remained virile. And yet virility takes on many meanings. Religious deeds mark one's strength.

Abraham Gave the Land to Isaac for Israel

The claim of Israel to the land, called into question along with much else in the fourth century, found validation in the deed of Abraham. In the time of Constantine and afterward, Christians purchased holy places in the land of Israel, which they called "the Holy Land," and imparted to the land the map that they had in their minds, just as Israel long had done. So the claim of Israel to the land now competed with the conception of the empire. The preoccupation with the right of Israel to the land of Israel brought our sages to see things in a very practical light.

LXI:VII.1.A. "But to the sons of his concubines, Abraham gave gifts, and while he was still living, he sent them away from his son Isaac, eastward to the east country" (Gen. 25:6):

227

B. In the time of Alexander of Macedonia the sons of Ishmael came to dispute with Israel about the birthright, and with them came two wicked families, the Canaanites and the Egyptians.

C. They said, "Who will go and engage in a disputation with them?"

D. Gebiah b. Qosem [the enchanter] said, "I shall go and engage in a disputation with them."

E. They said to him, "Be careful not to let the land of Israel fall into their possession."

F. He said to them, "I shall go and engage in a disputation with them. If I win over them, well and good. And if not, you may say, 'Who is this hunchback to represent us?' "

G. He went and engaged in a disputation with them. Said to them Alexander of Macedonia, "Who lays claim against whom?"

H. The Ishmaelites said, "We lay claim, and we bring our evidence from their own Torah: 'But he shall acknowledge the firstborn, the son of the hated' (Deut. 21:17). Now Ishmael was the firstborn. [We therefore claim the land as heirs of the firstborn of Abraham.]"

I. Said to him Gebiah b. Qosem, "My royal lord, does a man not do whatever he likes with his sons?"

J. He said to him, "Indeed so."

K. "And lo, it is written, 'Abraham gave all that he had to Isaac' (Gen. 25:2)."

L. [Alexander asked,] "Then where is the deed of gift to the other sons?"

M. He said to him, " 'But to the sons of his concubines, Abraham gave gifts [and while he was still living, he sent them away from his son Isaac, eastward to the east country]' (Gen. 25:6)."

N. [The Ishmaelites had no claim on the land.] They abandoned the field in shame.

O. The Canaanites said, "We lay claim, and we bring our evidence from their own Torah. Throughout their Torah it is written, 'the land of Canaan.' So let them give us back our land."

P. Said to him Gebiah b. Qosem, "My royal lord, does a man not do whatever he likes with his slave?"

Q. He said to him, "Indeed so."

R. He said to him, "And lo, it is written, 'A slave of slaves shall Canaan be to his brothers' (Gen. 9:25). So they are really our slaves."

S. [The Cannanites had no claim to the land and in fact should be serving Israel.] They abandoned the field in shame.

T. The Egyptian said, "We lay claim, and we bring our evidence from their own Torah. Six hundred thousand of them left us, taking away our silver and gold utensils: 'They despoiled the Egyptians' (Ex. 12:36). Let them give them back to us."

U. Gebiah b. Qosem said, "My royal lord, six hundred thousand men worked for them for two hundred ten years, some as silversmiths and some as goldsmiths. Let them pay us our salary at the rate of a denar a day."

V. The mathematicians went and added up what was owing, and they had not reached the sum covering a century before the Egyptians had to forfeit what they had claimed. They abandoned the field in shame.

W. [Alexander] wanted to go up to Jerusalem. The Samaritans said to him, "Be careful. They will not permit you to enter their most holy sanctuary."

X. When Gebiah b. Qosem found out about this, he went and made for himself two felt shoes, with two precious stones or twenty thousand pieces of silver set in them. When he got to the mountain of the house [of the temple], he said to him, "My royal lord, take off your shoes and put on these two felt slippers, for the floor is slippery, and you should not slip and fall."

Y. When they came to the most holy sanctuary, he said to him, "Up to this point, we have the right to enter. From this point onward, we do not have the right to enter."

Z. He said to him, "When we get out of here, I'm going to even out your hump."

AA. He said to him, "You will be called a great surgeon and get a big fee."

2.A.   "[But to the sons of his concubines, Abraham gave gifts, and while he was still living,] he sent them away from his son Isaac, eastward to the east country]' (Gen. 25:6):

B.   He said to them, "Go as far to the east as you can, so as not to be burned by the flaming coal of Isaac."

C.   But because Esau came to make war with Jacob, he took his appropriate share on his account: "Is this your joyous city, whose feet in antiquity, in ancient days, carried her afar off to sojourn? Who has devised this against Tyre, the crowning city?" (Is. 23:7).

D.   Said R. Eleazar, "Whenever the name of Tyre is written in scripture, if it is written out [with all the letters], then it refers to the province of Tyre. Where it is written without all its letters [and so appears identical to the word for enemy], the reference of scripture is to Rome. [So the sense of the verse is that Rome will receive its appropriate reward.]"

E.   [As to the sense of the word for] "the crowning city,"

F.   R. Abba bar Kahana said, "It means that they surrounded the city like a crown."

G.   R. Yannai, son of R. Simeon b. R. Yannai, said, "They surrounded it with a fence of thorns."

No. 1 is deposited here because of the case of the Ishmaelites, Abraham's children, deprived as they were of their inheritance. That issue pressed on the consciousness of the exegete compositors. No. 2 carries forward the eschatological reading of the incident. Israel's later history is prefigured in the gift to Isaac and the rejection of the other sons. The self-evidence that Esau's reward will be recompense for his evil indicates that the passage draws upon sarcasm to make its point.

Part Six

TOLEDOT:
Genesis Rabbah
Parashiyyot LXIII–LXVII

Esau and Jacob, Israel and Rome

When scripture speaks of Esau, our sages think of Rome. And why not, for they saw Jacob in a struggle with a powerful world-empire and found in the Torah's record the secret of the outcome. Then we ask how they made sense of the uneven struggle, and what lessons they learned from scripture to make sense of the world as they saw its history unfolding.

LXIII:VI.1.A. "And the children struggled together [within her, and she said, 'If it is thus, why do I live?' So she went to inquire of the Lord. And the Lord said to her, 'Two nations are in your womb, and two peoples, born of you, shall be divided; the one shall be stronger than the other, and the elder shall serve the younger']" (Gen. 25:22–23):

B. R. Yohanan and R. Simeon b. Laqish:

C. R. Yohanan said, "[Because the word 'struggle' contains the letters for the word 'run'] this one was running to kill that one and that one was running to kill this one."

D. R. Simeon b. Laqish: "This one releases the laws given by that one, and that one releases the laws given by this one."

2.A. R. Berekhiah in the name of R. Levi said, "It is so that you should not say that it was only after he left his mother's womb that [Esau] contended against [Jacob].

B. "But even while he was yet in his mother's womb, his fist was stretched forth against him: 'The wicked stretch out their fists [so Freedman] from the womb' (Ps. 58:4)."

3.A. "And the children struggled together within her":

B. [Once more referring to the letters of the word "struggled," with special attention to the ones that mean "run"] they wanted to run within her.

C. When she went by houses of idolatry, Esau would kick, trying to get out: "The wicked are estranged from the womb" (Ps. 58:4).

D. When she went by synagogues and study houses, Jacob would kick, trying to get out: "Before I formed you in the womb, I knew you" (Jer. 1:5)."

4.A. ". . . and she said, 'If it is thus, why do I live?' "

B. R. Haggai in the name of R. Isaac: "This teaches that our mother, Rebecca, went around to the doors of women and said to them, 'Did you ever have this kind of pain in your life?' "

C. "[She said to them,] 'If this is how it is: If this is the pain of having children, would that I had not gotten pregnant.'

D. Said R. Huna, "If I am going to produce twelve tribes only through this kind of suffering, would that I had not gotten pregnant."

5.A. It was taught on Tannaite authority in the name of R. Nehemiah, "Rebecca was worthy of having the twelve tribes come forth from her. That is in line with this verse:

B. " 'Two nations are in your womb, and two peoples, born of you, shall be divided; the one shall be stronger than the other, and the elder shall serve the younger.' When her days to be delivered were fulfilled, behold, there were twins in her womb. The first came forth red, all his body like a hairy mantle, so they called his name Esau. Afterward his brother came forth . . .' (Gen. 25:23–24).

C. " 'Two nations are in your womb': thus two.

D. " 'and two peoples': thus two more, hence four.

E. " '. . . the one shall be stronger than the other': two more, so six.

F. " '. . . and the elder shall serve the younger': two more, so eight.

G. " 'When her days to be delivered were fulfilled, behold, there were twins in her womb': two more, so ten.

H. " 'The first came forth red': now eleven.

J. " 'Afterward his brother came forth': now twelve."

K.   There are those who say, "Proof derives from this verse: 'If it is thus, why do I live?' Focusing on the word for 'thus,' we note that the two letters of that word bear the numerical value of seven and five respectively, hence, twelve in all."

6.A.   "So she went to inquire of the Lord":

B.   Now were there synagogues and houses of study in those days [that she could go to inquire of the Lord]?

C.   But is it not the fact that she went only to the study house of Eber?

D.   This serves to teach you that whoever receives an elder is as if he receives the presence of God.

Nos. 1–3 take for granted that Esau represents Rome, and Jacob, Israel. Consequently the verse underlines the point that there is natural enmity between Israel and Rome. Esau hated Jacob even while he was still in the womb. Jacob, for his part, revealed from the womb those virtues that would characterize him later on, eager to serve God as Esau was eager to worship idols. The text invites just this sort of reading. No. 4 and no. 5 relate Rebecca's suffering to the birth of the twelve tribes. No. 6 makes its own point, independent of the rest and tacked on.

Jacob Studies Torah, Esau Goes Hunting for Action

Rome, now Christian, carries forward the ancient tradition of the military empire. Israel, always Judaic, remains loyal to its tradition as well. That is the reading of the competition between Esau and Jacob. It would be daring indeed for people today to identify the enemies of the state of Israel with biblical figures—daring, but also a splendid act of faith.

LXIII:IX.1.A.   "When the boys grew up [Esau was a skilful hunter, a man of the field, while Jacob was a quiet man, dwelling in tents]" (Gen. 25:27):

B.   R. Phineas in the name of R. Levi: "The matter may be compared to the case of a myrtle and a wild rose,

growing side by side. When they had grown up, the one gave
forth its scent, the other its thorns.

C. "So too, all thirteen years [of immaturity] the two of
them would go to school and come home from school, but after thirteen years, the one went to the study houses, and the
other to temples of idolatry."

D. Said R. Eleazar b. R. Simeon, "A person has to take
responsibility for his son for thirteen years. From that time on,
he has to say, 'Blessed is he who has relieved me from the
penalties coming for the misdeeds of this one' [since he is
now responsible for himself]."

LXIII:X.1.A. "[When the boys grew up] Esau was a
skilful hunter [a man of the field, while Jacob was a quiet
man, dwelling in tents]" (Gen. 25:27):

B. He hunted people through snaring them in words [as
the Roman prosecutors do:] "Well enough, you did not steal.
But who stole with you? You did not kill, but who killed with
you?"

2.A. R. Abbahu said, "He was a trapper and a fields-
man, trapping at home and in the field.

B. "He trapped at home: 'How do you tithe salt?'
[which does not, in fact, have to be tithed at all!]

C. "He trapped in the field: 'How do people give tithe
for straw?' [which does not, in fact, have to be tithed at all!]"

3.A. R. Hiyya bar Abba said, "He treated himself as
totally without responsibility for himself, like a field [on
which anyone tramples].

B. "Said the Israelites before the Holy One, blessed be
he, 'Lord of all ages, is it not enough for us that you have
subjugated us to the seventy nations, but even to this one,
who is subjected to sexual intercourse just like a woman?'

C. "Said to them the Holy One, blessed be he, 'I too
will exact punishment from him with those same words: "And
the heart of the mighty men of Edom at that day shall be as
the heart of a woman in her pangs" (Jer. 49:22)."

4.A. ". . . while Jacob was a quiet man, dwelling in
tents" (Gen. 25:27):

B. There is a reference to two tents, that is, the school-house of Shem and the schoolhouse of Eber.

In the second paragraph nos. 1–3 deal with the description of Esau, explaining why he was like the field, nos. 2, 3. No. 2 follows up on no. 1, that is, hunting people and trapping them with words. In the one case Esau is compared to a Roman prosecutor, in the other, to a critic of the law. No. 3 then moves on to fresh material. Now Esau/Rome is condemned for yet another reason.

The Birthright and What it Meant

What precisely Esau sold now requires specification. Esau despises and rejects what was truly of worth, because Esau does not know what really matters.

LXIII:XIII.1.A. "Jacob said, 'First sell me your birth-right.' Esau said, 'I am about to die, of what use is a birth-right to me?' "

B. He said to him, "Sell me one day that is yours."

C. Said R. Aha, "Whoever knows how to reckon [the exile] will discover that for only one day Jacob lived under the shadow of Esau." [Freedman, p. 568, n. 4: The verse is translated as symbolically alluding to Israel in the diaspora, with Jacob demanding, "Sell me . . . yours," "leave me in peace if only for a short while," and R. Aha observes that that indeed has been the case.]

2.A. "Esau said, 'I am about to die, of what use is a birthright to me?' "

B. R. Simeon b. Laqish said, "He began to revile and blaspheme. What do I need it for: '. . . of what use is a birth-right to me?' "

3.A. Another explanation: "I am about to die:"

B. For Nimrod [the mighty hunter] was looking for him to kill him on account of the garment that had belonged to the first man [Adam] and had been inherited by Esau, for at the moment that Esau put it on and went out to the field, all the wild beasts and fowl in the world came and gathered around him [and that is why he was such a good hunter].

4.A. "Jacob said, 'Swear to me first.' So he swore to him and sold his birthright to Jacob" (Gen. 25:33):

B. Why did Jacob risk his life for the right of the first-born?

C. For we have learned in the Mishnah: Before the tabernacle was set up, the high places were permitted, and the rite of offering was carried out by the firstborn. Once the tabernacle was set up, the high places were forbidden, and the rite of offering was carried out by the priests [M. Zebahim 14:4].

D. He said, "Should that wicked man stand and make offerings?" Therefore Jacob risked his life for the right of the firstborn.

5.A. That is in line with the following verse: "I will prepare you for blood, and blood shall pursue you, surely you have hated blood, therefore shall blood pursue you" (Ez. 35:6).

B. But did Esau hate blood?

C. R. Levi in the name of R. Hama bar Hanina: "This is the blood of circumcision [which Esau did hate]."

D. R. Levi in the name of R. Samuel b. Nahman, "This refers to the blood of the offerings by the firstborn."

E. Rabbis say, "You have hated the blood of man when it is in his body, in line with this verse: 'Yes, he loved cursing and it came to him and he did not delight in blessing' (Ps. 109:17)."

F. R. Levi in the name of R. Hama bar Hanina, "He did not take pleasure in the birthright."

G. R. Huna said, "This refers to the blood of the offerings, which are called a blessing, in line with this verse: 'An altar of earth you shall make for me . . . I will come to you and bless you' (Ex. 20:21)."

No. 1 makes explicit what is at stake in the sale—namely, Israel's life under Esau's rule. Nos. 2, 3 revert to the body of the story and gloss details. No. 4 shows that what was at stake was a considerable issue. No. 5 takes up the cited intersecting verse, continuing the foregoing, the matter of the offerings. Esau had no right to make offerings, he had no respect for the temple and its cult. Rome for its part destroyed the temple, and, when in 360 of the century in which our document came to completion, the Roman emperor, an apostate from Christianity, permitted Israel to rebuild the temple, nothing came of it, and the Christian successors quickly called the project to an end. So Israel revered the birthright, and Esau despised it.

Esau and Intermarriage

So too Esau married wives among gentiles, not worshipers of the one true God, while Jacob would marry an heir of Abraham and Sarah.

LXV:I.1.A. "When Esau was forty years old, he took to wife Judith, the daughter of Beeri the Hittite, and Basemath the daughter of Elon the Hittite; and they made life bitter for Isaac and Rebecca" (Gen. 26:34–35):

B. "The swine out of the wood ravages it, that which moves in the field feeds on it" (Ps. 80:14).

C. R. Phineas and R. Hilqiah in the name of R. Simon: "Among all the prophets, only two of them spelled out in public [the true character of Rome, represented by the swine], Asaf and Moses.

D. "Asaf: 'The swine out of the wood ravages it.'

E. "Moses: 'And the swine, because he parts the hoof' (Deut. 14:8).

F. "Why does Moses compare Rome to the swine? Just as the swine, when it crouches, puts forth its hoofs as if to say, 'I am clean,' so the wicked kingdom steals and grabs, while pretending to be setting up courts of justice.

G. "So Esau, for all forty years, hunted married women, ravished them, and when he reached the age of forty, he presented himself to his father, saying, 'Just as father got married at the age of forty, so I shall marry a wife at the age of forty.'

H. "When Esau was forty years old, he took to wife Judith, the daughter of Beeri the Hittite, and Basemath the daughter of Elon the Hittite."

LXV:II.1.A. R. Yudan bar Simon commenced [discourse by citing the following verse]: "God makes the solitary to dwell in a house" (Ps. 78:7).

B. That accords with the view of R. Judah bar Simon, who has said, "Even if there is a *mamzer* at one end of the world, and a female-*mamzer* at the other end of the world, the Holy One, blessed be he, brings them together and matches them up. What is the scriptural proof of that view? '. . . God makes the solitary to dwell in a house' (Ps. 78:7). [A *mamzer*-man and woman can marry only someone in that same status, otherwise they must remain solitary.]

C. "So, since it is written, 'You shall utterly destroy them: the Hittite. . . .' (Deut. 20:17), therefore let this man [Esau], may his name be wiped out, come and marry this woman [Judith the Hittite], may her name be blotted out.

D. "When Esau was forty years old, he took to wife Judith, the daughter of Beeri the Hittite, and Basemath the daughter of Elon the Hittite."

LXV:IV.1.A. "And they made life bitter for Isaac and Rebecca" (Gen. 26:35):

B. Why Isaac first? Because, since Rebecca was the daughter of priests of idolatry, she paid no attention to the pollution of idolatry. But he was the son of holy parents, therefore he paid attention to it.

C. Therefore Isaac came first.

2.A. Another matter: Why Isaac first? Because she was responsible [for Esau's character]. For it is said, "And the Lord said to her, 'Two nations are in your womb' " (Gen. 25:23).

3.A. Another matter: Why Isaac first?

B. Because a woman ordinarily stays home and a man goes out to the market and learns understanding by circulating in public.

C. But this one, since his eyes were weak, stayed in the house, therefore, it was Isaac first.

4.A. Said R. Joshua b. Levi, "He was responsible that the Holy Spirit left [Isaac]."

The exegesis in the first paragraph of course identifies Esau with Rome. The roundabout route linking the fact at hand, Esau's taking a wife, passes through the territory of Roman duplicity. Whatever the government does, it claims to do in the general interest. But it really has no public interest at all. Esau for his part spent forty years pillaging women and then, at the age of forty, pretended to his father to be upright. That, at any rate, is the parallel clearly intended by this obviously unitary composition. The issue of the selection of the intersecting verse does not present an obvious solution to me; it seems to me only the identification of Rome with the swine accounts for the choice.

The point of the second of the three paragraphs is that Esau married the one woman in the world who was suitable for him—namely, a Hittite woman. His name and hers likewise were to be blotted out. This then illustrates God's unerring aim in mating up those who should marry, just as he matches the male-*mamzer*, who cannot marry an acceptable Israelite woman, with a female-*mamzer*. Thus they do have a chance to marry, just as Esau married someone suitable for him.

The question at hand in the third paragraph focuses upon the exposition of the framing of the base verse. Why Isaac realized the problem before Rebecca did generates a variety of explanations, each based on a distinct analogy. At the same time we have a link to what is to follow. For Isaac was ready to bless Esau instead of Jacob, even though he realized the corruption of the household. So Isaac appears to be a fool. He should have known better—that is the lesson at hand. The larger polemic favors Jacob over Esau, one need hardly add.

Old Age and Sickness

We think of old age as a time of sorrow, of sickness, and of chronic illness as things one would want to avoid. But these common sufferings of humanity may blemish creation. In the verse at hand—Isaac was old and sick and frail—we find out that Abraham, Isaac, and Jacob asked God for the very frailties that ordinary human beings would like to avoid. Why did they do so, and what did they achieve?

LXV:IX.1.A. "When Isaac was old, and his eyes were dim, so that he could not see, he called Esau his older son, and said to him, 'My son,' and he answered, 'Here I am' " (Gen. 27:1):

B. Said R. Judah bar Simon, "Abraham sought [the physical traits of] old age [so that from his appearance, people would know that he was old]. He said before him, 'Lord of all ages, when a man and his son come in somewhere, no one knows whom to honor. If you crown a man with the traits of old age, people will know whom to honor.'

C. "Said to him the Holy One, blessed be he, 'By your life, this is a good thing that you have asked for, and it will begin with you.'

D. "From the beginning of the book of Genesis to this passage, there is no reference to old age. But when Abraham our father came along, the traits of old age were given to him, as it is said, 'And Abraham was old' (Gen. 24:1)."

E. "Isaac asked God for suffering. He said before him, 'Lord of the age, if someone dies without suffering, the measure of strict justice is stretched out against him. But if you bring suffering on him, the measure of strict justice will not be stretched out against him. [Suffering will help counter the man's sins, and the measure of strict justice will be mitigated through suffering by the measure of mercy.]'

F. "Said to him the Holy One, blessed be he, 'By your life, this is a good thing that you have asked for, and it will begin with you.'

G. "From the beginning of the book of Genesis to this passage, there is no reference to suffering. But when Isaac came along, suffering was given to him: his eyes were dim.'

H. "Jacob asked for sickness. He said before him, 'Lord of all ages, if a person dies without illness, he will not settle his affairs for his children. If he is sick for two or three days, he will settle his affairs with his children.'

I. "Said to him the Holy One, blessed be he, 'By your life, this is a good thing that you have asked for, and it will begin with you.'

J. "That is in line with this verse: 'And someone said to Joseph, "Behold, your father is sick' " (Gen. 48:1)."

K. Said R. Levi, "Abraham introduced the innovation of old age, Isaac introduced the innovation of suffering, Jacob introduced the innovation of sickness.

L. "Hezekiah introduced the innovation of chronic illness. He said to him, 'You have kept a man in good condition until the day he dies. But if someone is sick and gets better, is sick and gets better, he will carry out a complete and sincere act of repentance for his sins.'

M. "Said to him the Holy One, blessed be he, 'By your life, this is a good thing that you have asked for, and it will begin with you.'

N. " 'The writing of Hezekiah, king of Judah, when he had been sick and recovered of his sickness' (Is. 38:9)."

O. Said R. Samuel b. Nahman, "On the basis of that verse we know that between one illness and another there was an illness more serious than either one."

Suffering, old age, sickness, and the like come to benefit humanity. That view leads to the inclusion of the base verse. Israel has to learn to accept God's measure, to submit and to endure—but also to thank God for caring, even by meting out punishment. That too is a mark of God's concern. The passage at hand, remarkable for its humanity, then translates the national policy of submission to God's will and preparation for redemption through penitence into a doctrine of virtue for the individual. People have to accept the human condition—sickness, old age, death—just as Israel has to accept Israel's condition. So Israel forms the model for humanity—contrary to the other model, the first man, Adam—and the condition of Israel comes to expression in the life of every individual. There is then a threefold set of correspondences: the individual, the nation, and nature. Just as the condition of nature testifies to Israel's sanctification every seventh day, so the condition of the nation expresses Israel's task, and so too the state of the individual, with illness, old age, and death the lot of all, restates the condition of the whole: all glorying in God as God's creatures, all accepting God's gifts, all awaiting God's salvation at the end of time. I cannot imagine a more complete harmony among all the dimensions of reality, natural and supernatural, historical and eternal, individual and national, than our sages have composed for Israel in the world.

Was Isaac Really Deceived? Did Jacob Really Lie?

We cannot admit that our father, Jacob, really lied, nor that our father Isaac could have been such a fool. As much as justifying old age, illness, and chronic ailments, so here too our sages found reason to justify what to our eyes appears beyond all apology. Isaac meant for Jacob to have the blessing, Jacob never lied. So the sages now argue.

LXV:XVIII.1.A. "So he went in to his father and said, 'My father,' and he said, 'Here I am. Who are you, my son? And Jacob said to his father, ' I am Esau your firstborn. [I have acted like the firstborn, because I have done as you told me; now sit up and eat of my game, that you may bless me']" (Gen. 27:18–19):

B. Said R. Levi, " 'I' am the one who will receive the Ten Commandments, but Esau is indeed your first born." [The "I" here is the one who will receive the Ten Commandments, which begin with the word "I."]

2.A. ". . . now sit up:"

B. Said R. Yohanan, "Said the Holy One, blessed be he, to Jacob, 'You have said, ". . . now sit up." ' By your life with that same language I shall pay you your just reward: "Rise up, O Lord, and let your enemies be scattered" (Num. 10:35)."

3. "But there is he who is swept away by want of righteousness" (Prov. 13:23) refers to Esau. Said the Holy One, blessed be he, to Esau, "You have said, 'Let my father arise'

(Gen. 27:31). By the fortune of my idol I adjure you to arise. By your life I shall pay you. I shall pay you back with that very same language: 'Rise up, O Lord, and let your enemies be scattered' (Num. 10:35)."

LXV:XIX.1.A. "But Isaac said to his son, 'How is it that you have found the game so quickly, my son?' [He answered, 'Because the Lord your God granted me success']" (Gen. 27:20):

B. "How come you found *the blessing* so quickly, my son? Your father was blessed at the age of seventy-five years, while you are only sixty-three."

2.A. "He answered, 'Because the Lord your God granted me success' " (Gen. 27:20):

B. R. Yohanan and R. Simeon b. Laqish:

C. One of them said, "If to provide a sacrifice for you the Holy One, blessed be he, provided what was required promptly, as it is written, 'And Abraham lifted up his eyes and looked and behold behind him a ram' (Gen. 22:13), how much the more so will he promptly provide food for you!"

D. The other of them said, "If to provide a mate for you, the Holy One, blessed be he, provided what was required promptly, as it is written, 'And he saw, and behold, there were camels coming' (Gen. 24:63), how much the more so will he promptly provide food for you!"

3.A. "He answered, 'Because the Lord your God granted me success' " (Gen. 27:20):

B. Said R. Yohanan, "The matter may be compared to the case of a raven bringing fire to his nest. [Freedman: He was courting disaster.] When he said, "Because the Lord your God granted me success," Isaac said, 'I know that Esau does not make mention of the name of the Holy One, blessed be he, while this one does make mention of God's name. This cannot be Esau but can only be Jacob."

C. "So when Jacob said this, he said, 'Come near, that I may feel you my son, to know whether you are really my son Esau or not' (Gen. 27:22)."

4.A. Said R. Hoshaiah, "When Isaac said, 'Come near, that I may feel you my son, to know whether you are really my son Esau or not' (Gen. 27:22), sweat poured down Jacob's thighs, and his heart melted like wax. So the Holy One, blessed be he, appointed two angels, one at his right hand, one at the left, to hold him up by his elbows, so that he would not fall.

B. "Thus it is written, 'Do not be dismayed' (Is. 41:10), meaning, 'Do not be like wax' [since the words 'dismay' and 'wax' share the same consonants]."

LXVII:XII.1.A. "Then Isaac called Jacob and blessed him [and charged him, 'You shall not marry one of the Canaanite women. Arise, go to Paddan-aram, to the house of Bethuel, your mother's father, and take as wife from there one of the daughters of Laban your mother's brother']" (Gen. 28:1–2):

B. [Isaac blessed Jacob] said R. Abbahu, "Because the blessings were still unsteady in his possession. When did the blessings become securely in his hand? 'Then Isaac called Jacob and blessed him.' "

C. Said R. Eleazar, "The validation of a writ is effected only through the confirmation of the signatures of the witnesses.

D. "So, if you might imagine that, had Jacob not deceived his father, he would not have taken the blessings, scripture states explicitly, 'Then Isaac called Jacob and blessed him.' "

E. R. Berekiah [in the name of R. Levi] said, "It may be compared to the case of a prince who was digging toward the king to receive a *litra* of gold. The king said to him, 'Why do it in secret? Come and take it for yourself in public.'

F. "So it is said, 'Then Isaac called Jacob and blessed him.' " [Thus he confirmed the original blessing and showed it was entirely by intention.]

2.A. ". . . and charged him, 'You shall not marry one of the Canaanite women:' "

B. He charged him concerning the daughters of Aner, Eshcol, and Mamre.

3.A. "Jacob obeyed his father and his mother [and went to Paddan-aram]" (Gen. 28:6):

B. "The way of a fool is straight in his own eyes, but he who is wise heartens to counsel" (Prov. 21:2):

C. "The way of a fool is straight in his own eyes" refers to Samson, who said, "Get her for me, for she pleases me very much" Judges 14:3).

D. ". . . but he who is wise heartens to counsel" refers to Jacob: "Jacob obeyed his father and his mother and went to Paddan-aram."

Nos. 1 and 2 in the first paragraph amplify the discourse, redirecting the statements of Jacob to the history of Israel in the future. Each statement then bears a deeper meaning, drawn from that history. No. 3 builds on the point of no. 2, using the same verse to Esau's disadvantage that has served as praise for Jacob.

In the second paragraph, nos. 1, 2 amplify Jacob's colloquy with Isaac. No. 3 begins the process of showing that Isaac knew just what he was doing. He realized that Esau would not talk that way, but he allowed the charade to proceed. No. 4 shows that Jacob was a poor liar, but that God helped him lie.

The thrust of no. 1 in the third paragraph is to prove that Jacob really received the blessings from Isaac, and that Isaac knew just what he was doing. No. 2 glosses, and no. 3 draws a parallel between Samson, who ordered his parents to select a woman of his choice, and Jacob, who accepted his parents' judgment.

The True Blessing that Isaac Gave to Jacob

We come now to the substance of the blessing. Our sages once more find in scripture evidence for the claim that their way of life, centering as it did on the study of Torah, came to them from the founders of Israel. Then the blessing of Isaac referred, in fact, to the study of the Torah that Jacob carried on.

LXVI:I.1.A. "May God give you of the dew of heaven [and of the fatness of the earth, and plenty of grain and wine. Let peoples serve you and nations bow down to you. Be lord over your brothers and may your mother's sons bow down to you. Cursed be everyone who curses you, and blessed be everyone who blesses you]" (Gen. 27:27–29):

B. "My root was spread out to the waters, and the dew lay all night on my branch" (Job 29:19).

C. Said Job, "It was because my doors were wide open that when everybody reaped dried ears, I reaped ears full of sap [fresh and ripe]."

D. What is the scriptural basis for that statement?

E. "My root was spread out to the waters, and the dew lay all night on my branch" (Job 29:19).

F. Jacob said, "Because I engaged in study of the Torah, which is compared to water, I had the merit of being blessed with dew."

G. "May God give you of the dew of heaven."

The reference to dew in the intersecting verse accounts for its inclusion with the base verse, and then the two verses are drawn together in a solid link. The main point is to introduce the theme of Torah study.

Part Seven

VAYESE:
Genesis Rabbah
Parashiyyot
LXVIII–LXXIV

Jacob Left Home Trusting in God

In many ways Jacob relives the unsteady life of Abraham. Like Abraham, Jacob was called upon to put his trust in God and undertake perilous journeys. But the route was the opposite, as if to complete the movement out with a voyage home. Jacob's pilgrimage brought him back to Babylonia, the home of his ancestors. Leaving the household of Isaac, disrupted as it was by the deception and the misplaced blessing, Jacob had nothing with him. All he could hope for was God's blessing, confirming the one his father had given him. Yet he trusted and did not fear. The message to fearful Israel hardly requires iteration.

LXVIII:I.1.A "Now Jacob left Beer-sheba" (Gen. 28:10):

B. R. Yudan in the name of R. Jonathan, R. Phineas in the name of R. Hinena bar Pappa commenced discourse by citing this verse: " 'Then you shall walk in your way securely, when you lie down, you will not be afraid, yes, you will lie down and your sleep shall be sweet' (Prov. 3:23–24):

C. " 'Then you shall walk in your way securely' refers to Jacob: 'Now Jacob left Beer-sheba.'

D. " '. . . when you lie down, you will not be afraid:' of Esau and Laban.

E. " '. . . yes, you will lie down and your sleep shall be sweet:' 'And he lay down in that place to sleep' (Gen. 28:11)."

LXVIII:II.1.A. R. Samuel bar Nahman commenced discourse by citing this verse: " 'A song of ascents. I will lift up my eyes to the mountains. From whence shall my help come? My help comes from the Lord, who made heaven and earth. He will not suffer your foot to be moved. He who keeps you will not slumber. Behold, he who keeps Israel neither slumbers nor sleeps. The Lord shall keep you from evil. He shall

guard your soul. The Lord shall guard your going out. . .'
(Ps. 121:1–7):

B. " '. . . to the mountains' means, to parents and
teachers [the word for mountains can be read, by a shift of
vowels, as either 'teachers' or 'those who conceived me'].

C. " 'Whence shall my help come?' [Jacob thus says]
'Concerning Eliezer [whose name contains the word for
'help'], when he went to bring Rebecca, it is written in his
regard: 'and the servant took ten camels' (Gen. 24:10). But I
do not have 'even a ring or a bracelet.' [That is why he wonders whence help will come.]"

D. R. Hinena said, "Isaac sent him out empty-handed."

E. R. Joshua said, "He sent him out with supplies, but
Esau went and seized them from him."

F. [Reverting to C., Samuel b. Nahman continues:] "Jacob then went and said, 'Shall I then lose hope in my creator?
God forbid, I shall not lose hope in my creator: My help
comes from the Lord, who made heaven and earth.'

G. " 'He will not suffer your foot to be moved:' unto
death.

H. " 'He who keeps you will not slumber. Behold, he
who keeps Israel neither slumbers nor sleeps. The Lord shall
keep you from evil:' from the wicked Esau and from Laban.

I. " 'He shall guard your soul': from the angel of death.

J. " 'The Lord shall guard your going out': 'Now Jacob
left Beer-sheba' (Gen. 28:10)."

2.A. R. Yudan in the name of R. Aibu [commenced discourse by citing the following verse]: " 'In the transgression of
the lips is a snare to the evil man, but the righteous comes
out of trouble' (Prov. 12:13):

B. "On account of the rebellion of Esau and Ishmael
against the Holy One, blessed be he, their downfall came.

C. " 'But the righteous comes out of trouble' (Prov.
12:13) refers to Jacob: 'Jacob left Beer Sheba' (Gen. 28:10)."

The intersecting verse presented in the opening paragraph
contains all three elements that the base verse contributes, the
leaving, the going without fear, and the lying down. Then the
themes that will come are given their preliminary statement.

The intersecting verses in the second paragraph are taken as a statement of Jacob upon leaving home. Since the cited verse refers to Israel, it is certainly an appropriate choice. Then each detail of the Psalm makes reference to a fact in connection with Jacob. No. 2 works out the same exercise with a different intersecting verse, now noting that Jacob said nothing to snare himself.

Why Does it Matter that Jacob Left Beer Sheba?

Scripture dwells on minor details of the lives of the patriarchs, so we ask why. What difference can it have made, that the narrative should make a point of informing us about trivialities?

LXVIII:VI.1.A. "Now Jacob left Beer-sheba" (Gen. 28:10):

B. Was he the only one who went [so that the statement is correctly made concerning Jacob alone]?

C. Did not any number of ass-drivers and camel-drivers go forth with him?

D. R. Azariah in the name of R. Judah bar Simon, R. Hanan in the name of R. Samuel bar R. Isaac: "When a righteous man is in a town, he is its glory, he is its praise, he is its honor. When he leaves there, its glory leaves there, its praise leaves there, its honor leaves there."

E. Along these same lines: "And she went forth out of the place where she was" (Ruth 1:7).

F. Was she the only one who went [that the statement is made concerning Ruth alone]?

G. Did not any number of ass-drivers and camel-drivers go forth with her?

H. R. Azariah in the name of R. Judah bar Simon, R. Hanan in the name of R. Samuel bar R. Isaac: "When a righteous man is in a town, he is its glory, he is its praise, he is its honor. When he leaves there, its praise leaves there, its honor leaves there."

I. That reply serves well in the case of Ruth, for she was alone, that righteous woman, as the ornament of the place. But was not Isaac there too?

J. R. Azariah in the name of R. Yudan b. R. Simon, "The merit attained by an individual righteous person cannot compare to that attained by two [so that even when one remains, the departure of the other is still noticeable (Freedman, p. 619, n. 4)]."

The composition stresses the importance of a righteous person to the place in which that person is located. The comparison of the statements concerning Jacob and Ruth then contributes to the larger argument.

The Meaning of Jacob's Dream

Jacob's leave-taking elicits comment, so too his dreaming. Why should we pay attention to dreams? It is because when Jacob dreams, he dreams of Israel in time to come.

LXVIII:XII.3.A. Bar Qappara taught on Tannaite authority, "There is no dream without a proper interpretation.

B. " 'That there was a ladder'": refers to the ramp to the altar.

C. " '. . . set up on the earth'": that is the altar, 'An altar of dirt you will make for me' (Ex. 20:24).

D. " '. . . and the top of it reached to heaven': these are the offerings, for their fragrance goes up to heaven.

E. " '. . . and behold, the angels of God': these are the high priests.

F. " '. . . were ascending and descending on it': for they go up and go down on the ramp.

G. " 'And behold, the Lord stood above it': 'I saw the Lord standing by the altar' (Amos 9:1)."

4.A. Rabbis interpreted the matter to prefigure Sinai: "And he dreamed:

B. " '. . . that there was a ladder': this refers to Sinai.

C. " '. . . set up on the earth': 'And they stood at the lower part of the mountain' (Ex. 19:17).

D. " '. . . and the top of it reached to heaven': 'And the mountain burned with fire into the heart of heaven' (Deut. 4:11).

E.   " '. . . and behold, the angels of God': these are Moses and Aaron.

F.   " '. . . were ascending': 'And Moses went up to God' (Ex. 19:3).

G.   " '. . . and descending on it': 'And Moses went down from the mount' (Ex. 19:14).

F.   " '. . . And behold, the Lord stood above it': 'And the Lord came down upon Mount Sinai' (Ex. 19:20)."

LXVIII:XIII.1.A.   R. Joshua b. Levi interpreted the verse at hand to speak of the exiles of Israel [symbolized in Jacob's exile from the land]:

B.   " 'And Jacob went out from Beer Sheba': 'Cast them out of my sight and let them go forth' (Jer. 15:1).

C.   " '. . . and went toward Haran': 'Wherewith the Lord has afflicted me in the day of his fierce anger' (Lam. 1:1) ["anger" using letters shared with the word for Haran].

D.   " 'And he lighted on a certain place': 'Til there be no place' (Is. 5:8).

E.   " '. . . and stayed there that night because the sun had set': 'She who has borne seven languishes, her spirit droops, her sun has set' (Jer. 15:9).

F.   " '. . . Taking one of the stones of the place': 'The hallowed stones are poured out at the head of every street' (Lam. 4:1).

G.   " '. . . he put it under his head': 'For your turbans are come down' (Jer. 13:18).

H.   " '. . . and lay down in that place to sleep': 'Let us lie down in our shame and let our confusion cover us' (Jer. 3:25).

I.   " 'And he dreamed': this alludes to the dream of Nebuchadnezzer [in the book of Daniel, as will now be spelled out].

J.   " '. . . that there was a ladder': this alludes to Nebuchadnezzar's image, for the word for image shares the same letters as the word for ladder.

K.   " '. . . set up on the earth': 'He set it up in the plain of Dura' (Dan. 3:1).

L.   " '. . . and the top of it reached to heaven': 'Whose height was three score cubits' (Dan. 3:1).

M. " '. . . and behold, the angels of God': Hananiah, Mishael, and Azariah.

N. " '. . . were ascending and descending on it': they were raising him up and dragging him down, dancing on him, leaping on him, abusing him: 'Be it known to you, O king, that we will not serve your gods' (Dan. 3:18).

O. " 'And behold, the Lord stood beside him and said': 'You servants of God, most high, come forth and come hither' (Dan. 3:26)."

2.A. Another interpretation: "And behold the angels of God. . . ." refers to Daniel.

B. ". . . ascending and descending on it": he went up and brought forth what it had swallowed from its mouth.

C. That is in line with this verse: "And I will punish Bel in Babylonia and I will bring forth out of his mouth that which he has swallowed up" (Jer. 51:44).

D. "And behold the Lord stood beside him" (Gen. 28:13): "O Daniel, servant of the living God" (Dan. 6:21).

In the opening paragraph, nos. 3 and 4 work out the specific dream before us. No. 3 reads the dream in terms of the temple cult, and no. 4 in terms of the revelation of the Torah at Sinai, while no. 5 has the dream refer to the partriarchs. At LXVIII:XIII we complete the interpretation of the base verse. The main theme is the link from Jacob to Israel's condition, with the rueful observations at Part 6, Paragraph I to make the point. The sources of interpretation are the temple, Sinai, the lives of the patriarchs, and the exile. It would be difficult to point to a more complete symbolic repertoire to evoke Israel's salvific life than one that encompasses Israel's cult, revelation, and salvation on the other side of the exile, that is, creation, celebrated in the cult, revelation, then redemption. The tripartite categories fully work themselves out in a rather complex structure.

Jacob Sees Rachel and Perceives All Judaism

The word "Judaism" stands for the whole of what we value, what binds us and defines us. How to define it? How to express it? That is the problem that faces both theologians and artists, musicians, painters, graphic artists, poets, writers, even scholars. For the task of saying everything all at once—that is a task that only the people who try to capture everything in one thing can accomplish. The enormous and elaborate statement that follows tells us, in a few paragraphs, how our sages discovered in humble passages all the Judaism that they espoused. At hand is Jacob's vision of the well. The story at hand concerns simple things, how a man saw and fell in love with his future wife. But the tale now turns to those who would come of the marriage: Israel, the people that Jacob would build out of his four wives. Our sages turn to the passage at hand and discover in Jacob's vision of the well the whole of that worldview and way of life that they taught as the Torah.

LXX:VIII.2.A. "Then Jacob lifted up his feet. . . . As he looked, he saw a well in the field" (Gen. 29:1):

B. R. Hama bar Hanina interpreted the verse in six ways [that is, he divides the verse into six clauses and systematically reads each of the clauses in light of the others and in line with an overriding theme]:

C. " 'As he looked, he saw a well in the field': this refers to the well [of water in the wilderness, Num. 21:17].

D. " '. . . and lo, three flocks of sheep lying beside it': specifically, Moses, Aaron, and Miriam.

E. " '. . . for out of that well the flocks were watered': from there each one drew water for his standard, tribe, and family."

F. "And the stone upon the well's mouth was great":

G. Said R. Hanina, "It was only the size of a little sieve."

I. [Reverting to Hama's statement]: " '. . . and put the stone back in its place upon the mouth of the well:' for the coming journeys. [Thus the first interpretation applies the passage at hand to the life of Israel in the wilderness.]

3.A. " 'As he looked, he saw a well in the field': refers to Zion.

B. " '. . . and lo, three flocks of sheep lying beside it': refers to the three festivals [Passover, Pentecost, Tabernacles, that is, *Pesah, Shavuot, Sukkot*].

257

C. " '. . . for out of that well the flocks were watered':
from there they drank of the holy spirit.

D. " '. . . The stone on the well's mouth was large': this
refers to the rejoicing of the house of the water drawing [on
Sukkot]."

E. Said R. Hoshaiah, "Why is it called 'the house of
the water drawing'? Because from there they drink of the
Holy Spirit."

F. [Resuming Hama b. Hanina's discourse:] " '. . . and
when all the flocks were gathered there:' coming from 'the
entrance of Hamath to the brook of Egypt' (1 Kgs. 8:66).

G. " '. . . the shepherds would roll the stone from the
mouth of the well and water the sheep': for from there they
would drink of the Holy Spirit.

H. " '. . . and put the stone back in its place upon the
mouth of the well': leaving it in place until the coming festival. [Thus the second interpretation reads the verse in light of
the temple celebration of the Festival of Tabernacles.]

4.A. " '. . . As he looked, he saw a well in the field':
this refers to Zion.

B. " '. . . and lo, three flocks of sheep lying beside it':
this refers to the three courts of the temple, concerning which
we have learned in the Mishnah: There were three courts
there, one at the gateway of the temple mount, one at the
gateway of the courtyard, and one in the chamber of the hewn
stones [M. San. 11:2].

C. " '. . . for out of that well the flocks were watered':
for from there they would hear the ruling.

D. " 'The stone on the well's mouth was large': this
refers to the high court that was in the chamber of the hewn
stones.

E. " '. . . and when all the flocks were gathered there':
this refers to the courts in session in the land of Israel.

F. " '. . . the shepherds would roll the stone from the
mouth of the well and water the sheep': for from there they
would hear the ruling.

G. " '. . . and put the stone back in its place upon the
mouth of the well': for they would give and take until they

had produced the ruling in all the required clarity." [The third interpretation reads the verse in light of the Israelite institution of justice and administration.]

5.A. " 'As he looked, he saw a well in the field': this refers to Zion.

B. " '. . . and lo, three flocks of sheep lying beside it': this refers to the first three kingdoms [Babylonia, Media, Greece].

C. " '. . . for out of that well the flocks were watered': for they enriched the treasures that were laid upon up in the chambers of the temple.

D. " '. . . The stone on the well's mouth was large': this refers to the merit attained by the patriarchs.

E. " '. . . and when all the flocks were gathered there': this refers to the wicked kingdom of Rome, which collects troops through levies over all the nations of the world.

F. " '. . . the shepherds would roll the stone from the mouth of the well and water the sheep': for they enriched the treasures that were laid upon up in the chambers of the temple.

G. " '. . . and put the stone back in its place upon the mouth of the well': in the age to come the merit attained by the patriarchs will stand [in defense of Israel]." [So the fourth interpretation interweaves the themes of the temple cult and the domination of the four monarchies.]

6.A. " 'As he looked, he saw a well in the field': this refers to the Sanhedrin.

B., " '. . . and lo, three flocks of sheep lying beside it': this alludes to the three rows of disciples of sages that would go into session in their presence.

C. " 'for out of that well the flocks were watered': for from there they would listen to the ruling of the law.

D. " '. . . The stone on the well's mouth was large': this refers to the most distinguished member of the court, who determines the law decision.

E. " '. . . and when all the flocks were gathered there': this refers to disciples of the sages in the Land of Israel.

F. " '. . . the shepherds would roll the stone from the mouth of the well and water the sheep': for from there they would listen to the ruling of the law.

G. " '. . . and put the stone back in its place upon the mouth of the well': for they would give and take until they had produced the ruling in all the required clarity." [The fifth interpretation again reads the verse in light of the Israelite institution of legal education and justice.]

7.*A.* " 'As he looked, he saw a well in the field': this refers to the synagogue.

B. " '. . . and lo, three flocks of sheep lying beside it': this refers to the three who are called to the reading of the Torah on weekdays.

C. " '. . . for out of that well the flocks were watered': for from there they hear the reading of the Torah.

D. " '. . . The stone on the well's mouth was large': this refers to the impulse to do evil.

E. " '. . . and when all the flocks were gathered there': this refers to the congregation.

F. " '. . . the shepherds would roll the stone from the mouth of the well and water the sheep': for from there they hear the reading of the Torah.

G. " '. . . and put the stone back in its place upon the mouth of the well': for once they go forth [from the hearing of the reading of the Torah] the impulse to do evil reverts to its place." [The sixth and last interpretation turns to the twin themes of the reading of the Torah in the synagogue and the evil impulse, temporarily driven off through the hearing of the Torah.]

LXX:IX.1.A. R. Yohanan interpreted the statement in terms of Sinai:

B. " 'As he looked, he saw a well in the field': this refers to Sinai.

C. " '. . . and lo, three flocks of sheep lying beside it': these stand for the priests, Levites, and Israelites.

D. " '. . . for out of that well the flocks were watered': for from there they heard the Ten Commandments.

E. " '. . . The stone on the well's mouth was large': this refers to the presence of God."

F. " '. . . and when all the flocks were gathered there":

G. R. Simeon b. Judah of Kefar Akum in the name of R. Simeon: "All the flocks of Israel had to be present, for if any one of them had been lacking, they would not have been worthy of receiving the Torah."

H. [Returning to Yohanan's exposition:] " '. . . the shepherds would roll the stone from the mouth of the well and water the sheep': for from there they heard the Ten Commandments.

I. " '. . . and put the stone back in its place upon the mouth of the well': 'You yourselves have seen that I have talked with you from heaven' (Ex. 20:19)."

The six themes read in response to the verse cover (1) Israel in the wilderness, (2) the temple cult on festivals with special reference to Tabernacles, (3) the judiciary and government, (4) the history of Israel under the four kingdoms, (5) the life of sages, and (6) the ordinary folk and the synagogue. The whole is an astonishing repertoire of fundamental themes of the life of the nation, Israel: at its origins in the wilderness, in its cult, in its institutions based on the cult, in the history of the nations, and, finally, in the twin social estates of sages and ordinary folk, matched by the institutions of the master-disciple circle and the synagogue. The vision of Jacob at the well thus encompassed the whole of the social reality of Jacob's people, Israel. Yohanan's exposition adds what was left out—namely, reference to the revelation of the Torah at Sinai.

Jacob Works for Rachel but is Deceived into Marrying Leah

Our sages find every opportunity to explain in their own terms and contexts the simple and domestic stories of scripture. Each thing bore a message for them. Nothing is left as mere history—let alone fiction.

LXX:XVIII.1.A. "Then Jacob said to Laban, 'Give me my wife, that I may go in to her, for my time is completed' " (Gen. 29:21):

B. Said R. Aibu, "Even if a man is totally dissolute, he would not use this kind of blunt language.

C. "But this is what he said, 'Thus has the Holy One, blessed be he, decreed for me, that I am to produce twelve tribes. Now I am eighty-four years old, and if I do not produce them now, when am I going to produce them?'

D. "Thus the scripture has to say, 'Then Jacob said to Laban, "Give me my wife, that I may go in to her, for my time is completed' " (Gen. 29:21)."

LXX:XIX.1.A. "So Laban gathered together all the men of the place and made a feast" (Gen. 29:22):

B. He brought together all the men of the place. He said to them, "You know that we were in need of water. But once this righteous man came, the water has been blessed. [So let's keep him around here.]"

C. They said to him, "What is good for you is what you should do."

D. He said to them, "Do you want me to deceive him and give him Leah, and, since he loves Rachel more, he will stay and work here with you for another seven years?"

E. They said to him, "What is good for you is what you should do."

F. He said to them, "Give me your pledge that none of you will inform him."

G. They gave him their pledge. Then he went and with the pledges the neighbors had given got them wine, oil, and meat.

H. What follows is that he was called Laban the deceiver, since he deceived even the people who lived in his own town.

I. All that day the people were praising him. When evening came, he said to them, "Why are you doing this?"

J. They said to him, "On your account benefits have been coming to us," and they sang praises before him, saying, *"Hey, Leah, Hey, Leah."*

K. In the evening they came to bring her in and they put out the lamps. He said to them, "Why so?"

L. They said to him, "Do you want us to be indecent the way you are? [Here we do not have sexual relations in the light.]"

M. All that night he would use the name of Rachel and she answered him. In the morning: "And in the morning, behold, it was Leah" (Gen. 29:24–25)!

N. He said, "How could you have deceived me, you daughter of a deceiver?"

O. She said to him, "And is there a book without faithful readers? [I know your story and so I followed your example.] Did not your father call you 'Esau,' and you answered him accordingly? So you called me by a name other than my own, and I answered you accordingly."

2.A. "And Jacob said to Laban, 'What is this that you have done to me? Did I not serve with you for Rachel? Why then have you deceived me?' And Laban said, 'It is not so done in our country, to give the younger before the firstborn. Complete the week of this one and we will give you the other also in return for serving me another seven years' " (Gen. 29:25–27):

B. Said R. Jacob bar Aha, "On the basis of this statement we learn the rule that people may not confuse one occasion for rejoicing with some other."

In the opening paragraph the exegete clarifies the rather coarse language imputed to Jacob. It is made into a statement of eagerness to carry out God's will. In the second paragraph, no. 1 presents a sustained amplification of details of the story, ending with a stunning and apt observation about the appropriate conduct of Leah with Jacob. No. 2, by contrast, just draws a moral.

Do Names Make a Difference?

The narrative carefully explains the names given to the children of Jacob, the founders and ancestors of the tribes of

Israel. Each name bears its significance. Stress on the importance of giving appropriate names would characterize Israel later on, whether the selected name was Moshe, Morris, or Marvin or Merwin, or Moti, it carried its message. And it always will.

LXXI:III.1.A. "And Leah conceived and bore a son and she called his name Reuben, for she said, 'Because the Lord has looked upon my affliction, surely now my husband will love me' " (Gen. 29:32):

B. Said R. Yose b. Haninah, "Four traits have been stated with respect to the categorization of names:

C. "There are those with nice names and nasty deeds, nasty names and nice deeds, nasty names and nasty deeds, nice names and nice deeds.

D. "There are those with nice names and nasty deeds: Esau, meaning, 'he does,' but he really did not do [God's will], and Ishmael, meaning, 'he will listen to God,' but he never did.

E. ". . . nasty names and nice deeds: the children of the exile: 'The children of Bakbuk, the children of Hakupha, the children of Harhur' (Ezra 2:51) [names meaning doubt, smiting, wrath, ague (Freedman)], but they had the merit of going up and building the house of the sanctuary.

F. ". . . nasty names and nasty deeds: the spies, Sethur, a man of destruction, Gaddi, wormwood, and death [Freedman].

G. ". . . nice names and nice deeds: these are the names of the tribes, such as Reuben, meaning, 'see grandchildren;' Simeon, meaning, 'one who listens to the voice of his father in heaven.' "

H. Said R. Yose bar Haninah, "The names of the tribes are not meant [Freedman, p. 654:] to stir up the recollection of their shortcomings [e.g., Reuben's or Judah's or Levi's sins, as the narrative will tell them] but to cover them up."

LXXI:IV.1.A. "She conceived again and bore a son and said, 'Because the Lord has heard that I am hated, he has given me this son also,' and she called his name Simeon" (Gen. 29:33):

B.   "This one is destined to produce an enemy [Zimri],
and who will heal his wound?

C.   " 'This son also': It is Phineas, who comes from
Levi."

2.A.   "Again she conceived and bore a son and said,
'Now this time my husband will be joined to me, because I
have borne him three sons,' therefore his name was called
Levi" (Gen. 29:34):

B.   R. Yudan said, " 'I accompany [since the Hebrew
letters for the word Levi can yield the word 'to keep someone
company'].' This one is destined to accompany the children to
their father in heaven."

3.A.   ". . . therefore his name was called Levi" (Gen.
29:34):

B.   In any passage in which we find the language,
"Therefore his name was called . . . ," the meaning is that
that tribe will become most populous.

4.A.   "And she conceived again and bore a son and said,
'This time I will praise the Lord,' therefore she called his
name Judah, then she ceased bearing" (Gen. 29:35):

B.   R. Berekhiah in the name of R. Levi: "The matter
may be compared to the case of a priest who went down to
the threshing floor, and someone gave him a *kor* of grain as
tithe, and the priest made no gesture of thanks, while another
gave him a basket of untithed produce, and the priest thanked
the man.

C.   [The one to whom no gesture of thanks was made]
said to him, "My lord, the priest, I gave you a *kor,* while the
other person gave you no more than a basketful, yet you
thanked him [and not me]!"

D.   "He explained, 'You gave me what is in fact my
share, while this one gave me his share [since he had to give
me only produce designated as tithe, but he gave me, in addition, the already tithed produce, that is not coming to the
priest].'

E.   "So too, since the matriarchs had the expectation
that this one would produce three sons and that one would

produce three and the other would produce three and the fourth would produce three, once she had given birth to a fourth son, she said, '*This* time [in particular] I will praise the Lord' [since it is more than I had coming to me]."

The several components of the paragraphs explain the meanings of the names. In the second paragraph, no. 4 in particular does a good job of amplifying the special thanks that are expressed in the name of Judah. No. 3 offers a more general proposition.

How One Talks to a Wife: Proper and Improper Ways

Our sages showed acute sensitivity to the feelings and special traits of women. They tried to impart to their disciples the attitudes of respect and courtesy for women. The contrast now drawn between Abraham's and Jacob's way of speaking to their wives teaches an important lesson.

LXXI:VII.1.A. "Jacob's anger was kindled against Rachel, and he said, 'Am I in the place of God, who has withheld from you the fruit of the womb?' " (Gen. 30:2):

B. Rabbis of the South [not the Galileans] in the name of R. Alexandri, Rabbana in the name of R. Abba bar Kahana: " 'Should a wise man make answer with windy knowledge and fill his belly with the east wind?' (Job 15:1).

C. " 'Should a wise man make answer with windy knowledge' refers to Abraham: 'And Abraham hearkened to the voice of Sarah' (Gen. 16:2).

D. " '. . . and fill his belly with the east wind?' speaks of Jacob: 'Jacob's anger was kindled against Rachel, and he said, "Am I in the place of God, who has withheld from you the fruit of the womb?' "

E. "Said the Holy One, blessed be he, to him, 'Is this the proper way to answer women in distress? By your life, your children are destined to stand before her son [Joseph].' " [Freedman, p. 658, n. 2: "This applies to Abraham:" Abra-

ham understood that a wise man should not make answer with
windy knowledge and so he obeyed Sarah, whereas Jacob did
not understand that a man should not fill his belly with the
east wind.]

2.A. "Am I in the place of God, who has withheld from
you the fruit of the womb?"

B. "From you he has withheld children, but from me he
has not withheld them."

C. She said to him, "Is this what your father did for
your mother? Did he not gird his loins for her?"

D. He said to her, "But he had no children at all, while
I have children."

E. She said to him, "And your grandfather had no children, but he girded his loins for Sarah."

F. He said to her, "Can you do deeds such as my grandmother did?"

G. She said to him, "And what did she do?"

H. He said to her, "She brought her rival, co-wife into
her own household."

I. She said to him, "If that's what is holding things up,
then: 'Here is my maid Bilhah, go in to her, that she may
bear upon my knees, and even I may have children through
her' (Gen. 30:3).

J. "Just as that one [Sarah] was given a household
through her rival, so I shall be given a household through my
rival [as a reward for bringing her into my household]."

3.A. "[So she gave him her maid Bilhah, as a wife, and
Jacob went in to her. And Bilhah conceived and bore Jacob a
son.] Then Rachel said, 'God has judged me [and has also
heard my voice and given me a son,' therefore she called his
name Dan]" (Gen. 30:5–6):

B. "He has judged me and declared me guilty, he has
judged me and declared me innocent.

C. "He has judged me and declared me guilty: 'But
Rachel was barren' (Gen. 29:31).

D. ". . . he has judged me and declared me innocent:
'. . . and has also heard my voice and given me a son,' therefore she called his name Dan."

4.A. " '. . . and has also heard my voice and given me a son,' therefore she called his name Dan:"

B. In any passage in which we find the language, "Therefore his name was called . . . ," the meaning is that that tribe will become most populous.

No. 1 contrasts Abraham and Jacob, thus a comment not on the verse at hand but on a larger theme. It is how Jacob talks with Rachel, showing the contrast between the improper and the proper way to treat one's wives. No. 2 then constructs a colloquy between Jacob and Rachel, explaining the direct connection between Sarah's and Rachel's actions with their handmaidens and therefore providing Rachel with a motivation for her actions. No. 3 does the same for Rachel, and no. 4 repeats a point already made.

God Remembered Rachel

The effort to draw comparisons and contrasts between Jacob and Abraham now moves on. Just as God remembered Sarah, so God remembered Rachel.

LXXIII:I.1.A. "Then God remembered Rachel, and God hearkened to her and opened her womb. She conceived and bore a son and said, 'God has taken away my reproach,' and she called his name Joseph, saying, 'May the Lord add to me another son!' " (Gen. 30:22–24):

B. "Remember me, O Lord, when you favor your people, O think of me at your salvation" (Ps. 106:4):

C. Said R. Eleazar, "On the New Year were Sarah, Rachel, and Hannah remembered: 'Then God remembered Rachel.' " [That is the passage of the Torah read in the synagogue on the New Year, with the passage on the birth of Samuel to Hannah read as the prophetic lection.]

LXXIII:II.1.A. "He has remembered his mercy and his faithfulness to the house of Israel; all the ends of the earth have seen the salvation of our God" (Ps. 98:3):

B. "He has remembered his mercy" refers to Abraham: "Mercy to Abraham" (Mic. 7:20).

C. ". . . and his faithfulness" refers to Jacob: "You will show faithfulness to Jacob" (Mic. 7:20).

D. ". . . to the house of Israel" the elder.

E. Who was the house of our father, Abraham? Was it not Rachel?

F. In regard to all of the others it is written, "And the children of Leah, the firstborn of Jacob was Reuben . . . and the children of Zilpah, Leah's maid, were Gad and Asher . . . and the children of Bilhah, Rachel's maid, were Dan and Naphtali" (Gen. 35:23–26).

G. But in connection with the children of Rachel it is written, "The sons of Rachel, Jacob's wife: Joseph and Benjamin" (Gen. 46:19). [Only Rachel is designated as Jacob's wife.]

2.A. Another matter: "He has remembered his mercy and his faithfulness to the house of Israel."

B. "Then God remembered Rachel [and God hearkened to her and opened her womb. She conceived and bore a son and said, 'God has taken away my reproach,' and she called his name Joseph, saying, 'May the Lord add to me another son!']" (Gen. 30:22–24).

The several exercises work out the theme of God's remembering Rachel. The important point comes when Rachel in particular is made subject to divine remembrance. This then forms the link between modern Israel and the matriarchs.

The Merit that Protected Jacob

Merit protects not only Israel in time to come, but the children and grandchildren of the patriarchs in their own day. Merit is what protected Jacob in his dangerous voyage to his family's country. Indeed, it is from the life of Jacob that we learn the lessons of merit. He states for himself exactly the doctrine of the merit of the fathers: "If the God of my father, the God of Abraham and the fear of Isaac, had not been on my side, surely now you would have sent me away empty-handed. God saw my affliction and the labor of my hand and rebuked you last night." I can imagine no more explicit statement of what our sages understand by merit than Jacob's declaration in scripture itself.

LXXIV:XII.1.A. "If the God of my father, the God of Abraham and the fear of Isaac, had not been on my side, surely now you would have sent me away empty-handed. God saw my affliction and the labor of my hand and rebuked you last night" (Gen. 31:41–42):

B. Zebedee b. Levi and R. Joshua b. Levi:

C. Zebedee b. Levi said, "Every passage in which reference is made to 'if' tells of an appeal to the merit accrued by the patriarchs. [Freedman, p. 684, n. 2: It introduces a plea for or affirmation of protection received for the sake of the patriarchs.]

D. Said to him R. Joshua, "But it is written, 'Except we had lingered' (Gen. 43:10) [a passage not related to the merit of the patriarchs]."

E. He said to him, "They themselves would not have come up except for the merit of the patriarchs, for if it were not for the merit of the patriarchs, they never would have been able to go up from there in peace."

F. Said R. Tanhuma, "There are those who produce the matter in a different version." [It is given as follows:]

G. R. Joshua b. Levi and Zebedee b. Levi:

H. R. Joshua b. Levi said, "Every passage in which reference is made to 'if' tells of an appeal to the merit accrued by the patriarchs except for the present case."

I. He said to him, "This case too falls under the category of an appeal to the merit of the patriarchs."

J. R. Yohanan said, "It was on account of the merit achieved through sanctification of the divine name."

K. R. Levi said, "It was on account of the merit achieved through faith and the merit achieved through Torah.

L. "The merit achieved through faith: 'If I had not believed. . . .' (Ps. 27:13).

M. "The merit achieved through Torah: 'Unless your Torah had been my delight' (Ps. 119:92)."

2.A. "God saw my affliction and the labor of my hand and rebuked you last night" (Gen. 31:41–42):

B. Said R. Jeremiah b. Eleazar, "More beloved is hard labor than the merit achieved by the patriarchs, for the merit achieved by the patriarchs served to afford protection for property only, while the merit achieved by hard labor served to afford protection for lives.

C. "The merit achieved by the patriarchs served to afford protection for property only: 'If the God of my father, the God of Abraham and the fear of Isaac had not been on my side, surely now you would have sent me away empty-handed.'

D. "The merit achieved by hard labor served to afford protection for lives: 'God saw my affliction and the labor of my hand and rebuked you last night.' "

The main interest is in the theology of merit. Precisely how do the lives of the patriarchs and matriarchs affect the future history of Israel? It is not a merely spiritual thing, not at all. Merit accruing to the ancestors for their faithfulness to God benefits the descendants. We have the analogy, then, of a family, in which the early generations accumulate wealth and hand it on to the later ones. But the wealth here is not money but *zekhut*, translated "merit." Then the point is clear: Exactly how did the ancestors gain merit? And how does Israel today gain merit? These are the questions that we find answered in the present passage. We note, by the way, the range of analogies and metaphors that serve to explain who is Israel. Israel here is a family—and that is a different metaphor from the one that describes Israel as a kingdom of priests and a holy people. No. 1 investigates the meaning of an expression used in the base verse, among other passages. The issue of the merit of the patriarchs comes up in the reference to the God of the fathers, and that accounts for the selection of the theme at hand.

Part Eight

VAYYISHLAH:
Genesis Rabbah
Parashiyyot
LXXV–LXXXIII

Do not Go Looking for Trouble—Jacob Should not have Sent Messengers to Esau

Our sages bear no brief for defending everything the patriarchs did. On the contrary, they often set a critical eye on the lessons to be learned from the patriarchs—and tell us to do the opposite. We see that thoroughly honest and sometimes skeptical approach here. Jacob sent messengers to Esau: Why? He erred. He should have allowed Esau to live his life without having to confront Jacob at all. Moreover, our sages are quick to tell us, in dealing with today's Esau, we err if we attract attention to ourselves.

LXXV:II.1.A. R. Judah b. R. Simon opened discourse by citing the following verse: " 'As a troubled fountain and a corrupted spring, so is a righteous man who gives way before the wicked' (Prov. 25:26):

B. "Just as it is impossible for a fountain to be forever muddied and for a spring to be forever spoiled, so it is impossible for a righteous man to be forever humbled before a wicked one.

C. "And like a fountain that is muddied or a spring that is spoiled, so is a righteous man who is humbled before a wicked man.

D. "Said the Holy One, blessed be he, to him, 'Esau was walking along his solitary way, and you had to go and send word to him and say to him, "Thus says your servant Jacob." ' "

LXXV:III.1.A. R. Huna cited the following: "He who passes by and meddles with strife not his own is like one who takes a dog by the ears" (Prov. 26:17).

B. Nahman b. Samuel said, "The matter may be compared to the instance of a bandit chief who went to sleep by

275

the way. Someone came back and woke him up from his nap. He said to him, 'Get up, get out of here, for there are bad people around here.'

D. "The bandit got up and started to beat the man up. The other said to him, '[God] rebuke this bad man.'

E. "He said to him, 'I was sleeping and you woke me up!'

F. "Thus said the Holy One, blessed be he, to him, 'Esau was walking along his solitary way, and you had to go and send word to him and say to him, "Thus says your servant Jacob." ' "

2.A. R. Judah b. R. Simon cited the following verse: " 'What will you say when he shall set the friends over you as head, whom you yourself have trained against you?' (Jer. 13:21).

B. "Thus said the Holy One, blessed be he, to him, 'Esau was walking along his solitary way, and you had to go and send word to him and say to him, "Thus says your servant Jacob." ' "

LXXV:XI.1.A. Another explanation of the statement, "And Jacob sent . . . ."

B. Why did he send out messengers to him?

C. This is what he was thinking, "I shall send messengers to him, perhaps he will return in repentance."

D. And he said to them, "This is what to say to him: 'Do not suppose that the way that Jacob went forth from the house of his father is the way he is coming back.' "

E. For it is said, "For with my staff I passed over this Jordan" (Gen. 32:11).

F. [Reverting to Jacob's message:] "For he did not take anything from his father. But [this is what the messengers were to say to Esau in Jacob's name:] It was for my salary [the messengers are to repeat to Esau] that I have acquired all these properties, through my own strength."

G. For it is said, "And now I have become two camps" (Gen. 32:11).

2.A. At the moment that Jacob referred to Esau as "my lord," the Holy One, blessed be he, said to him, "You have lowered yourself and called Esau 'my Lord' no fewer than eight times.

B. "I shall produce out of his descendants eight kings before your children [have any]: 'And these are the kings that reigned in the land of Edom before any king ruled the children of Israel' (Gen. 36:31)."

3.A. [In his message to Esau, Jacob said to him] "If you are ready for peace, I shall be your counterpart, and if you are ready for war, I shall be your counterpart.

B. "I have heroic, powerful troops, for I say something before the Holy One, blessed be he, and he grants what I ask: 'He will fulfil the desire of those who fear him' (Ps. 145:19)."

C. Therefore David came to give praise and glory before the Holy One, blessed be he, for he helped him when he fled from Saul, as it is said, "For lo, the wicked bend the bow" (Ps. 11:2), then, "When the foundations are destroyed, what has the righteous done?" (Ps. 11:3).

D. He said to him, "Lord of the age, if you had been angry with Jacob and had forsaken him and not helped him, and he was pillar and foundation of the world, in line with this verse, 'But the righteous is the foundation of the world' (Prov. 10:25), then 'what has the righteous done' (Ps. 11:3)?"

E. Concerning that moment it is said: "Some in chariots, some in horses, but we shall call on the name of the Lord our God" (Ps. 20:8). [Freedman, p. 697, n. 4: Jacob discomfited Esau by mentioning God, and David was saved from Saul by his trust in God.]

What exactly did Jacob send as his message to Esau? What troubles our sages is that Jacob spoke so obsequiously to Esau. Here, of course, they are looking for a model for themselves in their dealings with Rome. In the opening paragraph, no. 1 supplies a message for the messengers in place of that given at Gen. 32:3–4. No. 2 responds to the statement, Gen. 32:3: "Thus you shall say to my lord Esau." The effect is to link Jacob's encounter with Esau to Israel's history with Edom/Rome. There are no surprises here. The third paragraph works out a parallel between Jacob and David, as made explicit by Freedman. The message is this: Jacob should not have taken an initiative in dealing with Esau. The message of passivity in response to Rome can be seen as the subterranean polemic. The policy of the subjugated people is to resist passively and from day to day, and to understand that that too is honorable.

Esau and Israel's Enemies

In the simpler world of late antiquity, our sages could take a more sanguine view of history than can we. No generation, indeed, has lived in more difficult time than the generations beyond the Shoah. We all are survivors, bearing memories not inflicted on any prior generation of Jews, however desperate their days. So the message that follows tells us about the imagination of an easier day. But it bears remembering even now. For the basic conviction of our sages is that God protects Israel, sustains Israel, and alone justifies Israel's endurance through time.

LXXV:IX.1.A.   Someone else commenced discourse by citing this verse: "Do not grant, O Lord, the desires of the wicked, do not advance his evil plan" (Ps. 140:9).

B.   "Lord of all ages, do not give to the wicked Esau what his heart has devised against Jacob."

C.   What is the meaning of, "Do not advance his evil plan"?

D.   He said before him, "Lord of the ages, Make a bit for the mouth of the wicked Esau, so that he will not get full pleasure [from anything he does]." [The word for "evil plan" and for "bit" use the same consonants.]

E.   What sort of bit did the Holy One, blessed be he, make for Esau?

F.   Said R. Hama bar Haninah, "These are the barbarian nations, the Germans whom the Edomites fear. [The Romans face threats on their northern frontier from the German tribes. The city of Rome itself fell to the German invaders within a decade of the completion of this document, in the year 410. So the reference to the Edomites' fear of the Barbarians, meaning, the people over the frontier, is quite pointed. What is interesting is that Israel, for its part, does not fear them. In time to come Jews would find homes in the Germanic territories, becoming Europeans.]"

2.A.   Another interpretation of the verse, "Do not grant, O Lord, the desires of the wicked, do not advance his evil plan" (Ps. 140:9):

B.   Said Jacob before the Holy One, blessed be he, "Just as Laban had in mind to do evil to me and you did not let him do so, so undo the plans of Esau, so that he will not kill me."

2.A.   Another interpretation of the verse, "Do not grant, O Lord, the desires of the wicked, do not advance his evil plan" (Ps. 140:9):

B.   Said Jacob before the Holy One, blessed be he, "Just as Laban had in mind to do evil to me and you did not let him do so, so undo the plans of Esau, so that he will not kill me."

3.A.   Here we have one of three men who planned to do evil but did not succeed: Esau, Jeroboam, and Haman.

B.   In connection with Esau it is written: "And Esau said *in* his heart" (Gen. 27:41). With Jeroboam: "And Jeroboam said *in* his heart" (1 Kgs. 12:25). With Haman: "Now Haman said *in* his heart" (Est. 6:6). [All made plans in their hearts but did not get to carry them out.]

C.   What is the meaning of the statement, "And Esau said in his heart" (Gen. 27:41)?

D.   He thought, "Cain killed his brother, and the Holy One, blessed be he, did not do anything to him. In the end the first man produced other children and with him they inherited the world. So I shall kill father first, and then I shall kill my brother, so that I may inherit the entire world on my own."

E.   So it is said, "Let the days of mourning for my father be at hand" (Gen. 27:41).

F.   It does not say, "Let my father die," but rather, "Let the days of mourning for my father be at hand."

G. The meaning is that he planned, "I shall bring near the time of mourning for father first of all, and then I shall kill Jacob."

H. But the Holy One, blessed be he, did not give him the occasion to do what he planned. Therefore it is said, "Do not grant, O Lord, the desires of the wicked, do not advance his evil plan" (Ps. 140:9).

It would be difficult to be more explicit on current events than is no. 1, with its specific reference to the barbarian nations whom the Romans have to keep at bay. No. 2 presents no surprises. No. 3 presents a long essay on Esau's plans, which serves Gen. 27:41, not the present passage.

Jacob Should not have Feared. For a Jew it is a Sin to Despair, and the Hope of Israel is its Power to Hope

Scripture makes it explicit, once more, that Jacob feared. Our sages condemn Jacob for his lack of trust in God. He should not have feared. We who survive what we every day have to survive, memories and fears of a deeper and more tragic order than our sages, whatever their circumstances, could ever have imagined, have a lesson to learn too. It is that, for us above all generations, it is a sin to despair, and it is an act of courage to hope. Ours then is a generation that comes to scripture seeking grounds to hope. But what we learn is that fear too marks the faithful, and the greatest heroes came close to despair. That is not a lesson our generation can ignore.

LXXVI:I.1.A. "Then Jacob was greatly afraid and distressed" (Gen. 32:7):

B. R. Phineas in the name of R. Reuben opened by citing this verse: " 'Trust in the Lord with all your heart' (Prov. 3:5).

C. "To two men did the Holy One, blessed be he, give assurances, and both of them nonetheless were afraid, the select among the patriarchs and the select among the prophets.

D. "The select among the patriarchs was Jacob: 'For the Lord has chosen Jacob for himself' (Ps. 135:4).

E. "The Holy One, blessed be he, had said to him, 'Lo, I shall be with you' (Gen. 28:15), yet: 'Then Jacob was greatly afraid and distressed.'

F. ". . . and the select among the prophets: this was Moses, our master: 'Had not Moses, his chosen . . .' (Ps. 106:23).

G. "The Holy One, blessed be he, had said to him, 'Certainly I will be with you' (Ex. 3:12).

H. "But he was afraid: 'And the Lord said to Moses, "Do not fear him, for I have delivered him into your hand' " (Num. 21:34). Since he had to say, 'Do not fear him,' it is certain that he did fear him, for otherwise there was no need to make that statement."

2.A. R. Berekhiah and R. Helbo in the name of R. Samuel bar Nahman, "The Israelites were deserving of complete destruction in the time of Haman [for they lost hope], except that they took the position that had been taken by the elder, saying, 'If our father, Jacob, to whom the Holy One, blessed be he, gave assurances, was afraid, as to us, how much the more so!' "

B. "Then Jacob was greatly afraid" (Gen. 32:7).

No. 1 makes the obvious point that, after the promises God had made to Jacob, he should not have been afraid. This is then drawn into line with Moses' fear and shown to be perfectly natural. No. 2 makes essentially the same point, again linking Israel's history to Jacob's biography. The next compositions go over the same ground. The message to contemporary Israel is to have faith. As I said, we can do well to listen to our sages.

Jacob Goes to Meet Esau

How to meet Esau? With circumspection and deep caution. That is the lesson our father, Jacob, teaches us in our dealing with Rome, our sages say. It is enough to survive. For Israel today, the Jewish people too have to give thanks for little

things, like surviving the age of total war—to the measure that
we have survived, to hope a little, in an age of utter nihilism,
above all to keep faith in an age that believes in little and hopes
for nothing.

LXXVIII:VII.1.A.   "And Jacob lifted up his eyes and
looked, and behold, Esau was coming, and four hundred men
with him. So he divided the children among Leah and Rachel
and the two maids" (Gen. 33:1):

B.   Said R. Levi, "The lion got mad at the cattle and
the wild beasts of the world. They got together and said,
'Who will go and conciliate him?'

C.   "The fox said, 'I know three hundred parables, so I
shall go and conciliate him.'

D.   "They said, 'Well and good.'

E.   "He went a little way and stopped. They said to
him, 'Why are you stopping?'

F.   "He said to them, 'I forgot a hundred.'

G.   "They said to him, 'There are enough in two hundred to gain a blessing.'

H.   "He went a little way and stopped. They said to
him, 'Why are you stopping?'

I.   "He said to them, 'I forgot a hundred.'

J.   "They said to him, 'There are enough in one hundred to gain a blessing.'

K.   "Once they got to the lion, he said, 'I forgot them
all. So it's everyone for himself—each one had better conciliate the lion on his own.'

L.   "So was the case with Jacob."

2.A.   R. Judah bar Simon said, "[Jacob said,] 'I have
enough power to set forth prayer.' "

B.   R. Levi said, "[Jacob said,] 'I have enough power to
wage war.' "

C.   "But when he got there: 'he divided the children
among Leah and Rachel and the two maids.'

D.   "He said, 'Let the merit of each one sustain him.' "

LXXVIII:VIII.2.A.   "He himself went on before them":

282

B. "Just as a father has compassion upon his children" (Ps. 103:13):

C. R. Hiyya repeated on Tannaite authority: 'Just as the most compassionate of the fathers . . . .'

D. Who is that?

E. R. Judah bar Simon said, "It is Abraham: 'Far be it from you to do in such a manner' (Gen. 18:25).

F. R. Levi said, "It was Jacob: 'He himself went on before them'. He said, 'It is better that he lay hands on me and not on them.' "

4.A. ". . . bowing himself to the ground seven times, until he came near to his brother" (Gen. 33:3): Why seven times?

B. He said to him, "Regard yourself as if you are seated in an inner chamber, behind seven gratings, and in session and giving judgment, and I am subject to judgment before you, so be filled with mercy for me."

C. Said R. Hinena bar Isaac, "He did not stop prostrating himself and going along, then prostrating himself and moving along, until the attribute of divine justice gave way to the attribute of divine mercy [since these acts of bowing himself to the ground were addressed to God and not to Esau]."

Jacob is like the fox, who made his wives and children fend for themselves. In the first paragraph, no. 1 tells a wry parable to point out that, in the end, Jacob just walked along by himself, no longer accompanying the others in the encounter with Esau. No. 2 makes the same point, but in a way more honorable to Jacob. Now he maintains that he could overcome Esau on the basis of his own merit, but the merit of each of his household also will suffice. The joining of the two distinct statements seems to me a rather odd gesture on the part of the compositors.

In the second paragraph, no. 3 and no. 4 take up the matter of the prostrations. Both sets underline that Jacob did not humiliate himself before Esau or show himself obsequious. So the exegetical compositors once more revise the narrator's picture of Jacob.

Israel's Claim to the Land

Once more we revert to that obsession of our sages, the right of Israel to the land of Israel. The obsession bears remarkable relevance to our own day. Though tied to the land of Israel for the whole of its history, the Jewish people through much of its history has had to reestablish its claim and its right to what has always been Israel's and has never been relinquished by Israel. So our sages' return to this point testifies to a permanent and regrettable fact of Israel's life.

> *LXXIX:VII.1.A.* "And from the sons of Hamor, Shechem's father, he bought for a hundred pieces of money the piece of land on which he had pitched his tent. There he erected an altar and called it El-Elohe-Israel" (Gen. 33:19–20):
>
> *B.* Said R. Yudan bar Simon, "This is one of three passages on the basis of which the nations of the world cannot ridicule Israel, saying, 'You have stolen property.'
>
> *C.* "They are, first, the cave at Machpelah, second, the site of the temple, and third, the sepulcher of Joseph.
>
> *D.* "The cave at Machpelah: 'And Abraham weighed to Ephron the silver' (Gen. 23:16).
>
> *E.* ". . . second, the site of the temple: 'So David gave to Ornan for the place six hundred shekels of gold' (1 Chr. 21:25).
>
> *F.* ". . . and third, the sepulcher of Joseph: 'he bought for a hundred pieces of money the piece of land on which he had pitched his tent.' "

The Israelites had purchased the land on fair terms and have not stolen it. The Roman Christian presence in the land, the naming of places as holy because of events depicted in the New Testament in those places—these called into question in a sharp and religious way Israel's claim to the land. In Constantine's time, he and his mother had built churches all over the country, commemorating holy events in the life of Jesus. In the present day Christians began to make pilgrimages to the land. So the conflicting claims to the status of Israel involved, also, debate over who possesses the land of Israel, and the answer, given here, is that the children of Abraham, David, and Joseph possess the land.

Jacob Bore Responsibility for the Rape of Dinah

Jacob shows us how to act, but, as we have seen several times, also how not to act. In the present instance Jacob trusted in his own righteousness. God then showed him what that would avail. Jacob should have preserved modesty about his achievements. Instead he boasted, using language not appropriate to a man of faith. The result? A family calamity.

LXXX:IV.1.A. R. Judah bar Simon opened by citing this verse: " 'Do not boast about tomorrow' (Prov. 27:1). But you, Jacob, said 'So shall my righteousness bear witness for me tomorrow' (Gen. 30:33). [This expression of overconfidnece produced a dismal result.]

B. "Tomorrow your daughter will go out and get raped: 'Now Dinah went out' (Gen. 34:1)."

2.A. R. Huna in the name of R. Abba, the priest, of Bardelayya: "The Holy One, blessed be he, said to him, 'To him who is ready to faint, kindness is due from his neighbor' (Job 6:14).

B. "You have withheld kindness from your neighbor. When you gave her to Job in marriage, you did not convert him.

C. "And you did not seek to marry her off to someone who was circumcised [Esau]. Lo she will be married to an uncircumcised person.

D. " 'And you did not seek to have her married off in the acceptable way, so she will be taken in marriage in a forbidden way [merely through an act of sexual relations, not through the appropriate documentation].'

E. "That is in line with this verse: 'And Dinah went out' (Gen. 34:1)."

3.A. R. Simeon b. Laqish commenced discourse by citing this verse: "There he erected an altar and called it El-Elohe-Israel" (Gen. 33:20):

B. "He said to him, 'You are the God among those above, and I am the god among those below.' "

C. R. Huna in the name of R. Simeon b. Laqish: "[God said to him] 'Even the president of the community will not arrogate to himself that sort of authority, and yet do you take that sort of authority for yourself? Tomorrow your daughter will go out and get herself raped.'

D. "That is in line with this verse: 'Now Dinah, the daughter of Leah, whom she had borne to Jacob, went out' (Gen. 34:1)."

No. 1 places Jacob squarely into the scene. He was excessively confident and the rest followed. No. 2 blames Jacob in yet another way. No. 3 makes the same point a third time. Jacob expressed the wrong attitude and quickly found himself rebuked.

God's Love for Israel, Hamor's Lust for Dinah

To our sages God loves Israel. Since we are in God's image, our sages ask whether God's love compares to our love. What is the difference, they wonder, between love when God feels it and love when we do? This is the question they now answer, in an unusually profound reflection on the contrast between sacred, divine love and human desire and lust. The correspondence between human emotions and God's feelings forms one point of explaining how humanity is in God's image and after God's likeness.

LXXX:VII.1.A. "But Hamor spoke with them, saying ['The soul of my son Shechem longs for your daughter; I pray you give her to him in marriage. Make marriages with us; give your daughters to us, and take our daughters for yourselves. You shall dwell with us; and the land shall be open to you; dwell and trade in it; and get property in it']" (Gen. 34:8–10):

B. Said R. Simeon b. Laqish, "There are three expressions of love that the Holy One, blessed be he, used to express his affection for Israel: cleaving, loving, delighting in [and these expressions occur in three distinct verses]:

C. ". . . cleaving: 'But you who cleaved to the Lord your God' (Deut. 4:4).

D. ". . . loving: 'The Lord did not set his love upon you . . . because you were more in number than any people' (Deut. 7:7).

E. ". . . delighting in: 'And all nations shall call you happy, for you are a delightful land' (Mal. 3:12).

F. "But in the passage at hand, concerning a wicked person, we are able to denote them from verses of scripture:

G. ". . . cleaving: 'And his soul cleaved' (Gen. 34:4).

H. ". . . loving: 'The soul of my son Shechem loves for your daughter' (Gen. 34:8).

I. ". . . delighting in: 'Because he had delight in Jacob's daughter' (Gen. 34:19)."

J. R. Abba b. Elishib adds yet two more, "Love and speech."

K. "Love: 'I have loved you' (Mal. 1:2).

L. ". . . and speech: 'Speak to the heart of Jerusalem' (Is. 40:12).

M. "But in the passage at hand, concerning a wicked person, we derive all of them:

N. "Love: 'And he loved the girl' (Gen. 34:3).

O. "Speech: 'And he spoke to the heart of the girl' (Gen. 34:3)."

Specifically, the compositor wishes to contrast the love of a carnal nature, at which the nations are adept, with love of a supernatural character, which God bestows upon Israel. So the story at hand serves a much more profound purpose of supplying an analogy by means of contrast between God's love for Israel and Shechem's love of Dinah. It is a stunning and daring contrast—yet commonplace.

Jacob had Neglected his Vow

Jacob once more presents us with a negative lesson. When he left the land, he had promised that if he returned safely, he would build an altar to God. This vow he did not keep. What sages do is pick up the strands of the narrative and read them as a sequence of events. They further compare what is said at one point with what is done at another. This leads them to notice that Jacob had failed to carry out his vow.

LXXXI:1.1.A. "God said to Jacob, 'Arise, go up [to Bethel and dwell there, and make there an altar to the God who appeared to you when you fled from your brother Esau']" (Gen. 25:1):

B. "It is a snare to a man to eat consecrated food, and after vows to make examination" (Prov. 20:25).

C. "May a curse come upon someone who eats holy things in his throat" [Freedman, p. 745, n. 1: connecting the word for "snare" to the word for "to your throat" in Prov. 23:2].

D. R. Hiyya taught on Tannaite authority, "May a curse come on someone who derives secular benefit from holy things.

E. "And holy things refers only to Israel: 'Israel is holy to the Lord' (Jer. 2:3)."

F. ". . . and after vows to make examination" (Prov. 20:25):

G. Said R. Yannai, "If a man postpones carrying out a vow that he has made, the ledger that pertains to him is examined [in heaven]."

H. R. Hiyya bar Luliani said, "He requires flogging, in line with this verse: 'She shall be flogged' (Lev. 19:20). [The word for 'flogging' uses the consonants that can be read as 'to make examination.']

I. "You may know that that is the case, for our father Jacob, because he postponed carrying out his vow, found that the ledger pertaining to him was examined.

J. "God said to Jacob, 'Arise, go up to Bethel and dwell there, and make there an altar to the God who appeared to you when you fled from your brother Esau' (Gen. 25:1)."

The main point is that Jacob had long ago made a vow, which he had not yet carried out, and now it was time for him to do so. The narrative thus goes back to Gen. 28:20ff. and rejoins the threads of the story. Jacob was punished for not having carried out the vow right away, hence the story of Dinah.

Rachel Weeps for Israel

Rachel, mother of Israel, first love of Jacob, died, and Israel mourned for her. But Rachel in her day would mourn for Israel too—and will rejoice with Israel in the age of salvation.

LXXXII:X.1.A. "So Rachel died and she was buried on the way to Ephrath [that is, Bethlehem, and Jacob set up a pillar upon her grave; it is the pillar of Rachel's tomb, which is there to this day. Israel journeyed on and pitched his tent beyond the tower of Eder]" (Gen. 35:16–21):

B. Why did Jacob bury Rachel on the way to Ephrath?

C. Jacob foresaw that the exiles would pass by there [en route to Babylonia].

D. Therefore he buried her there, so that she should seek mercy for them: "A voice is heard in Ramah . . . Rachel weeping for her children. . . Thus says the Lord, 'Keep your voice from weeping . . . and there is hope for your future' (Jer. 31:15–16)."

The deeds of the patriarchs aim at the needs of Israel later on. The link between the lives of the patriarchs and the history of Israel forms a major theme in the exegetical repertoire before us.

Before a King Ruled in Israel

When scripture says that such and so happened "before a king ruled in Israel," modern scholars reasonably posit that that sentence was written after kings ruled in Israel. Hence, it must follow, that story derives not from the time of Moses—when there were no kings in Israel—but from the period after Saul and David had founded the monarchy. But that is not how our sages understand matters. Reading the same scriptures as do biblical scholars, they address their own concerns to the verse at hand. Not surprisingly, that point of anguish concerns Edom, who is Rome (as much as Esau is Rome). Then the fact that Edom/Rome had kings before Israel did produces a lesson bearing considerable comfort to Israel in time to come.

LXXXIII:II.1.A. "These are the kings who reigned in the land of Edom before any king reigned over the Israelites: Bela the son of Beor reigned in Edom, the name of his city being Dinhabah" (Gen. 36:31–32):

B. Said R. Aibu, "Before a king arose in Israel, kings existed in Edom: 'These are the kings who reigned in the land of Edom before any king reigned over the Israelites.' " [Freedman: "1 Kgs. 22:48 states, 'There was no king in Edom, a deputy was king.' This refers to the reign of Jehoshaphat. Subsequently in Jehoram's reign, Edom revolted and 'made a king over themselves' (2 Kgs. 8:20). Thus— Freedman explains—from Saul to Jehoshaphat, in which Israel had eight kings, Edom had no king but was ruled by a governor of Judah. Aibu observes that this was to balance the present period, during which Edom had eight kings while Israel had none. For that reason, Aibu employs the word for deputy when he wishes to say 'existed' thus indicating a reference to the verse in the book of Kings quoted above."]

C. R. Yose bar Haninah said, "[Alluding to a mnemonic, with the first Hebrew letter for the word for kings, judges, chiefs, and princes:] When the one party [Edom] was ruled by kings, the other party [Israel] was ruled by judges, when one side was ruled by chiefs, the other side was ruled by princes."

D. Said R. Joshua b. Levi, "This one set up eight kings and that one set up eight kings. This one set up Bela, Jobab, Husham, Samlah, Shaul, Hadad, Baalhanan, and Hadar. The other side set up Saul, Ishbosheth, David Solomon, Rehoboam, Abijah, Asa, and Jehoshaphat.

E. "Then Nebuchadnezzar came and overturned both [the Edomites and the Jews]: 'That made the world as a wilderness and destroyed the cities thereof' (Is. 14:17).

F. "Evil-merodach came and exalted Jehoiakin, Ahasuerus came and exalted Haman."

The passage once more stresses the correspondence between Israel's and Edom's governments, respectively. The reciprocal character of their histories is then stated in a powerful way, with the further implication that, when the one rules, the other waits. So now Israel waits, but it will rule. The simplest and least interesting fact of scripture, a rather pointless genealogy, turns out to contain a lesson of hope for Israel.

Part Nine

VAYESHEB:
Genesis Rabbah
Parashiyyot
LXXXIV–LXXXVIII

Jacob Should Have Enjoyed a Secure Old Age, Because He Trusted in God, but He Did Not, Because of the Troubles of Joseph

Just as we took stock in the life of Abraham, so, as we move into the tale of Joseph, we look back on the life of Jacob. Now he has reached old age. His favorite wife has died. His sons are growing up. He has wealth and influence. He should look forward to a long period of aging, enjoying the perspective of time and the satisfaction of achievement. But, in his long troubled life, the worst is yet to come. Having trusted in God, Jacob now undergoes new trials.

LXXXIV:I.1.A. "Jacob dwelt in the land of his father's sojournings, in the land of Canaan" (Gen. 37:1):

B. "When you cry, let those whom you have gathered deliver you. [The wind shall carry them all away, a breath shall bear them off. But he who takes refuge in me shall possess the land and shall inherit my holy mountain]." (Is. 57:13).

C. It has been taught on Tannaite authority: His gathering and the gathering of his sons saved him from the power of Esau.

D. "But the wind shall carry them all away, a breath shall bear them off:" this refers to Esau.

E. "But he who takes refuge in me shall possess the land and shall inherit my holy mountain:" this speaks of Jacob.

F. "Jacob dwelt in the land of his father's sojournings, in the land of Canaan" (Gen. 37:1).

LXXXIV:II.1.A. "The wicked flee when no one pursues, but the righteous are secure as a young lion" (Prov. 28:1).

B. The evil one runs away when there are no pursuers.

C. "And Esau went into a land because of his brother Jacob" (Gen. 36:1):

D. R. Eleazar, "It was because of a bond [that he owed to him]."

E. R. Joshua b. Levi said, "It was because of shame."

F. ". . . but the righteous are secure as a young lion":

G. "Jacob dwelt in the land of his father's sojournings, in the land of Canaan" (Gen. 37:1).

LXXXIV:III.1.A. "If the scourge slay suddenly, he will mock the calamity of the guiltless" (Job 9:23):

B. Antoninus asked our master, "What is the meaning of the verse, 'If the scourge slay suddenly . . .'?"

C. He said to him, "Decree that someone should have a hundred lashes, and they will be laid on him. But give orders that a hundred denars should be given to so and so, and what will happen? This one takes a piece, and that one takes a piece, and the one [you had in mind] will get nothing. [That is the sense of the passage:] 'he will mock the calamity of the guiltless.' [Those who in fact are guiltless and are assigned an advantage gain nothing. In a moment we shall see how Jacob's story illustrates that fact.]"

2.A. Said R. Aha, "When the righteous seek to dwell in peace in this world, Satan comes and opposes them, saying, 'It is not enough for them that so much is prepared for them in the coming age, that they want to live in peace in this world!'

B. "You may know that that is the case, for our father, Jacob, because he wanted to live in peace in this world, encountered the Satan assigned to Joseph: 'Jacob dwelt in the land of his father's sojournings, in the land of Canaan.' " [Jacob wanted to enjoy this world and the world to come, so the Satan who was assigned to dog Joseph's steps came and made trouble for Jacob as well. This shows that Israel should enjoy the world to come and accept its suffering in this world.]

3.A. "I was not at ease, neither was I quiet, and trouble came" (Job 3:26).

B. "I was not at ease": on account of Esau.

C. ". . . neither was I quiet": on account of Laban.

D. "and trouble came": on account of Joseph.

E. "Jacob dwelt in the land of his father's sojournings, in the land of Canaan."

In paragraph one, we reflect on Jacob and Esau. The fact that Esau took his leave from Jacob yields the intersecting verse's point, which is that Jacob dwelled securely and possessed the land because he trusted in God. We now expand upon that same point. Israel should not expect so much in this world. In the second paragraph, the point is the same as before. Jacob trusted in God so he lived securely. But Esau ran away when no one was pursuing him, surely not "because of Jacob." The third and final paragraph is the key to our sages' reflection on the life of Jacob. The composite seems to me to center on no. 2, which forms the pivot between no. 1, a general statement, and no. 3, an explicit application to the situation of Jacob. The main point is the reference of the intersecting verse to "the calamity of the guiltless." Once that forms the center, then the issue of Jacob's hope to dwell peacefully serves to illustrate the point that the guiltless often suffer. This is made explicit at no. 2, and then, as I said, no. 3 articulates the same point in concrete detail. Jacob should now have enjoyed security, but instead he confronted the troubles involved in Joseph's life. The application of our sages' comment to Israel's life later on hardly requires explication. Jacob did not, and Israel does not, always get what is coming. But trusting in God, Israel in the end will come through.

Joseph was the True Continuator of Jacob

The strength of our sages' reading of scripture lies in their capacity to see the whole in the parts. Modern biblical criticism accomplishes the equally striking work of analysis, showing the parts of which the whole is made up. In what follows sages expose the threads that unite discrete sections into a single, cogent statement.

LXXXIV:V.1.A. What comes prior to this statement?
[That is to say, can we see a relationship between the story at
hand and the one that has just concluded?] "And these are the
kings that reigned in the land of Edom" (Gen. 36:31), then
"Jacob dwelt in the land of his father's sojournings, in the
land of Canaan."

B. Said R. Hunia, "The man may be compared to the
case of someone who was walking along the way, and he saw a
pack of dogs and was afraid of them, so he sat down right in
the middle of the pack. So, since Jacob saw Esau and his commanders, he was afraid of them and settled right among them."

C. Said R. Levi, "The matter may be compared to the
case of a blacksmith whose shop was open into the middle of
the way, and his son, a goldsmith, had a shop open opposite
him. He once noted that large supplies of thorns were brought
to town. He said, 'Woe for the town, what is coming into it.'

D. "A smart fellow said to him, 'Are you afraid of
these? A single spark from your [forge] and one from your
son's and the two of you will burn up the thorns.'

E. "So too, when Jacob saw Esau and his commanders,
he was afraid. Said to him the Holy One, blessed be he, 'Are
you afraid of these? A single spark from your [forge] and one
from your son's and the two of you will burn them up.'

F. " 'And the house of Jacob shall be a fire, and the
house of Joseph a flame, and the house of Esau stubble, and
they shall burn them up' (Ob. 1:18)."

2.A. "These are the generations of the family of Jacob.
Joseph [being seventeen years old, was shepherding the flock
with his brothers]" (Gen. 37:2):

B. These generations came along only on account of the
merit of Joseph.

C. Did Jacob go to Laban for any reason other than for
Rachel?

D. These generations thus waited until Joseph was
born, in line with this verse: "And when Rachel had borne
Joseph, Jacob said to Laban, 'Send me away' " (Gen. 30:215).

E. Who brought them down to Egypt? It was Joseph.

F. Who supported them in Egypt? It was Joseph.

G. The reed sea split open only on account of the merit of Joseph: "The waters saw you, O God" (Ps. 77:17). "You have with your arm redeemed your people, the sons of Jacob and Joseph" (Ps. 77:16).

H. R. Yudan said, "Also the Jordan was divided only on account of the merit of Joseph." [The merit of Joseph in honoring his father and sustaining his people is what produced the splitting of the Jordan when the Israelites returned to the land.]

LXXXIV:VI.1.A "These are the generations of the family of Jacob. Joseph [being seventeen years sold, was shepherding the flock with his brothers]" (Gen. 37:2):

B. Said R. Samuel bar Nahman, "Surely scripture should say, 'These are the generations of the family of Jacob: Reuben . . .'!

C. "But the sense is this: Just as Jacob was born circumcised, so was Joseph born circumcised.

D. "Just as the mother of this one had been barren, so the mother of that one had been barren.

E. "Just as this one had given travail to his mother when he was born, so that one had given travail to his mother when he was born.

F. "Just as this one's mother had produced two sons, so that one's mother had produced two sons.

G. "Just as the brother of this one hated him, so the brothers of that one hated him.

H. "Just as the brother of this one tried to kill him, so the brothers of that one tried to kill him.

I. "This one was a shepherd and that one was a shepherd.

J. "This one was subjected to Satan's power and that one was subjected to Satan's power.

K. "This one was stolen two times, and that one was stolen two times.

L. "This one was blessed with riches, and that one was blessed with riches.

M. "This one went outside the land, and that one went outside the land.

N. "This one married a woman outside the land, and that one married a woman outside the land.

O. "This one produced children outside the land, and that one produced children outside the land.

P. "Angles accompanied this one, and angels accompanied that one.

Q. "This one was exalted through a dream, and that one was exalted through a dream.

R. "On account of this one was blessed the household of his father-in-law, and on account of that one was blessed the household of his father-in-law.

S. "This one went down to Egypt, and that one went down to Egypt.

T. "This one brought famine to an end, and that one brought famine to an end.

U. "This one imposed an oath [on his children] and that one imposed an oath [on his brothers].

V. "This one gave orders, and that one gave orders.

W. "This one died in Egypt, and that one died in Egypt.

X. "This one was embalmed, and that one was embalmed.

Y. "This one's bones came up from Egypt, and that one's bones came up from Egypt."

In the opening paragraph, the main point of no. 1 comes in Hunia's parable, which explains how Jacob could live near Esau. Levi's statement then explains why Jacob should not be afraid. No. 2 moves on to the next verse and asks why only Joseph is mentioned as the family of Jacob. The inner polemic is that the merit of Jacob and Joseph would more than suffice to overcome Esau/Rome. The second paragraph, providing the prologue to the Joseph story, draws the detailed parallels between Joseph's and Jacob's lives.

Joseph Brought Trouble on Himself by Being a Common Gossip

Guardians of the community, our sages saw inner dangers as well as threats from outside. Esau was not Jacob's only enemy.

Joseph also brought trouble on Israel. This he did by committing the sin our sages feared most beyond the mortal ones. And
that is the sin of common gossip. They find in Joseph's story an
example of how common gossip—speaking ill of others without
cause or reason—destroyed the family of Jacob, the community
of Israel.

LXXXIV:VII.1.A: "Joseph, being seventeen years old,
was shepherding the flock with his brothers; he was a lad [the
Hebrew word can also mean a fool] [and used to accompany
the sons of Bilhah and Zilpah, his father's wives, and Joseph
brought an ill report of them to their father]" (Gen. 37:2):

B. He was seventeen years old and you say that he was
a lad?

C. But he did childish deeds, decorating his eyes, curl-
ing his hair, and prancing along on his heels.

2.A. ". . . and Joseph brought an ill report of them to
their father":

B. R. Meir says, "Your sons are suspect of eating limbs
cut from living beasts."

C. R. Judah says, "They insult the sons of the handmaidens and they call them slaves."

D. R. Simeon says, "They stare at the daughters of the
land."

E. R. Judah bar Simon said, "In all three cases: 'A just
balance and scale are the Lord's' (Prov. 16:11). Said the Holy
One, blessed be he, to him, 'You have said, "Your sons are
suspect of eating limbs cut from living beasts." ' By your life,
even when they are engaged in doing the dastardly deed, they
nonetheless will perform the correct mode of slaughter. 'And
they ritually slaughtered a he-goat' (Gen. 37:31). [So you are
proved a liar.]

F. "[God continues] 'You have said, "They insult the
sons of the handmaidens and they call them slaves." ' Joseph
was sold as a slave (Ps. 105:17).

G. "[God continues] 'You have said, "They stare at the
daughters of the land." I will sick a bear on you.' 'His master's wife cast her eye upon Joseph' (Gen. 39:7)." [Joseph is

punished for his gossiping against his brothers, and the wife of Potiphar, the Egyptian, who lusted after him, would form his trial for what he said about his brothers.]

LXXXVII.III.2.A. What is written just prior to the passage at hand? "Now Joseph was handsome and good looking" (Gen. 39:6). Then: "And after a time his master's wife cast her eyes upon Joseph" (Gen. 39:7).

B. The matter may be compared to the case of a man who was sitting in the marketplace and penciling his eyes, fixing his hair, and prancing about. He said, "I am a real man."

C. They said to him, "If you are a real man, lo, there is a she-bear before you. Attack it."

The powerful comment of the first of the two paragraphs implicitly draws a link between Joseph's accusations against his brothers and things that actually happened to him. In this way the lesson of Joseph's life, that he brought on himself much that happened to him through his serving as a common gossip, is spelled out. A subterranean motif is the claim that whatever happened to Joseph was just and not capricious. God set a heavy hand over Joseph's life and intervened time and again, but always with good reason. The judge of all the world does justice all the time—if, at times, that fact becomes clear only under the aspect of eternity.

Judah/Tamar and the Redemption of Israel

The story of Judah and Tamar intervenes in the Joseph story. But, our sages maintain, it belongs there. The way in which they account for the story and its lesson yields their explanation, also, of the place of the tale in the larger narrative. The problem is not one of a literary character. It is an issue of religious interpretation of events, hence of explaining the sequence. Before suffering, redemption already is prepared. Before Israel sinks down to slavery in Egypt, the redeemer is born.

LXXXV:I.1.A. "It happened at that time that Judah went down from his brothers [and turned in to a certain Adullamite, whose name was Hirah. There Judah saw the daughter of a certain Canaanite, whose name was Shua; he married her and went in to her]" (Gen. 38:1):

B. "Judah has done treacherously [and an abomination is committed in Israel . . . for Judah has profaned the holiness of the Lord which he loves and has married the daughter of a strange god]" (Mal. 2:11).

C. [God] said to [Judah], "You have denied, Judah, you have lied, Judah."

D. ". . . and an abomination is committed in Israel . . . for Judah has profaned," which is to say, Judah has become unconsecrated.

E. ". . . the holiness of the Lord which he loves and has married a gentile [lit.: the daughter of a strange god]."

F. "It happened at that time that Judah went down from his brothers [and turned in to a certain Adullamite, whose name was Hirah. There Judah saw the daughter of a certain Canaanite, whose name was Shua; he married her and went in to her]."

2.A. "I will yet bring to you, O inhabitant of Mareshah, him who shall possess you, the glory of Israel shall come even to Adullam" (Mic. 1:15).

B. The reference is to the Holy One of Israel.

C. ". . . to Adullam shall come" the king of Israel.

D. "To Adullam he shall come:" "It happened at that time that Judah went down from his brothers and turned in to a certain Adullamite, whose name was Hirah. There Judah saw the daughter of a certain Canaanite, whose name was Shua; he married her and went in to her."

3.A. R. Samuel bar Nahman commenced discourse by citing this verse: " 'For I know the thoughts that I think toward you, says the Lord' (Jer. 29:11).

B. "While the fathers of the tribes were taken up with the sale of Joseph, Jacob was taken up with his sackcloth and fasting, and Judah was taken up with finding himself a wife, and the Holy One, blessed be he, was creating the light of the king Messiah.

C. "It happened at that time that Judah went down from his brothers [and turned in to a certain Adullamite,

303

whose name was Hirah. There Judah saw the daughter of a certain Canaanite, whose name was Shua; he married her and went in to her]."

4.A. "Before she travailed she brought forth" (Is. 66:7):

B. Before the final persecutor was born, the first redeemer was born:

C. "It happened at that time that Judah went down from his brothers [and turned in to a certain Adullamite, whose name was Hirah. There Judah saw the daughter of a certain Canaanite, whose name was Shua; he married her and went in to her]."

The interest of the exegete, no. 1, in the statement that Judah went down from his brothers, becoming less than they, is that he did so by marrying a Canaanite woman. No. 2 then follows up with attention to the place mentioned in the base verse. No. 3 draws the ironic contrasts among the activities of the heroes of the narrative. The messianic theme derives from the fact that the offspring of Judah and Tamar would be the Messiah. No. 4 goes over the same ground. Obviously, the linkage of the lives of the patriarchs to the history of Israel accounts for the point of special interest to the exegete. In some ways we have the equivalent of an operatic quartet, in which each character sings about a single strand of the drama, and in which all the strands form a whole greater than the sum of the parts. The messianic theme will now infuse all to follow, with contrasts and comparisons outlining the tragedy and the triumph of Israel.

Why God Favored Joseph in Particular

With Joseph in Egypt, the narrative dwells on the divine plan that works itself out in Joseph's life. Why Joseph in particular? That question demands an answer, as much as the question of why Israel in particular must atone through suffering for sin requires an explanation.

LXXXVI:IV.1.A. "The Lord was with Joseph [and he became a successful man; and he was in the house of his master, the Egyptian, and his master saw that the Lord was with him, and that the Lord caused all that he did to prosper in his hands]" (Gen. 39:2–3):

B. Was God with Joseph and not with the other tribal ancestors?

C. Said R. Yudan, "The matter may be compared to the case of a cowboy who had twelve cows carrying wine in the drove before him. One of the cows went into a gentile's store. The cowboy left the eleven cows and followed this one to retrieve it. People said to him, 'Why are you leaving the eleven and following this one?'

D. "He said to them, 'These are in the public domain, so I am not concerned that someone may touch the wine and turn it into prohibited wine [in the status of wine having been handled by a gentile and therefore assumed to have been used for a libation to an idol]. But as to this one, which has gone into a gentile's store, I am concerned that the gentile not touch the wine and turn it into libation wine.'

E. "So these are adults and they are in the domain of their father, but this one [Joseph] is the child and he is on his own. Therefore: 'The Lord was with Joseph [in particular].' "

2.A. ". . . and he became a successful man":

B. R. Berekhiah said, "[The word for prosperous uses the letters that occur in the word "rush," thus:] he was a man who rushed [away from sin], as in this verse: 'And they rushed into the Jordan before the king' (2 Sam. 19:18).

C. "The matter may be compared to the case of a she-bear who was standing in the marketplace, all adorned in precious stones and pearls. They said, 'Whoever rushes the bear can grab what she is wearing.'

D. "There was a certain smart fellow there, who said to them, 'You are looking at what is on her, but I am looking at [that which is in her mouth, namely,] her fangs.' "

E. Said R. Berekhiah, "[Freedman:] From that very she-bear he fled, and can there be a greater flight than this!"

No. 1 explains the emphatic statement that God was with Joseph in particular. No. 2 explains the sense of the word "prosperous," now joining the sense of the word to a judgment about Joseph's wisdom in avoiding the master's wife. Hence the threads of the tale are tightened. But only in a little while shall we see the full tale.

Joseph was Responsible for his own Situation. He Brought it on Himself

Once more we return to the main point of the Joseph story as our sages mediate it. Whatever happened to Joseph paid him back for what he had done, whether good or ill. Now we address the crisis of the encounter with the wife of his master: Why this particular form of trial?

LXXXVII:I.1.A. "And it came to pass after these things [that his master's wife cast her eyes upon Joseph and said, 'Lie with me.' But he refused and said to his master's wife, 'Lo, having me my master has no concern about anything in the house, and he has put everything that he has in my hand; he is not greater in this house than I am, nor has he kept back anything from me except yourself, because you are his wife; How then can I do this great wickedness and sin against God?']" (Gen. 39:7–9):

B. ["For at the window of my house I have looked out through my lattice, and I have seen among the simple, I have perceived among the youths, a young man without sense, passing along the street near her corner, taking the road to her house in the twilight, in the evening, in the time of night and darkness. And lo, a woman meets him, dressed as a harlot, wily of heart, she is loud and wayward, her feet do not stay at home, now in the street, now in the market, and at every corner she lies in wait. She seizes him and kisses him and with impudent face she says to him, 'I have to offer sacrifices, and today I have paid my vows; so now I have come out to meet you, to seek you eagerly and I have found you. I have decked my couch with coverings, colored spreads of Egyptian linen; I have perfumed my bed with myrrh, aloes, and cinnamon. Come let us take our fill of love till morning, let us delight ourselves with love. For my husband is not at home, he has gone on a long journey; he took a bag of money with him; at full moon he will come home' " (Prov. 7:6–20)]: "I have seen among the simple:" this refers to the tribal ancestors.

C. Said R. Levi, "In Arabia they call a youngster [by the same word as means 'the simple' in the cited verse]."

D. "I have perceived among the youths, a young man without sense": this refers to Joseph.

E. ". . . without sense": for he repeated gossip about his brothers.

F. Is there any greater senselessness than that?

G. "And lo, a woman meets him": this refers to the wife of Potiphar.

H. ". . . dressed as a harlot": for Joseph.

I. ". . . wily of heart": for her husband.

J. ". . . she is loud and wayward, her": she goes about crying.

K. ". . . her feet do not stay at home": but:

L. "now in the street, now in the market, and at every corner she lies in wait": asking people, "Have you seen Joseph?"

M. ". . . She seizes him and kisses him": "She caught him by his garment" (Gen. 39:11).

N. ". . . and with impudent face she says to him": "Come, lie with me" (Gen. 39:7).

O. "And it came to pass after these things [that his master's wife cast her eyes upon Joseph and said, 'Lie with me.' "]

The intersecting verse surely provides an ideal way of dealing with the base verse, since the components of the intersecting verse are readily joined to those of the base verse. The relevance is direct, the points of parallel apt. I see no way in which the intersecting verse clarifies a point relevant to the base verse, but the net effect is to underline the situation confronting Joseph. It is of his own doing. God's justice is exact—the main point the exegete wishes to underline in the Joseph story.

Why Joseph Resisted his Master's Wife

Joseph made himself important in his own eyes, so his brothers' envy led to his downfall. Had he learned his lesson? Sages, explaining why he was thrown into prison, construct a conversation to show he had not yet learned his lesson. Quite to the contrary, he continued in an arrogant way to overvalue himself and to regard himself as the center of things. So even at the crisis with the master's wife, he managed to do the right thing for the wrong reason.

LXXXVII:V.1.A. "But he refused [and said to his master's wife, 'Lo, having me, my master has no concern about anything in the house, and he has put everything that he has in my hand; he is not greater in this house than I am, nor has he kept back anything from me except yourself, because you are his wife; How then can I do this great wickedness and sin against God?']" (Gen. 39:7–9):

B. Judah son of Rabbi said, "If one exercises the right of refusal in a marriage that is based on right action, should one not also exercise the right of refusal in the case of a matter involving a sin?

C. "One exercises the right of refusal in a marriage that is based on right action: 'If her father utterly refuse to give her to him' (Ex. 22:16).

D. "Should one not also exercise the right of refusal in the case of a matter involving a sin?

E. "In a matter of carrying out a religious duty, one exercises the right of refusal: 'My husband's brother refuses . . .' (Deut. 25:7).

F. "Should one not also exercise the right of refusal in the case of a matter involving a sin [as Judah just said, B]? 'But he refused.' "

2.A. ". . . and said to his master's wife":

B. He said to her, "It is the custom of the Holy One, blessed be he, to choose the most precious of the house of my father to serve as a burnt offering.

C. "In the case of Abraham: 'Take your son.' Should I then listen to you? But perhaps I have been chosen to serve as a burnt offering, and through you I may be rendered unfit to serve as an offering."

3.A.   ". . . and said to his master's wife":

B.   He said to her, "It is the custom of the Holy One, blessed be he, to appear by night to the most precious of the house of my father.

C.   "As to Abraham: 'The word of the Lord came to Abram in a vision' (Gen. 15:1).

D.   "As to Isaac: 'And the Lord appeared to him' (Gen. 26:24).

E.   "As to Jacob: 'He dreamed, and lo, a ladder' (Gen. 28:12).

F.   "Should I listen to you? Then perhaps the Holy One, blessed be he, will appear to me, and he will find me unclean."

4.A.   "Lo . . . my master":

B.   He said to her, "I am afraid of 'behold, the man has become' (Gen. 3:22). [Freedman, p. 800, n. 2: "afraid of the punishment which overtook Adam for sin, that is, death and expulsion from paradise]."

C.   "The first man was driven out of the Garden of Eden on account of violating a religious duty of a minor order. On account of committing a most serious transgression [of having sexual relations with a married woman], all the more so [would I take an oath]!"

5.A.   "Lo . . . my master":

B.   "I am afraid on account of my father. Because Reuben had sexual relations with Bilhah, the birthright was taken from him and given to me. Should I then obey you and be driven from my birthright?"

6.A.   "Lo . . . my master":

B.   "I am afraid on account of my lord."

C.   She said, "I shall kill him."

D.   He said to her, "Is it not enough that I should be numbered in the company of adulterers, should I also be numbered in the company of murderers!"

E. "Yet if you still want it, 'Lo . . . my master.' There he is, standing right before you!"

F. Said R. Isaac, "The 'milk' of black goats and the milk of white goats are the same. [He can satisfy you as well as I can.]"

7.A. ["Lo . . . my master":] "I am afraid of the Holy One blessed be he."

B. She said to him, "But he is not around."

C. He said to her, "[Citing the verse of scripture, he answered her:] 'Great is the Lord, and much to be praised' (Ps. 48:2). [God will protect me from anything you try to do.]"

8.A. Said R. Abin, "She forced him from room to room and from chamber to chamber, until she got him into her bed. There was an idol incised above the bed, but she took a sheet and covered up its face.

B. "[Joseph said to her] 'The face of the idol you have covered up.' Concerning him about whom it is written, 'The eyes of the Lord that run to and fro through the whole earth' (Zech. 4:10), all the more so! [God will see no matter what you do.]"

9.A. ". . . he is not greater in this house than I am, nor has he kept back anything from me except yourself, because you are his wife; How then can I do this great wickedness and sin against God?" (Gen. 39:7–9):

B. R. Huna in the name of R. Idi: "Would something important have been left out of the verse, had the word 'against God' not been written? But 'against God' is written with letters that can be read. 'No! by God!' And that is the reply: 'By God! I shall not do this terrible thing.' "

The systematic exposition of the situation, the verses used, and the language of some of the verses vastly enrich the narrative. We start with a strikingly effective exercise on the word "refuse," in which exegetes give us two important examples in which it is a religious rite or duty to refuse, and then they contrast the exercise of refusal in the present case, a still more noble attainment. Nos. 2–7 bring us to the main point. They go through the list of those whom Joseph feared. The first two cover Joseph's own standing before God; he might have to serve as a burnt offering, he might receive a vision. In this way the narrative is tightened, with Joseph referring back to the religious experiences of his ancestors. But this reference also shows that Joseph remained important in his own eyes. Then comes the reference to Adam. The last three, nos. 5, 6, and 7, have Joseph express his fear of his father, master's wife, and God. It would be difficult to imagine a richer reading of the whole. No. 8 then provides Joseph with another argument, and no. 9 has him refuse in a most powerful oath. All this restates the story in line with its essentials, yet in a much deeper context than the narrative now enjoys. It would be difficult to point to a better example of the skills of both exegetes and authors of the individual passages and compositors of the whole.

In Prison Joseph Kept the Faith

How then did Joseph gain merit? It was through his steadfast faith, even in the face of threatened torture. Now the story in our sages' hands begins the shift to the redemption and true glory of Joseph. What he had demanded, he could not get for himself. What he in his misery could no longer imagine, he got. And all this why? Because of his trust in God.

LXXXVII:X.1.A. "But the Lord was with Joseph and showed him steadfast love and gave him favor in the sight of the keeper of the prison. [And the keeper of the prison committed to Joseph's care all the prisoners who were in the prison; and whatever was done there, he was the doer of it; the keeper of the prison paid no heed to anything that was in Joseph's care, because the Lord was with him; and whatever he did, the Lord made it prosper]" (Gen. 39:21–23):

B. R. Huna in the name of R. Hana: "His service pleased his master.

C. "When he would go out, Joseph would wash the dishes, lay out the tables, and make the beds. [But in trying to entice him, Potiphar's wife] said to him, 'In this matter I made your life miserable. By your life! I shall make your life miserable in other ways.'

D. "He would say to her, 'The Lord executes justice for the persecuted. [He gives bread to the hungry, the Lord looses those who are bound, the Lord raises up those who are bowed down, the Lord opens the eyes of the blind] (Ps. 146:7).' [We shall now see how, be his faith in God's justice and mercy as described in the verse of Psalms, Joseph found an answer to each of her threats.]

E. "She said to him, 'I shall have your rations cut in half.' He said to her, 'He gives bread to the hungry.'

F. "She said to him, 'I shall have you put in chains.' He said to her, '. . . the Lord looses those who are bound.'

G. "She said to him, 'I shall have you bowed down.' He said to her, '. . . the Lord raises up those who are bowed down.'

H. "She said to him, 'I shall have you blinded.' He said to her, '. . . the Lord opens the eyes of the blind.'"

I. To what extent [did she go]?

J. R. Huna in the name of R. Aha: "To such an extent that [Freedman:] she put an iron fork under his neck, so that he would have to cast his eyes on her.

K. "Even so, he would not look at her. That is in line with this verse: 'His feet they hurt with fetters, his person was laid in iron' (Ps. 105:18)."

2.A. ["'. . . the keeper of the prison paid no heed to anything that was in Joseph's care, because the Lord was with him; and whatever he did, the Lord made it prosper" (Gen. 39:22–23)]: "'. . . the keeper of the prison paid no heed to anything that was in Joseph's care, because the Lord was with him." Up to this point, we know that [the Lord was with him] in a time of distress.

B. How do we know that it was true, also, in a time of prosperity?

C. "'. . . and whatever he did, the Lord made it prosper."

No. 1 brings Potiphar's wife into the prison and sets the stage for no. 2. In prison Joseph kept the faith and trusted in

God, how much the more so in time of prosperity! The message to Israel cannot have been missed.

The Real Meaning of the Dream:
Israel's Redemption

Finding Israel's history in the patriarchs' biography, our
sages naturally undertook on their own an exercise of dream
interpretation. Specifically, they read the dream explained by
Joseph, but now they asked about Israel. The message of redemption recurs wherever our sages look. Israel did not descend into Egypt before Israel's salvation from Egypt had been
made ready.

LXXXVIII:V.1.A. ["So the chief butler told his dream to
Joseph and said to him, 'In my dream there was a vine before
me, and on the vine there were three branches; as soon as it
budded, its blossoms shot forth, and the clusters ripened into
grapes. The pharaoh's cup was in my hand, and I took the
grapes and pressed them into the pharaoh's cup and placed
the cup in the pharaoh's hand.' (Gen. 39:11–13)]. ". . . there
was a vine before me": this refers to Israel: "You plucked up
a vine out of Egypt" (Ps. 80:9).

B. ". . . and on the vine there were three branches":
this refers to Moses, Aaron, and Miriam.

C. ". . . as soon as it budded, its blossoms shot forth":
specifically, the blossoming of the redemption of Israel.

D. ". . . and the clusters ripened into grapes": as soon
as the vine budded, it blossomed, and as soon as the grapes
blossomed, the clusters ripened.

2.A. " 'Pharaoh's cup was in my hand, and I took the
grapes and pressed them into pharaoh's cup and placed the
cup in pharaoh's hand.' '. . . you shall place pharaoh's cup in
his hand' ":

B. On what basis did sages ordain that there should be
four cups of wine for Passover?

C. R. Hunah in the name of R. Benaiah: "They correspond to the four times that redemption is stated with respect

to Egypt: 'I will bring you out . . . and I will deliver you . . . and I will redeem you . . . and I will take you' (Ex. 6:6–7)."

D.   R. Samuel b. Nahman said, "They correspond to the four times that 'cups' are mentioned here: 'Pharaoh's *cup* was in my hand, and I took the grapes and pressed them into pharaoh's *cup* and placed the *cup* in pharaoh's hand.' "

E.   R. Levi said, "They correspond to the four kingdoms."

F.   R. Joshua b. Levi said, "They correspond to the four cups of fury that the Holy One, blessed be he, will give the nations of the world to drink: 'For thus says the Lord, the God of Israel, to me, "Take this cup of the wine of fury' " (Jer. 25:15). 'Babylon has been a golden cup in the Lord's hand' (Jer. 51:7). 'For in the hand of the Lord there is a cup' (Ps. 75:9). 'And burning wind shall be the portion of their cup' (Ps. 11:6).

G.   "And in response to these, the Holy One, blessed be he, will give Israel four cups of salvation to drink in the age to come: 'O Lord, the portion of my inheritance and of my cup, you maintain my lot' (Ps. 16:5). 'You prepare a table before me in the presence of my enemies, you have anointed my head with oil, my cup runs over' (Ps. 23:5). 'I will lift up the cup of salvations and call upon the name of the Lord' (Ps. 116:13).

H.   "What is said is not 'cup of salvation' but 'cup of salvations,' one in the days of the Messiah, the other in the time of Gog and Magog."

3.A.   Joseph said to him, "[Since the dream refers to Israel's coming redemption] you have brought me a good gospel, so I shall now give you a good gospel: 'within three days pharaoh will lift up your head and restore you to your office.' "

5.A.   ". . . that they should put me into the dungeon":

B.   Said R. Abin, "The meaning is that they put [One] with me in prison. [Freeman, p. 817, n. 4: The divine presence accompanied me.]"

How shall we relate the vision at hand to Israel's present concerns? At no. 1 we read the vision in light of the story of

Israel's redemption from Egypt. Then, at the next paragraph, marked no. 2, we bring the point home, by linking Israel's redemption specifically to aspects of the language of the vision. The power of the statement of Samuiel b. Nahman is to link the symbolism of the cups to the larger story, but Hunah and Levi do still better, for they show that, even in the tale of Joseph's dream interpretation, we see the redemption of Israel, on the one side, and the corresponding oppression of the four kingdoms—or governing empires—to which Israel would be subjected, on the other. So even before the fact, Israel's ultimate redemption was secure. Here is yet another example of sage's finding in the tales of Genesis the meaning of events in their own day.

God's Role in Joseph's Life

The point of emphasis of course requires repetition. Everything that happened to Joseph formed part of God's plan for Israel. Each detail contributed its small proof of that proposition.

LXXXVIII:VII.1.A. "But the chief butler did not remember Joseph, but forgot him" (Gen. 40:20–23):

B. For that entire day he was making resolutions [to inform pharaoh], but the angel came and reversed them. He tied knots [so as to remember] and the angel came and untied them.

C. Said the Holy One, blessed be he, to him, "You may have forgotten him, but I have not forgotten him."

The forgetfulness now becomes part of the divine plan. So the message is clear and powerful. Whatever happens to Israel, good or bad, comes from God and conforms to a larger plan. Israel now may not know that plan. But in time to come, Israel will understand how all things fit together into the pattern of salvation.

Part Ten

MIQQES:

Genesis Rabbah
Parashiyyot
LXXXIX–XCII

God's Role in Joseph's Life

Every detail of Joseph's life reveals God's plan. That fundamental proposition guides our sages through the reading of Joseph's life, in one detail after another. For our sages find little merit in understatement. They are out to prove a point, and the more examples, arguments, and above all, facts, they find to prove the point, the better. The corollary? God's plan is just—and what is more important, has been revealed to Israel in the Torah. So if we read scripture properly, we shall discern the rules that govern our lives as individuals and also the history of Israel as a people.

LXXXIX:I.1.A. "And it came to pass at the end of two years [the pharaoh dreamed that he was standing by the Nile]." (Gen. 41:1):

B. "He sets an end to darkness . . . the stones of thick darkness and the shadow of death" (Job 28:3):

C. A span of time has been assigned to the world, decreeing how many years it would spend in darkness.

D. What is the scriptural evidence? "He sets an end to darkness . . . the stones of thick darkness and the shadow of death" (Job. 28:3).

E. For all that time that the impulse to do evil is in the world, darkness and gloom are in the world. When the impulse to do evil is uprooted from the world, darkness and deep gloom will pass from the world.

2.A. Another interpretation of the verse: "He sets an end to darkness . . . the stones of thick darkness and the shadow of death" (Job. 28:3):

B. A span of time was assigned to Joseph, decreeing how many years he would spend in prison.

319

C. Once the end came, the pharaoh had his dream: "And it came to pass at the end of two years [the pharaoh dreamed that he was standing by the Nile]" (Gen. 41:1).

The cited verse introduces at no. 1 the theme of the prevailing interpretation of Joseph's life, which has emphasized his power to sin and his regeneration. So the underlying point is that Joseph's impulse to do evil reached the end of its allotted span of time, at which point the end of his period of suffering also came. In this period the story of Mordecai's and Esther's salvation of Israel in the time of Ahasueros took on special meaning. In the synagogue at Dura-Europos, for example, a painter in the year 245, just a century earlier, had covered a good part of the west wall with pictures of Israel's salvation in the time of Queen Esther. Joseph produced the tribe from which Mordecai, therefore also Esther, derived, and so we shall see the linkage between Joseph's salvation and Mordecai's and Esther's an important theme from here on out. Since Joseph's story has repeatedly been linked to Israel's history, with strong emphasis on the links between Joseph and Mordecai, the deeper message addresses Israel's condition and links its impulse to sin with its degraded condition.

Joseph Got What was Coming to Him— in a Good Sense too

Joseph did good, not only evil. So we begin the quest for evidence that God responds to the man's good deeds as well.

XC:III.1.A. "And the pharaoh said to Joseph, 'Behold I have set you over all the land of Egypt.' Then the pharaoh took his signet ring from his hand and put it on Joseph's hand and arrayed him in garments of fine linen and put a gold chain about his neck and he made him to ride in his second chariot, and they cried before him, '*Abrech* [Bow the knee]!' Thus he set him over all the land of Egypt" (Gen. 41:43–44):

B. R. Yudan in the name of R. Benjamin bar Levi: "Joseph was given what belonged to him.

C. "The mouth that had not kissed sin, 'That no one will kiss me [in obeisance] except for your authority for him to do so.'

D. "The neck, which did not cleave to transgression: '. . . and put a gold chain about his neck.'

E. "The hands, that did not reach out in transgression: 'Then the pharaoh took his signet ring from his hand and put it on Joseph's hand.'

F. "The body, which did not cleave in transgression: '. . . and arrayed him in garments of fine linen.'

G. "The feet, which did not take a step in transgression, will step aboard the royal chariot: '. . . and he made him to ride in his second chariot.'

H. "The intellect, which did not obsess about transgression, will come and gain the title of wisdom: *'Abrech,'* meaning [reading its consonants as two distinct words] 'father' *(ab)* but young *(rach)* in years.

I. "But Nebuchadnezzar was called *tafsar,* a word that yields through its consonants 'fool in wisdom' but a 'prince' only in years."

No. 1 links the details of the pharaoh's charge to the virtues of Joseph, item by item. So we prove, in one detail after another, that Joseph got what was coming to him, both when he suffered and when he rose to glory.

In Despair, Hope: In Egypt, Redemption

The worst of times point to the opposite: in suffering, look for redemption, in slavery, freedom, in the triumph of the enemy sibling, the true hope for Israelite salvation in time to come. Our sages' power lies in seeing the opposite of what things seem to be, in seeing to the depths and the truth of matters. The suffering of Israel is prefigured in the descent into Egyptian slavery. So when our sages find hope in Egypt, they remind Israel not to despair, even in time of trouble. In reading one thing in the light of something else, they find a message of consolation for the troubled people.

XCI:I.1.A. "When Jacob learned that there was grain in Egypt, he said to his sons, 'Why do you look at one another?' And he said, 'Behold I have heard that there is grain in Egypt, go down and buy grain for us there that we may live and not die' " (Gen. 42:1):

B. "Happy is he whose help is the God of Jacob, whose hope is in the Lord his God" (Ps. 146:5).

C. Said R. Yohanan, "[Since the word for 'grain,' which is *sheber*, and the word for hope, *seber*, are comparable but for a shift in one letter, we interpret as follows: 'Happy is he whose help is the God of Jacob, whose hope is in the Lord his God.' Thus: 'When Jacob learned that there was *hope* in Egypt.' "

2.A. "Behold he breaks down and cannot be built up again. He shuts up a man and there can be no opening" (Job. 12:14):

B. Once the Holy One, blessed be he, had destroyed the scheme of [Joseph's brothers, who are referred to as] the tribal ancestors, it would not be built up again.

C. "He shuts up a man and there can be no opening":

D. This refers to the ten tribal ancestors, who came and went to Egypt and did not know that Joseph was alive.

E. But to Jacob it was revealed that Joseph was alive: "When Jacob learned that there was *hope* in Egypt."

3.A. "Who commands the sun and it does not rise, and seals the stars" (Job. 9:7):

B. "Who commands the sun and it does not rise": refers to Jacob.

C. ". . . and seals the stars": this refers to the tribal ancestors, who came and went to Egypt and did not know that Joseph was alive.

E. But to Jacob it was revealed that Joseph was alive: "When Jacob learned that there was *hope* in Egypt."

4.A. [We now take the two meanings imputed to the word at hand:] "That there was *sheber*," means [not grain but] famine.

B. "That there was *seber*," that is, plenty.

C. "That there was disaster": "And Joseph was brought down to Egypt" (Gen. 39:1).

D. "That there was hope": "And Joseph was the governor" (Gen. 42:6).

E. "That there was disaster": "And they shall serve them, and the Egyptians shall afflict them" (Gen. 15:13).

F. "That there was hope": "And afterward they shall come out with great substance" (Gen. 15:14).

At the outset we gain the basis for the interpretations to follow. The key word bears a number of meanings, and we shall read matters in light of each of them in succession. Nos. 2–4 form a single sustained discourse, one of considerable power. A situation of disaster contains hope, and redemption came out of Egypt. By choosing an intersecting verse that opens up that question, our sages show the story in a wholly new light. So, as we saw, sages show that things are precisely the opposite of what they seem, and the triumph of Christianity is its disaster. But their vision would be a long time in coming true, for only in our own day have some Christians recognized the extraordinary costs to Christianity exacted by worldly power.

Joseph Finds his Brothers; The Details of the Narrative

Having seen time and again how our sages read one story in the light of another, we do well to pause and follow them as they lead us through the details of a single important event. In what follows we gain insight into the power of our sages to open the narrative in its own terms. Now they broaden our understanding of what is said, but they do not introduce those grand themes of sin and suffering, redemption and salvation, that occupy them throughout. So we work our way through the account, noticing what sages choose to emphasize, following their minds as they encounter the story unadorned.

XCI:VI.1.A. Another interpretation of the verse, "When Jacob learned that there was grain in Egypt" (Gen. 42:1):

B. Now was Jacob down in Egypt, that he saw grain in Egypt? For scripture has said, "When Jacob learned that there was grain in Egypt"?

C. And did he not say to his sons, "Behold I have heard that there is grain in Egypt?" [So he had to rely on rumor, and he did not know the facts.]

D. But from the day on which Joseph was kidnapped, the Holy Spirit was taken away from him. He would see but not see, hear but not hear.

2.*A.* And why is it not said, "There is grain," *(yesh bar)* meaning, "there is food" in Egypt? Rather it says, *seber,* instead of *sheber.*

B. The sense is this: He saw in his glass that his hope *(sibro)* was in Egypt.

C. And who was this? It was Joseph.

3. "[When Jacob learned that there was grain in Egypt,] he said to his sons, 'Why do you draw attention to yourselves [RSV: look at one another]?' [And he said, 'Behold I have heard that there is grain in Egypt, go down and buy grain for us there that we may live and not die']" (Gen. 42:1):

B. [Following the sense, "do not make yourselves conspicuous"] he said to him, "My sons, you are all strong and you are all brothers.

C. "[Do not go forth with food in hand] do not all enter through a single gate, and do not stand together in one place."

D. "[. . . do not all enter through a single gate] on account of the evil eye.

4.A. ". . . go down":

B. Why does the verse use the word "go down there," rather than, "go there"?

C. It is because he foresaw that they would decline and be enslaved in Egypt.

5.A. Another explanation: ". . . go down":

B. On the basis of this verse you learn that whoever has to buy grain in the marketplace is one who has declined in status. [People of status grow their own grain.]

6.A. "So ten of Joseph's brothers went down to buy grain in Egypt" (Gen. 42:3):

B.   Scripture could well have said, "the sons of Jacob." Why say, "the brothers of Joseph"?

C.   In the beginning they did not treat him in a fraternal way, but they sold him, and in the end they regretted it.

D.   Every day they would say, "Let us go and find out what happened to him and bring him back to his father."

E.   When Jacob said to them, "Go down to Egypt," they all decided to treat him in a fraternal way.

7.*A.*   Said R. Judah bar Simeon, "So too Joseph knew that his brothers were coming down to Egypt. What did he do? He set up guards on the ten gates and said to them, 'Write down the name of everyone who enters.' In the evening they brought him their notes. This one was called 'Reuben son of Jacob,' and that one, 'Simeon son of Jacob,' and the other, 'Levi, son of Jacob,' and the other, 'Judah, son of Jacob.'

B.   "He said to them, 'Close all the granaries and keep only one of them open.' He gave their names to the one who was in charge of the open granary.

C.   "He said to him, 'When the ones whose names are written down come to you, bring them to me.'

D.   "Some days passed, and they did not come. He sent for them and found them in the red-light district. Now what in the world were they doing there? They had said, 'It may be that, because Joseph was unusually handsome, they put him in a tent [like whore, to work as a male hustler].'

E.   "They arrested them and brought them to Joseph."

8.*A.*   "Joseph saw his brothers and knew them, but he treated them like strangers":

B.   What is the meaning of the word, "he treated them like *strangers*"?

C.   The meaning is that to them he appeared to be a gentile. [He had become assimilated to the dress and style of the Egyptians.]

9.*A.*   He took his cup and [to practice magic] struck it and said to them, "You are spies" (Gen. 42:7).

B.   They said to him, "We are sons of one man" (Gen. 42:11).

C. "If you are sons, why did you not enter through a single gate?"

D. They said to him, "Father gave us orders."

E. "And what were you doing in the red-light district?"

F. "We lost something and we were looking for it."

G. He said to them, "I see in my cup that two of you destroyed a great city and sold your brother to Arabs."

H. ". . . They were frightened, and said to him, 'We are twelve.' "

I. "Then where are the other two?"

J. ". . . the youngest is this day with our father, and one is no more. . . ."

K. He said to them, "Go, bring him to me."

L. They went to their father and told him everything that had happened to them.

M. He said to them, "Where is Simeon?"

N. They said to him, "They seized him on our account."

O. He said to them, "You have only added to my sadness."

P. "And Jacob their father said to him, 'You have bereaved me of my children; Joseph is no more, and Simeon is no more; and now you would take Benjamin; all this has come upon me' " (Gen. 42:36).

Q. "Then Reuben spoke to his father, 'Slay my two sons if I do not bring him back to you; put him in my hands and I will bring him back to you' " (Gen. 42:2 37).

R. He said to him, "Are your sons not my sons?"

S. Said Judah to them, "Wait on the elder until the bread is all gone from the house."

T. When the bread was all gone from the house, Judah said to him, "If Benjamin comes with us, it is possible that he will be arrested and it is possible that he will not be arrested. But if he does not go with us, we shall all assuredly die. It is not good to ignore what is subject to doubt and to seize on what is absolutely sure to happen."

U. Jacob said, "Who will be surety for him?"

V. He said to him, "I shall serve as pledge for him" (Gen. 43:9).

W. He then sent them off.

X. When Joseph saw him, he was happy, for Benjamin looked like his mother.

XCI:VI.1.A. "[And Joseph's brothers came and bowed themselves before him with their faces to the ground. Joseph saw his brothers and knew them, but he treated them like strangers and spoke roughly to them. 'Where do you come from?,' he said. They said, 'From the land of Canaan, to buy food.' Thus Joseph knew his brothers, but they did not know him. And Joseph remembered the dreams which he had dreamed of them and he said to them, 'You are spies, you have come to see the weakness of the land.' They said to him, 'No, my lord, but to buy food have your servants come. We all are sons of one man, we are honest men, your servants are not spies.' He said to them, 'No, it is the weakness of the land that you have come to see.' And they said, 'We, your servants, are twelve brothers, the sons of one man in the land of Canaan, and behold, the youngest is this day with our father, and one is no more.' But Joseph said to them, 'It is as I said to you, you are spies. By this you shall be tested: by the life of the pharaoh, you shall not go from this place unless your youngest brother comes here. Send one of you and let him bring your brother, while you remain in prison, that your words may be tested, whether there is truth in you, or else, by the life of pharaoh, surely you are spies.' And he put them all together in prison for three days" (Gen. 42:6–17)]: "Joseph saw his brothers and knew them, but he treated them like strangers":

B. R. Joshua bar Nehemiah: "He turned into a gentile to them."

2.A. "Thus Joseph knew his brothers":

B. When they fell into his hand [he acknowledged them as brothers].

C. ". . . but they did not know him":

D. When he fell into their hand [they did not acknowledge him as a brother].

E. Rabbis say, "He, who left them when they had full beards: 'Thus Joseph knew his brothers.'

F. "But they, who left him before he had a full beard: '. . . but they did not know him.' "

3.A. "We all are sons of one man, we are honest men, your servants are not spies":

B. The Holy Spirit glowed in them when they said to him, "*We,*" meaning, "You." That is "We [including you] are all the sons of one man."

4.A. "We, your servants, are twelve brothers, the sons of one man in the land of Canaan, and behold, the youngest is this day with our father, and one is no more":

B. He said to them, "And where is the one [who is no more]?"

C. They said to him, "We sold him."

D. "And how much did you sell him for?"

E. "For five *sela*s."

F. "If someone were to say to you, 'Give me five *sela*s, and I'll give him back to you,' would you do it?"

G. "Yes."

H. "And if someone said to you, 'Give me twice that,' would you do it?"

I. "Yes."

J. "And if someone should said to you, 'Even if you give any amount of money at all, I shall not give him back to you,' what would you do?"

K. "That is why we have come down here, either to kill or be killed."

L. He said to them, "That is precisely what I said to you" (Gen. 42:14).

5.A. "By this you shall be tested: by the life of pharaoh, you shall not go from this place unless your youngest brother comes here. Send one of you and let him bring your brother, while you remain in prison, that your words may be tested, whether there is truth in you, or else, by the life of pharaoh, surely you are spies:"

B. When he wanted to take an oath falsely, he would say, "By the life of pharaoh."

C. Said R. Levi, "The matter may be compared to the case of a sheep who fled from the pasture, and came into the house of a widow.

D. "What did she do? She slaughtered the sheep and flayed it and put its hide on the bed and covered it with a sheet.

E. "When people came looking for the sheep and asked her about it, she said, 'May it be so that this woman will cut off and eat of the meat of that sheep if I know anything at all about it!'

F. "So did Joseph say, 'By the life of pharaoh.' "

6.*A.* "And he put them all together in prison for three days" (Gen. 42:6–17)]:

B. The Holy One, blessed be he, never leaves the righteous in distress for more than three days.

7.*A.* "On the third day Joseph said to them, 'Do this and you will live' (Gen. 42:18)":

B. That is in line with this verse: "After two days he will revive us, on the third day he will raise us up, that we may live in his presence" (Hos. 6:2).

C. That is, on the third day as in the case of the tribal fathers.

In the opening paragraph, no. 1 presents an acute observation, based on the disparity between two verses. No. 2 goes over a familiar etymological lesson. No. 3 reviews equally familiar ground, leading us to conclude that we are dealing with a composition originating somewhere other than the one that has already told us these things. Nos. 4, 5 derive lessons from the word choice at hand. No. 6 proceeds in the same way, now introducing the theme of the repentance of Joseph's brothers. No. 7 takes up the narrative and embellishes it, adding details here and there, and that is the same purpose in nos. 8, 9. No. 7–9 form a single unfolding discourse.

What we have in the second paragraph also is a sequence of glosses of verses in sequence, each of the glosses underlining a given point or enriching the narrative. The net effect is to deepen the story by giving details otherwise unstated, or by providing a more elaborate picture. The reference to resurrection on the third day cannot be missed. It is Israel—"the tribal fathers [of 7.C] that will return to life "on the third day." Israel stands for all else, and the resurrection of the dead will begin with Israel's return to full life. The response to Christian doctrine is explicit.

Jacob Loses Sight of God's Purpose

Once more we return to Jacob, ringing the changes on the familiar theme that Jacob should have had more faith than he did. The proposition seems to alternate with the one that holds that Jacob enjoyed serenity because he trusted in God. But here, Jacob loses sight of what is happening: the working out of God's plan.

XCI:X.1.A. "But if you will not send him, we will not go down, for the man said to us, 'You shall not see my face unless your brother is with you' " (Gen. 43:5):

B. He said to him, "What will happen if he tells us the truth, while we answer him nonsense [saying that we could not bring him down because the trip is dangerous]."

2.A. "And Israel said, 'Why did you treat me so ill as to tell the man that you had another brother?' " (Gen. 43:6):

B. R. Levi in the name of R. Hama bar Haninah: "In his entire life Jacob said something nonsensical only in this place. Said the Holy One, blessed be he, 'I am busy trying to make his son king of Egypt,' and he says, 'Why did you treat me so ill!'

C. "That is in line with this verse: 'Why do you say, O Jacob, and speak, O Israel,' 'My way is hid from the Lord' " (Is. 40:27)."

3.A. "And they said, 'The man questioned us carefully about ourselves and our kindred, saying, "Is your father still alive? Have you another brother?" What we told him was in answer to these questions. Could we in any way know that he would say, "Bring your brother down"?' " (Gen. 43:7):

B. Said R. Abba, "He was even able to tell us what sort of wood our beds were made of!"

4.A. "And Judah said to Israel his father, 'Send the lad with me, and we will arise and go, that we may live and not die, both we and you and also our little ones' " (Gen. 43:8):

B. "It is better that one soul should be subject to doubt, and that all of us not be assuredly subject to death."

5.A. "I will be surety for him, of my hand you shall require him. If I do not bring him back to you and set him before you, then let me bear the blame forever" (Gen. 43:9–10):

B. This refers to the age to come, which is entirely day [and never night].

No. 1 brings Jacob under criticism, and no. 2 underlines the contempt of the storyteller, as interpreted, for Jacob's reluctance. Jacob should have had faith in God, a message we noted earlier as well. The other glosses simply underline main traits of the story or introduce minor improvements.

Jacob Accepted Divine Chastisement

Now comes the other aspect of Jacob: his acceptance of suffering as God's punishment. That proposition yields the view that suffering may bring good. In our sage's day, no less than in our own time, examples to the contrary abounded. But they nonetheless introduced the consideration at hand: whatever happens, happens because God wants it to happen, and, it must follow, people must accept suffering as a means of atonement.

XCII:I.1.A. "May God almighty grant you mercy before the man, that he may send back your other brother and Benjamin. If I am bereaved of my children, I am bereaved" (Gen. 43:14):

B. R. Phineas in the name of R. Hanan of Sepphoris opened discourse by citing the following verse: " 'Happy is the man whom you chasten, O Lord.' And if someone should come along to object, then: '. . . and whom you teach out of your Torah' (Ps. 94:12).

C. "What is written with respect to Abraham? 'And I will bless you and make your name great' (Gen. 12:2).

D. "But when he went forth, famine leaped upon him, but he did not complain or object.

E. "[Thus Jacob said to his sons] 'So too you, if troubles come upon you, do not object or complain.' "

2.A. Said R. Alexandri, "You have no one without troubles. Happy is the person whose Torah bring about his sufferings [that is, because of his hard work in studying the Torah]."

B. Said R. Joshua b. Levi, "All sufferings that come upon a person and prevent him from his Torah study constitute sufferings that serve to rebuke. But all forms of suffering that do not prevent a person from studying the Torah are sufferings that come out of love [that a person may suffer in this world and joy all the more the age to come]."

3.A. Rabbi saw a blind man who was laboring in Torah study. He said to him, "Peace to you, free man."

B. He said to him, "Did you hear that I used to be a slave?"

C. He said to him, "No, but you will be a free man in the age to come."

4.A. Said R. Yudan, "It is written, 'And if he smite out his slave's tooth or his slavewoman's tooth, he shall let him go free for his tooth's sake' (Ex. 21:27).

B. "He upon whom troubles come, how much the more so!"

5.A. R. Phineas in the name of R. Hoshaia: " 'Happy is the man whom you chasten, O Lord.' The word 'Lord' is not written out in the four-lettered name of God, but only with the two letters, YH. The matter may be compared to one who is judged before the court and said, 'May it be so.' [Freedman, p. 848, n. 3: Yah is by a play on words interpreted as a shortened form of yehi, 'let it be so, but no more.' Thus even the man who is happy in God's chastisement yet prays to be spared further suffering.]

B. "So it was with our father, Abraham: 'He who in the future is destined to say to suffering, "Enough," may he say to my suffering now, "Enough." '

C. " 'And God Almighty give you mercy' (Gen. 43:14). [The word for 'Almighty,' *shaddai*, contains letters, *dai*, which, read by themselves, mean 'enough.']"

The sustained exposition of the problem of suffering deals with a number of distinct themes. We take up the matter of suffering brought on by God's love as distinct from suffering aimed at chastisement. The point is made to impute to Jacob both acceptance of divine punishment and the prayer that that will be enough. The message to Israel—patience but hope— requires no comment. When we consider how frequently and emphatically our sages repeat that main point, we realize what brought them to the book of Genesis to begin with. Here, after all, is where it all began. Here we should find out what it all means.

Part Eleven

VAYYIGASH:
Genesis Rabbah
Parashiyyot XCIII–XCV

Judah Found the Right Words and the Right Way

Judah led the way to the reconciliation of the brothers and Joseph. How did he do it? He found the right words. The way to make peace is to say the right thing. Israel now lacked all means of coercion. All Jews had were words. So they had best find the ones that appeal to a shared logic, a common reason.

XCIII:IV.1.A. "Counsel in the heart of man is like deep water, but a man of understanding will draw it out" (Prov. 20:5):

B. The matter may be compared to a deep well, full of cold water, and the water was sweet, but no one could drink from it. Someone came and tied one rope to another, one thread to another, and then let a bucket down and drew water up from the well and drank it.

C. Everyone then began to draw water and drink it.

D. So Judah did not stop answering Joseph, word for word, until he reached his heart: "Then Judah went up to him and said, 'O my lord, let your servant, I pray you, speak a word in my lord's ears, and let not your anger burn against your servant, for you are like pharaoh himself' " (Gen. 44:18).

XCIII:VI.1.A. "Then Judah went up to him and said, 'O my lord, let your servant, I pray you, speak a word in my lord's ears, and let not your anger burn against your servant, for you are like pharaoh himself' " (Gen. 44:18):

B. R. Judah, R. Nehemiah, and Rabbis [discussed the sense of this "going up" or "drawing near"]:

C. R. Judah said, "This was a drawing near as for battle, as it says, 'So Joab and the people who were with him drew near to battle' (2 Sam. 10:13)."

D. R. Nehemiah said, "It was a drawing near for conciliation, in line with the usage in this verse: 'Then the children of Judah drew near to Joshua' (Joshua 14:6). The purpose was to conciliate him."

E. Rabbis say, "It was a drawing near for prayer, in line with the usage in this verse: 'And it came to pass at the time of the offering of the evening offering, that Elijah the prophet came near' and said, 'O Lord, God of Abraham, Isaac, and Israel, this day let it be known that you are God in Israel' (1 Kgs. 18:36)."

F. Said R. Eleazar, "Interpret the verse to bear this meaning: 'If it is for war, I am coming. If it is for conciliation, I am coming. If it is for prayer, I am coming.' "

2.A. "[Then Judah sent up to him and said] 'O my lord [let your servant, I pray you, speak a word in my lord's ears, and let not your anger burn against your servant, for you are like pharaoh himself']" (Gen. 44:18):

B. [Since the Hebrew for "O my Lord" contains the letters that can be read "me, my Lord," we interpret] "Take me, not him.

C. "If it is to draw water, let it be me; if it is to serve, let it be me; if it is to chop wood, let it be me."

3.A. Another interpretation: [Since the words at hand can be read to mean "a wrong, my lord," we interpret] "You do us a wrong, my lord. For you said to us, 'Bring him down to me, that I may set my eyes upon him' (Gen. 44:21). Is this what you call 'setting eyes'?"

B. Said R. Simon, "What he said was this: 'According to our laws, it is written, "He shall surely pay. But if he cannot pay, then let him be sold in exchange for what he has stolen" (Ex. 22:2).' But this one is able to pay [so should not be enslaved]."

4.A. "[Then Judah sent up to him and said, 'O my lord] let your servant, I pray you, speak a word in my lord's ears [and let not your anger burn against your servant, for you are like pharaoh himself']" (Gen. 44:18):

B. He said, "Let my words enter your ears. As to this young one's grandmother because pharaoh took her for a single night, he and his household were punished with plagues:

'And the Lord plagued pharaoh and his house witge; 5

watch out that you are not smitten with *saraat*. [That is, the punishment of those pharaohs that harm Israel is the skin-ailment called *saraat*.]

C. "This one's mother died only oaccount of the curse of his father, as it is said, 'With whomever you find your gods, he shall not live' (Gen. 31:32). So watch out that he not hurl a single curse at you and you die.

D. "So too, two of us went into a great city and destroyed it, in the one case on account of a woman.

E. "In the present case, on account of a [Benjamin] man the beloved of the eyes, the one who is in charge of the abode of the Holy One, blessed be he [Freedman, p. 860, n. 2: God's temple would be in Benjamin's territory, thus Benjamin gave hospitality to God]: 'Of Benjamin he said, "The beloved of the Lord shall dwell in safety by him, he covers him all the day, and he dwells between his shoulders' " (Deut. 33:12). As to this one, how much the more so!"

5.A. "[Then Judah went up to him and said, 'O my lord] let your servant, I pray you, speak a word in my lord's ears [and let not your anger burn against your servant, for you are like pharaoh himself']" (Gen. 44:18):

B. Said R. Jeremiah bar Shemaiah, " 'If I only say a word (*davar*, DBR), I shall bring a plague (*dever*, DBR) on them.' "

C. Said R. Hanan, "When Judah got mad, the hair of his chest would protrude through his clothes, and if he put iron bars in his mouth, he would spit them out like dust."

6.A. "[Then Judah went up to him and said, 'O my lord, let your servant, I pray you, speak a word in my lord's ears, and let not your anger burn against your servant] for you are like pharaoh himself' " (Gen. 44:18):

B. "Just as pharaoh makes a decree but does not carry it out, so you make a decree and do not carry it out.

C. "Just as pharaoh lusts after homosexual sex, so you lust after homosexual sex.

D. "Just as pharaoh is king and you are second to him, so my father [Jacob, really] is king in the land of Canaan and I am second to him.

E. "And if I unsheathe my sword, I shall begin with you and end with pharaoh."

F. If he had said, "I shall begin with pharaoh and end with you." Joseph would have abided him. But when he said, "And if I unsheathe my sword, I shall begin with you and end with pharaoh," Joseph gave a sign to Manasseh and he stamped one foot on the floor, and the whole place trembled.

G. Judah said, "Oy! Such a temper can come only from my father's house!"

H. When Judah realized the true state of affairs, he began to speak more gently: "My lord asked . . . and we said to my lord" (Gen. 44:19–20).

XCIII:V.1.A. "Behold the days come, says the Lord, that the plowman will overtake the reaper, and the treader of grapes him who sows seed. And the mountains shall drop sweet wine . . ." (Amos 9:13):

B. "The days come says the Lord, that the plowman will overtake" refers to Judah.

C. "The reaper" speaks to Joseph: "For behold, we were binding sheaves" (Gen. 37:7).

D. ". . . and the treader of grapes": this is Judah: "For I have trodden Judah for me" (Zech. 9:13).

E. ". . . him who sows seed:" this is Joseph, who sowed the seed of his father and brought them down to Egypt.

F. ". . . And the mountains shall drop sweet wine": refers to the tribal progenitors, who said, "If kings contend with one another, what difference does it make to us? It is appropriate for a king to contend with another king [Judah, the founder of Israelite royalty, with the king of Egypt]."

G. "Then Judah went up to him and said, 'O my lord, let your servant, I pray you, speak a word in my lord's ears, and let not your anger burn against your servant, for you are like pharaoh himself' " (Gen. 44:18).

In the opening paragraph, the analogy is well composed, and Judah is represented as a man of understanding, who, linking one thing to the next, managed to touch Joseph. So Judah's capacity to make his case through words, not deeds, finds praise. In the concluding paragraph, no. 1 works out the meanings for the word "drawing near," citing the present passage as evidence in its inquiry. But the exegesis of our passage is not taken up. Nos. 2, 3 work on the meaning of the word "O my lord," that is, a further exercise. But now the available meanings serve the exegesis of the verse at hand. No. 3 produces an expansion of Judah's statement, making his speech considerably more forceful than scripture's version, and also linking the present story to ones that have gone before. Nos. 5, 6 carry forward the program of no. 4, but at the end we produce a more conciliatory speech for Judah—only after he begins to recognize the fact that Joseph was his brother. The net effect is to represent Judah as a proud monarch, not as servile.

The Power of Repentance

At issue is whether the brothers learned their lesson and repented for the evil deed they had done. That is what Joseph must find out. His entire quest attests to the power of repentance to overcome sin and achieve reconciliation. And why not? For when we repent, we specify what lesson we have learned, and we therefore can undertake not to repeat the sin or bad deed that has brought trouble. Without repentance we can well repeat what we have done, for we have never acknowledged it is wrong.

XCIII:IX.1.A. R. Hiyya bar Abba said, "In every statement that you find that Judah made to Joseph in the presence of his brothers, up to the point, 'Then Joseph could not control himself before all those who stood by him [and he cried, "Make everyone go out from me." So no one stayed with him when Joseph made himself known to his brothers' (Gen. 45:1)], contains words meant to conciliate Joseph, conciliate his brothers, and conciliate Benjamin.

B. ". . . to conciliate Joseph: 'See how he is ready to give his life for the children of Rachel.'

C. ". . . conciliate his brothers: He said, 'See how he gives his life for his brothers.'

D. ". . . and conciliate Benjamin: He said to him, 'Just as I gave my life for your brother, so I give my life for you.' ''

2.A. "Then Joseph could not control himself before all those who stood by him, and he cried, 'Make everyone go out from me.' [So no one stayed with him when Joseph made himself known to his brothers]" (Gen. 45:1):

B. R. Hama bar Hanina and R. Samuel bar Nahmani:

C. R. Hama bar Hanina said, "Joseph did not act properly [in leaving himself without his retinue for protection], for if one of the brothers had kicked him, he would have died forthwith."

D. R. Samuel bar Nahmani said, "He acted in a right and proper way. He knew the truly righteous character of his brothers. He thought, 'God forbid, my brothers are not suspect of intent to murder.' ''

No. 1 supplies fresh dialogue for Judah, as though the narrative did not give enough, and no. 2 further lays the groundwork for the reconciliation of Joseph and his brothers. The tendency of the compositors is to include materials that show Judah as strong, wise, and prudent. Joseph for his part is shown carefully studying whether the brothers have truly repented. He signals his view that they have by allowing them access to his person. This he would not have done had he feared they would murder him upon discovering his identity. So the exegete-compositors underline the deeper significance of the details at hand. The story is now an account of the power of repentance, for the brothers, and forgiveness and reconciliation, for Joseph.

The Brothers Reveal their True Character

Now we shall see that the brothers did repent. How do we know it? Because, faced with the chance to commit the same sin they had done long ago, they overcame the temptation. They faced the loss of Benjamin. Had they learned their lesson? Indeed so. They offered themselves instead of their brother. That now demonstrates their regeneration. So too Israel, facing the occasion of committing the sin for which it now suffered, would demonstrate their regeneration by not committing that same sin. The sin, sages maintained, had been rebellion against God's will. The regeneration? Submission and acceptance of God's will.

XCIII:VIII.1.A. Another matter: "My lord asked [his servants, saying, 'have you a father or a brother?' And we said to my lord, 'We have a father, an old man, and a young brother, the child of his old age, and his brother is dead, and he alone is left of his mother's children, and his father loves him' " (Gen. 44:19–20):

B. Judah said to him, "You should know that this proves you had improper intentions in dealing with us.

C. "How many other countries have come down here to buy food. But did you ask them questions the way you asked us?

D. "Are we here to try to make a marriage with your daughter, or do you want to marry our sister?

E. "Nonetheless, we did not hide a thing from you."

2.A. "And we said to my lord, 'We have a father, an old man, and a young brother, the child of his old age, and his brother is dead, and he alone is left of his mother's children, and his father loves him' ":

B. Could a man so reliable as Judah say something of which he was not certain? How could he have said, ". . . and his brother is dead"?

C. But this is what he thought to himself, "If I say to him that he is alive, he will say to me, 'Go and bring him,' just as he said to me concerning Benjamin."

D. "Therefore I shall tell him, '. . . and his brother is dead.' "

3.A. "If you take this one also from me, and harm befalls him, you will bring down my gray hairs in sorrow to Sheol" (Gen. 44:29):

B. This is what Jacob, our father, said, "In the beginning, when Benjamin was living with me, I felt serene about his brother and his mother. But now it appears to me as if all three of them have been taken from me all at once."

C. To what may our father, Jacob, be compared in respect to Benjamin?

D. To a lamp with three windows. If someone wanted to put out the flame through one of them, he put out the entire lamp.

4.A. ". . . and harm befalls him, you will bring down my gray hairs in sorrow to Sheol":

B. He thought, "Woe is me! Perhaps a decree has been issued against Rachel, that both she and her children will perish on the way. For she died while en route, and Joseph died while en route, and now, if this one dies en route, I shall die for pining after him."

5.A. Said Joseph to Judah, "Judah, Why are you the spokesman? Do you not have brothers who are older than you?"

B. He said to him, "Nonetheless, all of them stand outside the realm of responsibility, but, for my part, my very stomach aches with anguish."

C. He said to him, "Why so?"

D. He said to him, "Because I am the surety for him."

E. He said to him, "On what basis are you surety for him? If it is a matter of silver, I'll provide it for you. If it is a matter of gold, I'll provide it for you."

F. He said to him, "It is not a matter of silver or gold. But this is what I said to father, I shall be subject to ostracism in the age to come, which is called 'days.' "

G. For it is said, "I will be surety for him; of my hand you shall require him. If I do not bring him back to you and set him before you, then let me bear the blame for all days; for if we had not delayed, we would now have returned twice" (Gen. 43:9–10).

6.A. [Judah] said to him, "What do you want of Benjamin? If it is for size, lo, I am greater than he, and if it is for strength, I am stronger than he.

B. "It is better for me to serve as a slave in his stead and not give pain to father."

C. For it is said, "For how can I go back to my father if the lad is not with me? I fear to see the evil that would come upon my father" (Gen. 44:34).

D. When Judah mentioned his father's pain, Joseph could not contain himself, but, nonetheless, he found the strength and remained seated. He said to them, "Where is your brother, whom you said that he died? Where is he? Is he certainly dead?"

E. He said to him, "Yes."

F. He said to him, "Why are you telling lies? Did you not sell him to me, and I bought him from your hands? I shall call him and he will answer me."

G. Then he called out, "Joseph son of Jacob! Joseph son of Jacob!"

H. And they looked in all four corners of the house.

I. He said to them, "Why are you looking around? I am Joseph, your brother."

J. But they would not believe him until he had exposed himself and shown them the mark of the circumcision.

The power of the entire composite lies in its expansion of the narrative through added discourse. At each detail the motives or further thoughts of the participants come to expression. The exposition is smooth and follows a continuous path. The intent of the authors of each item is simply to heighten the effect of the narrative, and the compositors who selected and organized the whole have clearly followed suit.

Why Jacob Believed that Joseph Really Lived

When Jacob heard that Joseph lived, he did believe it— before he laid eyes on Joseph. Why? Because Joseph sent him a piece of information which, Jacob knew, only he could have known. At this point our sages once more remind us of their way of life, centered as it was in the study of the Torah. Since Jacob had taught Torah to Joseph, Joseph told Jacob what portion he had been studying at the point at which he was taken away. That persuaded Jacob that Joseph did live.

XCIV:III.1.A. "So they went up out of Egypt and came to the land of Canaan, to Jacob their father. And they told him, 'Joseph is still alive and he is ruler over all the land of Egypt.' And his heart fainted, for he did not believe them. But when they told him all the words of Joseph, which he had said to them, and when he saw the wagons which Joseph had sent to carry him, the spirit of their father Jacob revived. And Israel said, 'It is enough; Joseph my son is still alive; I will go and see him before I die' " (Gen. 45:25–28):

B. Taught R. Hiyya on Tannaite authority, "Look at what happens to a liar. Even when he tells the truth, people do not believe him. [So too Jacob did not want to believe the brothers, since they had lied to him before.]"

2.A. "But when they told him all the words of Joseph, which he had said to them, and when he saw the wagons which Joseph had sent to carry him, the spirit of their father Jacob revived. And Israel said, 'It is enough; Joseph my son is still alive; I will go and see him before I die' " (Gen. 45:25–28):

B. On the wagons that pharaoh had sent to carry him there was an idol incised. Judah went and burned it.

C. That is the tribe that is accustomed to burn idols. [The heirs of Judah would be zealots in the war against idolatry.]

3.A. [Making reference to the word for "wagons," which uses consonants that yield the word for "heifers"] R. Levi in the name of R. Yohanan bar Shaulah, "He said to them, 'If he believes you, well and good.'

B. " 'And if not, you say to him, "When I left you, I was studying the passage concerning the heifer whose neck is broken [in the case of the finding of a neglected corpse, as specified at Deut. 21:1–9]." ' "

C. "That is the point of the statement: 'when he saw the wagons.' [When Jacob saw the wagons, he knew that Joseph had sent him a hint that, when they had parted from one another, they were studying the subject involving the consonants of the word for wagons, that is, the subject of the heifer whose neck is to be broken.]"

4.A. "And Israel said, 'It is enough; Joseph my son is still alive; I will go and see him before I die' " (Gen. 45:28):

B. [Since the word for "enough" can be read as "great," hence, "Great is Joseph my son," Jacob's statement may be interpreted as follows:] "The power of Joseph my son is great, For how many troubles overwhelmed him, and yet he endured in his righteousness.

C. "I have expressed, more than he ever did, distress: 'My way is hid from the Lord' (Is. 40:27). But now I am certain that I have a share in your ample goodness."

No. 1 makes a routine observation, not particular to our story. Nos. 2, 3 enrich the story with details. No. 3 is particularly interesting, because it draws on a detail of the story to explain why Jacob did believe the message. No. 4 provides Jacob with a moving statement in praise of Joseph.

Torah in Egypt

Once the theme of Torah study makes its appearance, we naturally ask what arrangements Jacob and his sons made for the study of the Torah in Egypt. In fact our sages find evidence for the creation of schools for the purpose even before Israel came to Egypt.

XCV:III.1.A. "He sent Judah before him to Joseph, to appear before him in Goshen, and they came into the land of Goshen" (Gen. 46:28):

B. What is the meaning of the word "to appear" [which is built on the root that means "to teach"]?

C. Said R. Nehemiah, "It was his task to set up a study house there, so that he would teach Torah, in which the tribal fathers would recite the Torah.

D. "You may know that that is the case, for when Joseph went his way from him, Jacob knew that passage of the Torah that he was studying when he departed, and he had been reviewing it with him. When the brothers of Joseph came and told him, 'Joseph is still alive . . . his heart fainted, for he did not believe them' (Gen. 45:26), Jacob remembered from what passage Joseph had departed.

E.   "So Jacob thought, 'I know that it was from studying the passage on the heifer whose neck is broken in the case of the finding of the neglected corpse that Joseph took his leave of me.'

F.   "He said to them, 'He will give you some sign that indicates the passage of the Torah that he left off studying when he left me. Then I shall believe you.'

G.   "And Joseph too remembered the passage that he had left off studying. What did Joseph do? He gave them wagons, as it is said, 'And Joseph gave them wagons' (Gen. 45:21) [and the word for 'wagon' and the word for 'heifer' use the same consonants].

H.   "This serves to teach you that wherever he went, he engaged in study of the Torah, just as his fathers did, even though, up to that moment, the Torah had not yet been given."

2.A.   Now lo, it is written with respect to Abraham, "Because Abraham hearkened to my voice and kept my Torahs" (Gen. 26:5). Whence did Abraham study Torah?

B.   Said R. Simeon b. Yohai, "[His father did not teach him, he never had a master. Whence did he learn Torah?] The Holy One, blessed be he, designated his two kidneys like two full jugs, and they flowed and taught him wisdom, in line with the following verse: 'I will bless the Lord, who has given me counsel, yes, in the night seasons my kidneys instruct me' (Ps. 16:7)."

C.   R. Levi said, "He studied Torah on his own, as it is said, 'The dissembler in his heart shall have his fill from his own ways, and a good man shall be satisfied from himself' (Prov. 14:14)."

D.   Said R. Samuel b. Nahman in the name of R. Jonathan: "Even the laws governing the commingling of domain in courtyards [for purposes of creating a single domain for carrying on the Sabbath] did Abraham know. [These laws,

involving rules not found explicitly stated in the Torah but
only in the traditions of sages, taught how several domains, or
properties, can be united into a single domain, so that people
living on the property may carry objects into the shared and
common area. Ordinarily, as is well known, people may not
carry objects on the Sabbath from private to public domain, so
by mingling the ownership of the common domain, they en-
able themselves to do so.]"

E.   For it is said, "[I will multiply your descendants as
the stars of heaven and will give to your descendants all these
lands; and by your descendants all the nations of the earth
shall bless themselves] because Abraham obeyed my voice and
kept my charge, my commandments, my statutes, and my
laws" (Gen. 26:4–5).

F.   How old was Abraham when he recognized his creator?

G.   R. Hananiah said, He was one year old when he recognized his creator."

H.   R. Levi in the name of R. Simeon b. Laqish: "He
was three years old."

I.   "How do we know? It is stated, 'because Abraham
obeyed my voice and kept my charge,' that is, he listened to
the voice of his creator and kept his charge [for the years
numbered by the numerical value of the consonants in the
word] 'because' and since he lived 175 years, and the letters
of the word for 'because' bear the numerical value of 172, he
was three years of age when he converted."

J.   And he observed even the most minor details of the
Torah and taught Torah to his sons, as it is said, "For I have
known him to the end that he may command his children"
(Gen. 18:19).

K.   Said the Holy One, blessed be he, to him, "You
have taught Torah to your son in this world. But in the
world to come, I in my majesty will teach them the Torah,
as it is said, 'And all your children shall be taught of the
Lord' (Is. 54:13)."

The point made earlier, that Joseph sent a sign to Jacob
that only Jacob would understand, now recurs, but in an interesting revision. Once more the eschatological dimension is

probed, with no. 2 making the point explicit. So the settlement in the land of Goshen is treated as a foretaste of the end of days, and the Torah study center that Jacob sent Judah to create is explicitly linked to what is to come. What follows is that the compositors have selected three successive items to make their point. The main point is to restate the thing that links all Israel, then and now, into one entity before God. It is the fact that Israel is one family, and the latter generations enjoy the *zekhut*, or merit, attained by the former generations, the matriarchs and patriarchs. So Jacob is like Abraham, the first sage, and Israel now—in the fourth century—is like Jacob and Abraham when it accepts the teachings of our sages. All form one family, all share one destiny, all rely on one body of merit, and all hope in one God.

Part Twelve

VAYEHI:
Genesis Rabbah
Parashiyyot XCVI–C

Neither is there Dominion on the Day of Death

Our sages took death into the pattern of life, understanding that whoever is born dies. They did not take a romantic view of death, nor did they view it as a tragedy. But they did point to the reality that, at death, all one's power and pretension fall away: "Neither is their dominion in the day of death" struck them as a perfectly correct observation, demanding exemplification.

XCVI:III.1.A. "And when the time drew near that Israel must die [he called his son Joseph and said to him, 'If now I have found favor in your sight, put your hand under my thigh and promise to deal loyally and truly with me. Do not bury me in Egypt, but let me lie with my fathers; carry me out of Egypt and bury me in their burying place.' He answered, 'I will do as you have said.' And he said, 'Swear to me.' And he swore to him. Then Israel bowed himself upon the head of his bed]" (Gen. 47:29–31):

B. "There is no man that has power of the spirit . . . neither is there dominion in the day of death" (Qoh. 8:8).

C. Said R. Joshua of Sikhnin in the name of R. Levi, "As to the trumpets that Moses made in the wilderness, when Moses lay on the point of death, the Holy One, blessed be he, hid them away, so that he would not blow on them and summon the people to him.

D. "This was meant to fulfill this verse: '. . . neither is there dominion in the day of death' (Qoh. 8:8).

E. "When Zimri did his deed, what is written? 'And Phineas went after the man of Israel into the chamber' (Num. 25:8). So where was Moses, that Phineas should speak before he did?

F. " '. . . neither is there dominion in the day of death' (Qoh. 8:8).

G. "But the formulation expresses humiliation. Salvation was handed over to Phineas [and Moses] abased himself.

H. "So too with David: 'How king David was old' (1 Kgs. 1:1). What is stated about him when he lay dying? 'Now the days of David drew near, that he should die' (1 Kgs. 21:1).

I. "What is said is not '*king* David,' but merely 'David.'

J. "The same applies to Jacob, when he was on the point of death, he humbled himself to Joseph, saying to him, 'If now I have found favor in your sight.' [So he abased himself, since there is no dominion on the day of death.]

K. "When did this take place? As he drew near the end: 'And when the time drew near that Israel must die.' "

What strikes the exegete is the unprepossessing language used by Jacob in speaking to Joseph. The intersecting verse makes clear that, on the day of one's death, one no longer rules. Several examples of that fact are given, Moses, David, finally Jacob. So the proposition about the loss of power on the occasion of death derives proof from a number of sources, and the passage has not been worked out to provide the exegesis of our base verse in particular. The exposition is all the more moving because the exegete focuses upon his proposition, rather than on the great personalities at hand. His message obviously is that even the greatest lose all dominion when they are going to die. In this way the deeds of the founders define the rule for the descendants.

On not Worshiping the Patriarchs

Why did Jacob care that he not be buried in Egypt? In an age of the veneration of saints, our sages found the answer obvious. Jacob did not want to be turned into an idol and worshiped, because the idol, as much as the worshiper, must suffer punishment.

XCVI:V.1.A. "[And when the time drew near that Israel must die] he called his son Joseph" (Gen. 47:29–31):

B. Why did he not call Reuben or Judah? Reuben, after all, was firstborn, Judah was king [that is to say, the later kings of Israel would come from the tribe of Judah], but he ignored them and called Joseph. Why so?

C. It was because Joseph had the power to do the job, therefore: "he called his son Joseph."

3.A. ". . . Do not bury me in Egypt [but let me lie with my fathers; carry me out of Egypt and bury me in their burying place.' He answered, 'I will do as you have said.' And he said, 'Swear to me.' And he swore to him. Then Israel bowed himself upon the head of his bed]" (Gen. 47:29–31):

B. [Jacob explained] "Why [not bury me in Egypt]? Because Egypt is going to be smitten with vermin, which will swarm under my body. Therefore: 'Do not bury me in Egypt.' "

4.A. Another reason: On what account did Jacob not want to be buried in Egypt? That they not make him into an idol.

B. For just as punishment is exacted from those that worship idols, so punishment is exacted from the idol as well, as it is said, "And against all the gods of Egypt I will execute judgment" (Ex. 12:12).

C. So you find in the case of Daniel, when he had interpreted the dream of Nebuchadnezzar, what does scripture say?

D. "Then the king Nebuchadnezzar fell upon his face and worshiped Daniel and commanded that they should offer an offering and sweet fragrance to him" (Dan. 2:46).

E. So the king gave orders to make an offering to him, but Daniel did not want it.

F. He said, "For just as punishment is exacted from those that worship idols, so punishment is exacted from the idol as well."

G. So you find in the case of Hiram, once he had declared himself a god, what is written in his regard? "Because your heart is lifted up, and you have said, 'I am a god' " (Ez. 28:2), the Holy One, blessed be he, said to him, "Behold, you are wiser than Daniel" (Ez. 28:3).

H. [God said to him] "You find in the case of Daniel that Nebuchadnezzar wanted to make him an offering, but he did not want it, while you made yourself into a god."

I. What happened in the end to him? "I have cast you to the ground, I have laid you before kings, that they may gaze upon you" (Ez. 28:17).

J. Jacob did not want the Egyptians to err: "It is written in connection with the Egyptians, 'Whose flesh is as the flesh of asses' (Ez. 23:20). They are compared to asses. But I am compared to sheep: 'Israel is a scattered sheep' (Jer. 50:17). 'And the firstling of an ass you shall redeem with a lamb' (Ex. 34:20)."

K. [So, Jacob thought] "It is so that they will not effect redemption through me."

L. It is for that reason that it is stated: ". . . Do not bury me in Egypt [but let me lie with my fathers; carry me out of Egypt and bury me in their burying place]."

4.A. Why is it that all the patriarchs demand and highly prize burial in the land of Israel?

B. Said R. Eleazar, "There is a reason for it."

C. Said R. Hanina said R. Joshua b. Levi, "What is the meaning of the statement, 'There is a reason for it'?

D. " 'I shall walk before the Lord in the land of the living' " (Ps. 115:9) [which is the land of Israel]."

To understand the passage at hand, we have to recall two facts. First, Egypt was a land in which the dead were venerated and their bodies preserved. We have also to keep in mind that, in the age now dawning, not only the deeds but also the bones of the very bodies of saints would be venerated, so that, in time to come, the bone of a saint would be a treasure. Indeed, the veneration of the saints, for Christians, corresponded to the veneration of the patriarchs, for Jews, and the notion of merit, or *zekhut*, found its counterpart in the store of grace imputed to saints and inhering, some held, even in their bones. Accordingly, the passage at hand presents a striking polemic. It is against the veneration of the bones of the patriarchs, speaking of Egypt but meaning Christian Rome. The rather satisfying repertoire of readings of the base verse raises all the important questions of detail and also focuses upon the main point. Why Joseph? Because he could do the job, so no. 1. Nos. 3, 4 then ask the main question, which is why Jacob was so eager not to be buried in Egypt. If we knew for sure that the author of the passage knew about the cult of the saints and of the dead popular among Christians at the point that the document at hand reached closure, we could find in no. 3 a stunning polemic. The view of no. 4 of the land as the place where life takes place of course is well documented.

God's Judgment and Jacob's Blessing

Our sages read Jacob's blessing as a judgment upon his sons. So they compare the setting—the father blessing his sons—to the Day of Atonement. The blessing then serves to prefigure the last judgment.

XCVIII:I.1.A.   "Then Jacob called his sons [and said, 'Gather yourselves together, that I may tell you what shall befall you in days to come. Assemble and hear, O sons of Jacob, and hearken to Israel, your father. Reuben, you are my first-born, my might and the first fruits of my strength, preeminent in pride and preeminent in power. Unstable as water, you shall not have preeminence, because you went up to your father's bed, then you defiled it, you went up to my couch!']" (Gen. 49:1–4):

B.   "I will cry to God Most High [unto God who completes it for me]" (Ps. 57:3):

C.   "I will cry to God Most High": on the New Year.

D.   ". . . unto God who completes it for me": on the Day of Atonement.

E.   To find out which [goat] is for the Lord and which one is for an evil decree. [The reference is to Leviticus 16, with its rite of the two goats, one bearing the sins of Israel into the wilderness, the other offered to the Lord as an atonement offering.]

2.A.   Another matter: "I will cry to God Most High [unto God who completes it for me]" (Ps. 57:3):

B.   "I will cry to God Most High": refers to our father, Jacob.

C. ". . . unto God who completes it for me": for the Holy One, blessed be he, concurred with him to give each of the sons a blessing in accord with his character.

D. "Then Jacob called his sons [and said, 'Gather yourselves together, that I may tell you what shall befall you in days to come]."

XCVIII:II.1.A. "The lot is cast into the lap, but the decision is wholly from the Lord" (Prov. 16:33):

B. [The high priest on the Day of Atonement casts lots, choosing which goat for the wilderness, which for the altar. So here too:] "The lot is cast into the lap": this refers to the Day of Atonement.

C. ". . . but the decision is wholly from the Lord": To find out which [goat] is for the Lord and which one is for an evil decree.

2.A. Another matter: "The lot is cast into the lap": this refers to the lot of the tribal fathers.

B. ". . . but the decision is wholly from the Lord": for the Holy One, blessed be he, concurred with him to give each of the sons a blessing in accord with his character.

C. "Then Jacob called his sons [and said, 'Gather yourselves together, that I may tell you what shall befall you in days to come.]"

3.A. "Then Jacob called his sons":

B. R. Yudan and R. Phineas:

C. R. Yudan said, " 'Then Jacob called' God to be with 'his sons.' "

D. R. Phineas said, "He invited him for his sons."

E. Said R. Abun, "He made him guardian for his sons."

4.A. "Then Jacob called his sons and said, 'Gather yourselves together, that I may tell you what shall befall you in days to come":

B. "Gather yourselves together" from the land of Israel, "and assemble and hear" in Raameses.

C. "Gather yourselves together" the ten tribes.

D. "And assemble and hear" the tribes of Judah
and Benjamin.

E. He commanded them to treat the tribes of Judah and
Benjamin with honor.

5. R. Aha said, "Gather together" means 'purify' in line
with this verse: 'And they gathered themselves together . . .
and they purified themselves' (Neh. 12:28)."

6.A. Rabbis say, "It means that he commanded them
[his sons] about dissension. He said to them, 'All of you
should form a single gathering.'

B. "That is in line with this verse: 'And you, son of
man, take one stick and write upon it, "For Judah and for the
children of Israel his companions" ' (Ez. 37:16).

C. "What is written is 'his companion,' meaning, that
when the children of Israel form a single assembly, then they
prepare themselves for redemption.

D. "For what is written afterward? 'And I will make
them one nation in the land' (Ez. 37:22)."

7.A. "Then Jacob called his sons and said, 'Gather yourselves together, that I may tell you what shall befall you in
days to come':

B. R. Simon said, "He showed them the fall of Gog, in
line with this usage: 'It shall be in the end of days . . . when
I shall be sanctified through you, O Gog' (Ez. 38:15). 'Behold, it shall come upon Edom' (Is. 34:5)."

C. R. Judah said, "He showed them the building of the
house of the sanctuary: 'And it shall come to pass in the end
of days that the mountain of the Lord's house shall be established' (Is. 2:2)."

D. Rabbis say, "He came to reveal the time of the end
to them, but it was hidden from him."

E. R. Judah in the name of R. Eleazar bar Abina: "To
two men the secret of the time of the end was revealed, but
then it was hidden from them, and these are they: Jacob
and Daniel.

F. "Daniel: 'But you, O Daniel, shut up the words and
seal the book' (Dan. 12:4).

G. "Jacob: 'Then Jacob called his sons and said, "Gather yourselves together, that I may tell you what shall befall you in days to come. Assemble and hear, O sons of Jacob, and hearken to Israel, your father. Reuben, you are my firstborn.' "

H. "This teaches that he came to reveal the time of the end to them, but it was hidden from him."

I. The matter may be compared to the case of the king's ally, who was departing this world, and his children surrounded his bed. He said to them, "Come and I shall tell you the secrets of the king." Then he looked up and saw the king. He said to them, "Be most meticulous about the honor owing to the king."

J. So our father looked up and saw the presence of God standing over him. He said to them, "Be most meticulous about the honor owing to the Holy One, blessed be he."

The intersecting verse in the opening paragraph invites the comparison of the judgment of the Days of Awe to the blessing of Jacob, and that presents a dimension of meaning that the narrative would not otherwise reveal. Just as God decides which goat serves what purpose, so God concurs in Jacob's judgment of which son/tribe deserves what sort of blessing. So Jacob stands in the stead of God in this stunning comparison of Jacob's blessing to the day of judgment. But Jacob will give way to God, who will replace him in the parental role. God is the true parent of Israel. The link between Jacob's biography and the holy life of Israel is fresh.

The same point is repeated in the second paragraph at no. 1–2 with a different intersecting verse. No. 3 clarifies a minor detail. No. 4 interprets the language at hand both in its immediate context and in the larger setting of Israel's history. No. 5 goes over the same language, and no. 6 introduces, in the identical context, an eschatological dimension. No. 7 successfully carries forward this final theme, which surely is invited by the base verse, so that the personal history of the individual, dealt with at the opening compositions, gives way to the national history of Israel.

Israel's Unity and God's Unity

The quest in Jacob's blessing for points of contact with the sages' own religious life moves from sin and atonement to the theological affirmation of God's unity. Israel on earth stands for God in heaven. When Israel on earth is united, that affirms the unity of God in heaven.

XCVIII:III.2.A. ". . .and hearken to Israel, your father":

B. R. Yudan and R. Phineas:

C. R. Yudan said, "Listen to the God of Israel your father."

D. R. Phineas said, "Your father, Israel, is [like] God.

E. "Just as the Holy One, blessed be he, creates worlds, so your father creates worlds. Just as the Holy One, blessed be he, divides worlds, so your father divides worlds."

3.A. Eleazar son of his brother said, "On the basis of the statement at hand the Israelites acquired the merit of reciting the *Shema*.

B. "When Jacob our father was departing the world, he called his twelve sons and said to them, 'Is the God of Israel who is in heaven your father? Is it possible that you have in mind dissension against the Holy One, blessed be he?'

C. "They said to them, 'Hear O Israel' (Deut. 6:4), our father, just as in your mind there is no dissension against God, so there is not in our hearts any dissension against God, but rather: "the Lord is our God, the Lord is one" (Deut. 6:4).'

D. "Then he too expressed with his lips: 'Blessed is the name of the glory of his kingdom forever and ever.' "

E. R. Berekhiah and R. Helbo in the name of R. Samuel: "That is why Israel proclaims morning and night, 'Hear O Israel,' our father, buried in the cave of Machpelah, that very matter that you commanded us remains the custom among us: 'the Lord our God, the Lord is one.' "

No. 2 moves into deeper ground, explaining the language of Jacob with stress on the use of the word "hear," which brings God and Jacob into the same category. No. 3 pursues the same point about the use of the word "hear." Once more we find an effort to link Israel's liturgical life to the death of Jacob.

The Blessing of Judah in Particular, the Messianic Question in General

Judah stands for the coming Messiah, so our sages search out with special care the meaning of what is said to him. They seek guidance on what is going to be when the Messiah comes. Stress on Messianic question surely accords with the issue forced by the triumph of Christianity: How shall we know when the real Messiah comes?

XCVIII:VII.1.A. ["Judah is a lion's whelp, from the prey, my son, you have gone up. He stooped down, he couched as a lion."] "Judah is a lion's whelp":

B. This teaches that he gave him the might of the lion and the daring of the young lion.

2.A. ". . . from the prey, my son, you have gone up":

B. From the prey of my son Joseph you went up and were exalted, from the mauling of Tamar you went up and were exalted.

3.A. ". . . He stooped down, he couched as a lion":

B. From Perez to David: "He couched, he lay down as a lion" (Num. 24:9).

C. From David to Zedekiah: "He stooped down, he crouched as a lion."

4.A. Some say: ". . . He stooped down, he crouched as a lion":

B. From Perez to Zedekiah, "He stooped down."

C. From Zedekiah to the king Messiah, ". . . he crouched as a lion."

5.A. ". . . He stooped down, he crouched as a lion":

B. In this world, "He stooped down."

C. In the age to come, ". . . he crouched as a lion."

6.A. "He stooped down, he crouched as a lion":

B. When he has no enemies, "He stooped down."

C. Until the enemies perished, ". . . he crouched as a lion."

What is important here is the reading of the verse in line with Israel's hope of a Messiah to come from the house of Judah.

Issachar and Zebulun, Torah and Making a Living

A recurrent concern of our sages, study of Torah, makes its appearance as well. Sages maintained that Issachar accomplished much in the study of Torah, and Zebulun made it possible by supporting him while he studied. They worked out the fantasy that others would work so they could study, crediting Zebulun with the merit attained by Issachar. Here, as much as in the blessing of Judah, they discovered matters of deep concern to themselves.

XCVIII:XII.1.A. ["Issachar is a strong ass, crouching between the sheepfolds; he saw that a resting place was good, and that the land was pleasant; so he bowed his shoulder to bear, and became a slave at forced labor" (Gen. 49:14–15).] "Issachar is a strong ass": Just as in the case of an ass, its bones are visible, so the Torah learning of Issachar was visible to him.

B. ". . . crouching between the sheepfolds": This refers to the two rows of disciples of sages who are in session before them.

C. ". . . he saw that a resting place was good": this refers to the Torah, as it is said, "For I have given you a good portion" (Prov. 4:2).

D. ". . . and that the land was pleasant": this is the Torah: "The measure thereof is longer than the land" (Job 11:9).

E. ". . . so he bowed his shoulder to bear": the yoke of the Torah.

F. ". . . and became a slave at forced labor": these are the two hundred heads of sanhedrins who derived from the tribe of Issachar.

G. That is in line with the following verse: "And of the children of Issachar, men that had understanding of the times; the heads of them were two hundred, and all their brethren were at their commandment" (1 Chr. 12:33).

H. What is the meaning of "the times"?

I. R. Tanhuma said, "The seasons."

J. R. Yose bar Qisrai says, "The rules of intercalation of the calendar."

K. ". . . the heads of them were two hundred," for two hundred heads of sanhedrins were produced by the tribe of Issachar.

L. ". . . and all their brethren were at their commandment" (1 Chr. 12:33): for all their brethren made the law accord with their instruction, and he provided for them rulings in accord with the law revealed to Moses at Sinai.

M. And how come all of this glory came to Issachar?

N. It was on account of Zebulun, for he would conduct business affairs and provide for Issachar, who was a master of Torah. [That is to say, Zebulun supported Issachar, so that the one did business and made a living for both, while the other studied the Torah and also—for both—made a living, the one in this world, the other in the world to come.]

O. That is in line with this verse: "Zebulun will dwell at the shore of the sea" (Gen. 49:13).

P. Now when Moses came to bestow a blessing on Israel, he gave precedence to the blessing for Zebulun over the blessing for Issachar: "Rejoice, Zebulun, in your going out, and Issachar in your tents" (Deut. 33:18).

Q. The meaning is this: Because of "Issachar in your tents" ["Rejoice, Zebulun, in your going out"].

R. And some say, "Issachar is in the tents of Zebulun."

3.A. "Issachar is a strong ass": the produce of Issachar was sizable. The tribe of Zebulun would take it and set sail, and the nations of the world would see it and find it astonishing. The Israelites would say to them, "Are you amazed at these? If you saw the masters of this produce, engaged in study of the Torah, you would have something about which to be amazed." As a result, many proselytes came and converted.

B. R. Simon in the name of R. Aha said, " 'Issachar is a strong ass' means Issachar is an ass for proselytes. [This is a play on the word for large-boned and proselytes, both of which use the same consonants.]"

No. 1 works out the theme of Issachar's Torah study, and no. 3 makes the familiar point that masters of Torah must reach out and bring gentiles to the knowledge of God and the Torah.

Jacob and Pharaoh, Israel and the Nations

We end by comparing Jacob and pharaoh, each standing for his nation. What marks Israel is worship of God, while in Egypt pharaoh is worshiped as a god. Israel knows the difference, therefore, between earthly monarchs and their Father in heaven. The exaltation of the emperor in Constantinople then forms a contrast to Israel's exaltation of God alone.

C:I.1.A. "When Jacob finished charging his sons, he drew up his feet into the bed and breathed his last and was gathered to his people" (Gen. 49:33):

B. "Know that the Lord—he is God. It is he who has made us, and we did not create ourselves" (Ps. 100:3).

C. R. Judah bar Simon and R. Aha:

D. R. Judah bar Simon said, " 'Know that the Lord—he is God. It is he who has made us, 'and we did not create ourselves.' That is not like the view of pharaoh, who said, 'The river belongs to me myself, and I have made it for myself' (Ez. 29:3)."

E. R. Aha said, " 'Know that the Lord—he is God. It is he who has made us.' and to him we commit our souls."

F. "When Jacob finished charging his sons, he drew up his feet into the bed and breathed his last and was gathered to his people."

The opening unit introduces an intersecting verse to emphasize the difference between Jacob and pharaoh. Jacob understood that God, not man, creates man and ends human life when he chooses.

The Merit of the Nations

The nations, for their part, enjoy this world, but, in it, they gain some merit too. Where and how? The nations enjoy whatever benefit they have because of some good deed. Whatever reward they have coming they get here and now, and not in the eternal age to come. So the nations get this world, and Israel, the world to come. Here is how our sages state that proposition.

C:VI.1.A. "When they came to the threshing floor of Atad, which is beyond the Jordan, they lamented there with a very great and sorrowful lamentation, and he made a mourning for his father seven days" (Gen. 50:10):

B. Said R. Samuel bar Nahman, "We have reviewed the entire scripture and found no other place called Atad. And can there be a threshing floor for thorns [the Hebrew word for thorn being *atad*]?

C. "But this refers to the Canaanites. It teaches that they were worthy of being threshed like thorns. And on account of what merit were they saved? It was on account of the acts of kindness that they performed for our father, Jacob [on the occasion of the mourning for his death]."

D. And what were the acts of kindness that they preformed for our father, Jacob?

E. R. Eleazar said, "[When the bier was brought up there] they unloosened the girdle of their loins."

F. R. Simeon b. Laqish said, "They untied the shoulder-knots."

G. R. Judah b. R. Shalom said, "They pointed with their fingers and said, 'This is a grievous mourning to the Egyptians' (Gen. 50:11).

H. Rabbis said, "They stood upright."

I. Now is it not an argument a fortiori: now if these, who did not do a thing with their hands or feet, but only because they pointed their fingers, were saved from punishment, Israel, which performs an act of kindness [for the dead] with their adults and with their children, with their hands and with their feet, how much the more so [will they enjoy the merit of being saved from punishment]!

J. Said R. Abbahu, "Those seventy days that lapsed between the first letter and the second match the seventy days that the Egyptians paid respect to Jacob. [Seventy days elapsed from Haman's letter of destruction until Mordecai's letter announcing the repeal of the decree (cf. Est. 3:12, 8:9). The latter letter, which permitted the Jews to take vengeance on their would-be destroyers, should have come earlier, but it was delayed seventy days as a reward for the honor shown by the Egyptians to Jacob (Freedman, p. 992, n. 6).]"

The Egyptians gained merit by honoring Jacob in his death, so Abbahu. This same point then registers for the Canaanites. The connection is somewhat farfetched, that is, through the reference to the threshing floor, but the point is a strong one.

Joseph and his Brothers: The Last Act

The story of Israel's beginnings is drawing to a close. The final drama brings Joseph together with his brothers. We now see that Israel's sons did achieve complete reconciliation. Peace within Israel is the highest good.

C:VIII.1.A. "After he had buried his father, Joseph returned to Egypt with his brothers and all who had gone up with him to bury his father. When Joseph's brothers saw that their father was dead, they said, 'It may be that Joseph will hate us and pay us back for all the evil which we did to him' " (Gen. 50:14):

B. R. Levi and R. Isaac:

C. R. Levi said, "it was because he did not invite them to a banquet."

D. Said R. Tanhuma, "His intent was only for the sake of heaven. He said, 'In the past father would seat me above Judah, who is king, and above Reuben, who is firstborn. But now it is not right that I should sit above them. But that is not what they were thinking. Rather: 'It may be that Joseph will hate us.' "

E. R. Isaac said, "He had gone and looked into that pit [and that is why they were afraid.]"

F. Said R. Tanhuma, "His intent was only for the sake of heaven. But that is not what they were thinking. Rather: 'It may be that Joseph will hate us.' "

2.A. "So they sent a message to Joseph, saying, 'Your father gave this command [before he died, 'Say to Joseph, "Forgive I pray you the transgression of your brothers and their sin, because they did evil to you." And now, we pray you, forgive the transgression of the servants of the God of your father.' Joseph wept when they spoke to him]" (Gen. 50:16–17):

B. It has been taught on Tannaite authority: R. Simeon b. Gamaliel said, "Great is peace, for even the fathers of the tribes told lies so as to bring peace between Joseph and the fathers of the tribes."

C. "For so it is said, 'Your father gave this command [before he died] "Say to Joseph, 'Forgive I pray you the transgression of your brothers and their sin, because they did evil to you.' " But where did he give such orders? We do not find that he ever gave such orders."

3.A. "Say to Joseph, "Forgive I pray you the transgression of your brothers and their sin, because they did evil to you." And now, we pray you, forgive the transgression of the servants of the God of your father.' Joseph wept when they spoke to him" (Gen. 50:16–17):

B. He said, "Can my brothers even now suspect me of such things?"

4.A. "His brothers also came and fell down before him and said, 'Behold, we are your servants' " (Gen. 50:18):

B. They said to him, "You wanted one of us as a slave, but lo, we are all your slaves."

C:IX:1.A. "But Joseph said to them, 'Fear not, for am I in the place of God? As for you, you meant evil against me, but God meant it for good, to bring it about that many people should be kept alive, as they are today. So do not fear; I will provide for you and your little ones.' Thus he spoke to their heart and comforted them" (Gen. 50:19–21):

368

B. Can someone speak to the heart? But the sense is that he spoke words to them that comforted them.

C. He said to them, "You are to be compared to the dust of the earth. As with the dust of the earth, who can wipe out the dust of the earth? You have been compared to the wild beast of the field. As with the wild beast of the field, who can wipe out the wild beasts of the field? You have been compared to the stars. Who can wipe out the stars? Ten stars tried to destroy one star and could not overcome it. As to twelve tribes, how can I change the order of the world that one star can destroy twelve stars?

D. "For the twelve stars correspond to the twelve hours of the day and the twelve constellations of the heavens" [Freedman].

E. Said R. Simlai, "You are the body and I am the head: 'Let the blessing come upon the head, Joseph' (Deut. 33:16). If you take away the body, what good is the head?

F. "[Joseph further said to his brothers] 'Furthermore, if you had not come down here, they would have called me a slave. Now that you have come down here, my birth as a free man has become known. So if that is the case, shall I kill you?

G. "If I kill you, people will say that this one does not keep his word: 'If he did not keep his word with his brothers, with whom will he keep his word?' "

H. "[He further said to his brothers] 'They will also say, "They were not really his brothers, but he picked up a gaggle of boys and called them his brothers. You may know that that is the fact, for in the end he trumped up charges against them and killed them." '

I. "Joseph further said, 'Should I become my father's nemesis, with his fathering and with my burying the brothers? Or shall I become a nemesis of God, with God's blessing [my brothers] and my cutting down [my brothers]?' "

J. Thus: "He spoke to their heart and comforted them."

2.A. Now if Joseph, who spoke mild words to the hearts of the tribal fathers and thereby comforted them, when the Holy One, blessed be he, comes to comfort Jerusalem, how much the more so:

B. "Comfort, comfort my people" (Is. 40:1).

The expansion dwells on what Joseph said to reassure the brothers. No. 2 provides an important link to the eschatological salvation of Israel, so that the present scene prefigures Israel's future history. Our sages find in the book of Genesis a single, recurring, and powerful message of salvation.

General Index

Index of Biblical and Talmudic References